Religious Studies for GCSE

Also from Polity:

Religion and Ethics for OCR: The Complete Resource for the New AS and A Level Specification, Mark Coffey & Dennis Brown

This book is dedicated with affection to my special friends Ann, and Ann, Fiona and Lord Bert

RELIGIOUS STUDIES FOR GCSE

PHILOSOPHY AND ETHICS
APPLIED TO CHRISTIANITY, ROMAN CATHOLICISM & ISLAM

DENNIS BROWN

polity

The right of Dennis Brown to be identified as Author of this Work has been asserted in accordance with the UK Copyright, Designs and Patents Act 1988.

First published in 2016 by Polity Press

Polity Press
65 Bridge Street
Cambridge CB2 1UR, UK

Polity Press
350 Main Street
Malden, MA 02148, USA

ISBN-13: 978-1-5095-0436-7
ISBN-13: 978-1-5095-0437-4 (pb)

A catalogue record for this book is available from the British Library.

Library of Congress Cataloging-in-Publication Data

Names: Brown, Dennis, 1955- author.
Title: Religious studies for GCSE : philosophy and ethics applied to
   Christianity, Roman Catholicism and Islam / Dennis Brown.
Description: Malden, MA : Polity, 2016. | Includes bibliographical references
   and index.
Identifiers: LCCN 2016000848| ISBN 9781509504367 (hardcover : alk. paper) |
   ISBN 1509504362 (hardcover : alk. paper) | ISBN 9781509504374 (pbk. : alk.
   paper) | ISBN 1509504370 (pbk. : alk. paper)
Subjects: LCSH: Christianity and other religions--Islam--Examinations. |
   Islam--Relations--Christianity--Examinations. | Catholic
   Church--Examinations. | General Certificate of Secondary Education.
Classification: LCC BP172 .B7725 2016 | DDC 261.2/7--dc23 LC record available at https://lccn.loc.
gov/2016000848

Typeset in 9.5 on 13 pt Utopia Regular by Servis Filmsetting Ltd, Stockport, Cheshire
Printed and bound in the UK by Clays Ltd, St Ives PLC

For further information on Polity, visit our website: politybooks.com

Contents

Tables

Acknowledgements

I am very happy to thank the many people involved in the production of this book. Particular thanks go to my editor, Jonathan Skerrett, for his enthusiasm, patience, attention to detail and many helpful and encouraging comments on various drafts of each chapter, and to others in the Polity family, notably India Darsley and Caroline Richmond, who have helped to produce the book to a very high standard despite working to a tight deadline.

I also owe a debt of gratitude to my colleagues in the Religion & Philosophy department at the Manchester Grammar School. I offer them my heartfelt thanks for their constant support and encouragement during this project, even if it has at times meant yet more conversations about 'the book'! A particular thank you also goes to the 'guinea-pigs' in my Year 11 class of 2015–16, especially to Joel, Josh, Sam, Ted, Tom and Will, who were subjected to several draft chapters and 'encouraged' to go beyond the strict remit of the specification in order to provide feedback to me. I applaud their perseverance and perspicacity and am grateful to them for their help.

Introduction

For students

Welcome to the study of philosophy and ethics! This is something of an unusual book in several ways. Most textbooks you might see are designed to cover only one specification from one awarding organization (or AOs, formerly known as exam boards). This book, however, covers specifications from four AOs: AQA, OCR, Edexcel and WJEC Eduqas. Within each of these, there are 'full' courses and 'short' courses, as well as one international one. In total, there are *twelve* different specifications.

The specifications also allow for the study of different religions. This book approaches each topic from the viewpoints of Christianity, Roman Catholic Christianity (or Roman Catholicism) and Islam. Every chapter has clear sections for each of these religions, and you may find the labels in the margin helpful in order to go directly to the religion you are studying or revising. It is worth clarifying what 'Christianity' and 'Roman Catholicism' mean, as used in this book, since Roman Catholicism is, after all, a denomination of Christianity. In some topics (for example, euthanasia, terrorism and human rights), there is no difference between the 'Roman Catholic' view and that of other Christian denominations. In these cases, there are just 'Christian' views. I have provided separate discussion and explanation of Roman Catholic views only when there is a significant difference between those and other Christian views. Examples of where this is important include abortion and divorce. In each case where this occurs, the different sections are labelled clearly.

The book is also large, covering lots of topics in philosophy and ethics. You should not be put off, though, because the good news is that you will not have to study everything detailed here! You can find which parts you will need by consulting the grid later in this introduction. If you don't know which specification you are doing, ask your teacher.

Within each chapter, too, you will find 'Taking it Further' boxes. These are optional sections or paragraphs that provide a little more information or more detail on a topic, a different angle or an extra scholarly view. You won't necessarily need to learn this material for your exams, and you can simply skip these boxes without interrupting the rest of your reading; however, you may wish to study them if you are keen on getting top grades.

I hope that you will find the topics you study interesting. As you make your way through the material, you will get used to the way language is used and how the concepts link to issues in the real world and, perhaps, to the other subjects you are studying.

The final chapter in the book (chapter 14) is about exam technique. It will give you hints about how best to answer the types of question on your specification and help you to focus on what you need to achieve the highest grade possible.

I hope that you have a great time studying philosophy and ethics!

For teachers

The scope of the book

This book covers all of the philosophy and ethics elements of each of the major awarding organizations (or AOs, formerly known as exam boards): AQA, Edexcel (including the IGCSE), OCR and WJEC Eduqas. It is suitable for both full-course and short-course GCSEs.

I have taken an 'all-inclusive' approach to the variety of philosophy and ethics topics offered by all the AOs, and this book therefore contains all of the philosophy and ethics sections that students need to know, regardless of which specification they are studying. Some students may decide to delve into a topic that interests them, even though it may not be part of their course of study. If this happens, and it does not detract from their understanding of their 'necessary' topics, it can only be a positive thing.

The book approaches each topic from the viewpoints of Christianity, Roman Catholic Christianity and Islam. It is worth clarifying what 'Christianity' and 'Roman Catholic Christianity' (or 'Roman Catholicism') mean, as used in this book. In some topics – for example, euthanasia, terrorism and human rights – there is no difference between the 'Roman Catholic' view and that of other Christian denominations. In these cases, there are just 'Christian' views. I have provided separate discussion and explanation of Roman Catholic views only when there is a significant difference between those and other Christian views. Examples of where this is important include abortion and divorce. In each case where this occurs, the different sections are labelled clearly. Any centre offering Roman Catholic Christianity as one of their religious traditions, therefore, will be able to direct their students to these sections.

Use of Biblical and Qur'anic translations

I have deliberately used different versions of the Bible from which to quote. The most frequently used is the New Revised Standard Version (NRSV), as this provides an accurate translation, though, when it makes the sense of a passage clearer for students, I have also used the New International Version (NIV).

For quotations from the Qur'an, I have generally drawn on the classic translation by N. J. Dawood. I have sometimes used one or more online versions if they are easier to understand for GCSE students. All quotations from other Muslim documents and authorities have been sourced from freely available online sites.

Citations from modern scholars are referenced directly after the quotation.

Level of challenge

One of the 'highlights' of this book is the academic level at which it is pitched. I have deliberately written it at a level that is designed to stretch students so that they will complete the GCSE course with a good understanding of all the relevant topics they study. For many students, this course will mark the end of their formal education in religious studies. I believe it is important that both teachers and students see religious studies as having value as an academic subject, in line with other subjects, so it needs to be rigorous and challenging.

One aspect of this challenge is the 'Taking it Further' boxes that appear in each chapter. These are optional sections or paragraphs, suitable for some students but not for all. They can easily be skipped over and do not interrupt the flow of the arguments or the points made in the main body of the text; rather, they provide a little more information or more detail on a topic, a different angle or an extra scholarly view. They are intended to enhance a student's understanding of the topic under consideration.

Another reason for pitching the level of the book is that the Department for Education declared that it wanted to see real academic challenge in each revised subject. The 'Taking it Further' boxes are a specific case in point where this academic challenge may be explicitly seen.

One final point about the academic level of the book and the 'Taking it Further' boxes concerns the new grading system. The 9–1 numerical system replaces the A*–G nomenclature. A grade 9 is pitched above an A*, and it may well be that the increased level of detail generally in this book may assist students to achieve the highest grade of which they are capable.

'Extra' chapter

Chapter 1, 'Religious Texts and Other Sources of Authority', is not technically required for study. It has been included because it is central to an understanding of some of the important discussions on philosophy and ethics contained in the rest of the book. For example, one of the crucial reasons why Christians disagree on ethical issues such as abortion is because of the way they interpret the biblical passages that are thought to be relevant in this debate.

So, although it is not specifically required by the Department for Education's regulations or by AOs, discussion of this topic will inevitably arise in classroom debates in whichever specification students study. It will obviously be up to teachers to determine whether or how they use this chapter in their courses. This is why I have included it for all specifications in the grid.

Sample questions

At the end of each chapter (with the exception of chapter 1), there are some sample questions. Because each of the AOs has designed their own style of questions to fit their specifications, AQA type questions will be different from OCR type questions, and from those of the other AOs, and so on. Each question will be clearly labelled with regard to which AO it is designed for. This will mean that, for some chapters, there will be sample questions for some AOs but not for others, because different specifications offer different topics. For example, for chapter 6, 'Religion and Science', and chapter 11, 'Global Relationships', there are sample questions for AQA, Edexcel and WJEC Eduqas, but not for OCR.

Specifications

Below are some of the basic details of the current GCSEs (and the IGCSE) offered by AQA, Edexcel, OCR and WJEC Eduqas, showing how the materials in this book match up to the philosophy and ethics components of these specifications. The grid can be used to locate which chapters satisfy each specification: identify your specification in the left-hand column and then simply look across the grid to see which chapters are required.

AQA Religious Studies A (8062)

Component 1: The study of religions: beliefs, teachings and practices
Component 2: Thematic studies
  Either four religious, philosophical and ethical studies themes or two religious, philosophical and ethical studies themes and two textual studies themes
  Religious, philosophical and ethical studies themes:
    Theme A: Relationships and families (**Chapter 9**)
    Theme B: Religion and life (**Chapters 6, 7, 8 and 11**)
    Theme C: The existence of God and revelation (**Chapters 2, 3, 4 and 5**)
    Theme D: Religion, peace and conflict (**Chapter 12**)
    Theme E: Religion, crime and punishment (**Chapter 13**)
    Theme F: Religion, human rights and social justice (**Chapters 9, 10 and 11**)
  Textual studies themes:
    Theme G: St Mark's Gospel – the life of Jesus
    Theme H: St Mark's Gospel as a source of religious, moral and spiritual truths

AQA Religious Studies B (8063)

1 Catholic Christianity
2 Perspectives on faith
  One religion chosen from either Islam or Judaism and either two religious, philosophical and ethical studies themes chosen from:
    Theme A: Religion, relationships and families (**Chapters 8 and 9**)
    Theme B: Religion, peace and conflict (**Chapter 12**)
    Theme C: Religion, human rights and social justice (**Chapters 9, 10 and 11**)
  or two textual studies themes:
    Theme D: St Mark's Gospel – the life of Jesus
    Theme E: St Mark's Gospel as a source of spiritual truth

Edexcel Religious Studies A: Faith & Practice in the 21st Century (1RA0)

Students must complete Area of Study 1 and Area of Study 2, and then either Area of Study 3 or Area of Study 4

Area of Study 1: Study of Religion
Area of Study 2: Study of Second Religion
Area of Study 3: Philosophy and Ethics
    Students must select one religion from a choice of three religions (Catholic Christianity, Christianity, Islam):
    Arguments for the Existence of God **(Chapters 2, 3, 4 and 5)**
    Religious Teachings on Relationships and Families in the 21st Century **(Chapter 9)**
Area of Study 4: Textual Studies

Edexcel Religious Studies B: Beliefs in Action (1RB0)

Two areas of study: Students must select a different religion for each area of study that they follow. Students who select Catholic Christianity for an area of study are not permitted to select Christianity for their second area of study and vice versa.

Area of Study 1: Religion and Ethics
    Beliefs
    Marriage and the Family – of the chosen religion **(Chapter 9)**
    Living the Religious Life
    Matters of Life and Death **(Chapters 6, 7, 8 and 11)**
Area of Study 2: Religion, Peace and Conflict
    Beliefs
    Crime and Punishment **(Chapters 5 and 13)**
    Living the Religious Life – of the chosen religion
    Peace and Conflict **(Chapter 12)**
Area of Study 3: Religion, Philosophy and Social Justice
    Beliefs
    Philosophy of Religion **(Chapters 2, 3, 4 and 5)**
    Living the Religious Life – of the chosen religion
    Equality **(Chapters 10 and 11)**

Edexcel International GCSE Religious Studies (4RS0)

Part 1: Beliefs and Values
    The universe, human beings and their destiny **(Chapters 5, 6, 7, 8, 11 and 12)**
    Ultimate reality and the meaning of life **(Chapters 2, 3, 4, 5 and 8)**
    Relationships, families and children **(Chapter 9)**
    Rights, equality and responsibilities **(Chapters 9, 10 and 11)**
Part 2: The Religious Community

OCR Religious Studies (J625)

Component Group 1: Beliefs and teachings & Practices
Component Group 2: Religion, philosophy and ethics in the modern world from a religious perspective
    Relationships and families **(Chapter 9)**
    The existence of God, gods and the ultimate reality **(Chapters 2, 3, 4 and 5)**
    Religion, peace and conflict **(Chapter 12)**
    Dialogue between religious and non-religious beliefs and attitudes **(Chapters 8 and 10)**

WJEC Eduqas Religious Studies

Component 1: Religious, Philosophical and Ethical Studies in the Modern World
    Theme 1: Issues of Relationships **(Chapter 9)**
    Theme 2: Issues of Life and Death **(Chapters 6, 7, 8 and 11)**
    Theme 3: Issues of Good and Evil **(Chapters 5 and 13)**
    Theme 4: Issues of Human Rights **(Chapters 10 and 11)**
Component 2: Study of Christianity
Component 3: Study of a World Faith

AQA Religious Studies Short Course (8061)

Section A: The study of religions: beliefs and teachings
Section B: Thematic studies: religious, philosophical and ethical studies
    Theme A: Relationships and families **(Chapter 9)**
    Theme B: Religion, peace and conflict **(Chapter 12)**

Edexcel Religious Studies B Short Course: Beliefs in Action (3RB0)

Students must select a different religion for each area of study that they follow. Students who select Catholic Christianity for an area of study are not permitted to select Christianity for their second area of study and vice versa.

Area of Study 1: Religion and Ethics
    Religious Belief
    Marriage and the Family **(Chapter 9)**
Area of Study 2: Religion, Peace and Conflict
    Religious Belief
    Peace and Conflict **(Chapters 5 and 12)**

OCR Religious Studies Short Course (J125)

Section A: Beliefs and teachings
Section B: Relationships and families. **(Chapter 9)**
Section C: Dialogues between religious and non-religious beliefs and attitudes
(Chapters 8 and 10)

WJEC Eduqas Religious Studies Short Course

Component 1: Religious, Philosophical and Ethical Studies in the Modern World
   Theme 1: Issues of Relationships **(Chapter 9)**
   Theme 2: Issues of Life and Death **(Chapters 6, 7, 8 and 11)**
Component 2: Study of Christianity
Component 3: Study of a World Faith

Awarding Organization (AO)	FULL COURSES	AQA	AQA	Edexcel	Edexcel	Edexcel	OCR	WJEC Eduqas	SHORT COURSES	AQA	Edexcel	OCR	WJEC Eduqas
Specification		Spec A (8062)	Spec B (8063)	Spec A (1RA0)	Spec B (1RB0)	IGCSE (4RS0)	(J625)			(8061)	Spec B (3RB0)	(J125)	
Chapter 1: Religious Texts and Other Sources of Authority		✓	✓	✓	✓	✓	✓	✓		✓	✓	✓	✓
Chapter 2: The Existence of God		✓		✓	✓	✓	✓						
Chapter 3: The Nature and Characteristics of God		✓		✓	✓	✓	✓						
Chapter 4: Revelation and Religious Experience		✓		✓	✓	✓	✓						
Chapter 5: The Problem of Evil		✓		✓	✓	✓	✓	✓			✓		
Chapter 6: Religion and Science		✓			✓	✓		✓					✓
Chapter 7: Death and Life after Death		✓			✓	✓		✓					✓
Chapter 8: Human Nature		✓	✓		✓	✓	✓	✓				✓	✓
Chapter 9: Relationships and Families		✓	✓	✓	✓	✓	✓	✓		✓	✓	✓	✓
Chapter 10: Religion, Human Rights and Social Justice		✓	✓		✓	✓	✓	✓				✓	
Chapter 11: Global Relationships		✓	✓		✓	✓		✓					✓
Chapter 12: War and Peace		✓	✓		✓	✓	✓			✓	✓		
Chapter 13: Crime and Punishment		✓			✓			✓					
Chapter 14: Study Skills, Revision and Exams		✓	✓	✓	✓	✓	✓	✓		✓	✓	✓	✓

Religious Texts and Other Sources of Authority

In this chapter, you will learn about what is meant by authority in the context of Christianity and Islam, what religious texts there are in Christianity and Islam, why they are sources of authority for believers, and what other sources of authority there are in these two religions.

In Christianity, you will be learning about the Bible and ways of interpreting it, as well as sources of authority for Christians, such as Jesus and the Apostles, tradition, religious leaders, religious experience, natural law and conscience. In Islam, you will learn about the Qur'an, the Sunnah, ahadith, religious experience and Fiqh as sources of authority.

What do we mean by authority?

Authority, in terms of religion, means the power or the right to say what is right and wrong, what followers should or should not do, and what to believe or not believe. When Christians or Muslims talk about the sources of authority that they accept and use, they generally use the word in one of two ways – *internal* authority and *external* authority.

Internal authority is the kind of authority that the person (or thing) has in him- or herself. For example, anyone who is especially intelligent or exceptionally good at a particular skill (sport, art, etc.) is said to have internal authority because of who they are. For example, Mahatma Gandhi, without first holding any official position, showed an authority that people recognized and followed. Jesus never held an official position during his life, and neither did the Prophet Muhammad. The authority they had derived from who they were, not from any official public office they held.

External authority comes from holding an office or position. For example, a police officer has authority, even if he or she is not a pleasant person, simply because he or she is in that position. The symbol of their office is a particular type of uniform, and this is how their authority may be recognized. In religious terms, examples of authority figures include the Pope, priests and imams.

> **Task**
>
> Is the authority held today by Jesus for Christians or the Prophet Muhammad for Muslims internal authority or external authority? Explain your answer.

Authority
is what makes things important. **Internal authority** is what makes someone or something important for who or what they are. **External authority** is given to people because of the position they hold.

The **Bible**
is the Christian holy book, consisting of 66 separate books, 39 in the Old Testament, 27 in the New Testament. Roman Catholics hold 7 extra books in their Bible (the Apocrypha) that Protestants reject.

Sources of authority in Christianity and Roman Catholic Christianity

Table 1.1 shows the sources of authority in Christianity and Roman Catholic Christianity that will be discussed in this chapter.

CHRISTIANITY ROMAN CATHOLICISM

The Bible

The Holy Book – or religious text with authority – in Christianity is the **Bible**, which is made up of two parts, the Old Testament and the New Testament. The word 'testament' means 'witness', so the Bible is a witness to God's interaction with humans and a record of the special relationship God has with them. This is why it is such an important source of authority for Christians.

The Old Testament

The Protestant Christian Old Testament contains thirty-nine books, while the Roman Catholic **canon** includes seven others. Together, the books provide a collection of writings that trace the story of God's creation of the universe and humans, their rebellion against God, God's judgement on them, and the long process by which God

Canon
comes from the Greek word for 'measure' and is the name given to the books in the Bible and are the 'measure' of Christian belief.

Table 1.1 Sources of authority in Christianity and Roman Catholic Christianity

The Bible	The Holy Book of Christianity, the (inspired) word of God
Jesus	The Son of God, whose life and resurrection showed God's saving power
The Apostles	Followers of Jesus to whom he gave authority to lead the Church
Religious experiences	Conversions, mystical experiences, revelations and visions from God
Tradition	Teachings and ways of doing things passed down over the ages, traced back to Jesus and the Apostles
Religious leaders	The Pope is 'Prince of Apostles' in Roman Catholicism and has God's authority to guide the Church
Natural law	God's laws are naturally visible in the world because God created it
Conscience	A God-given capacity to help humans decide what is right and wrong

It is traditionally believed that the first five books of the Bible were communicated to Moses directly by God. This German manuscript illumination from 840 shows God handing the scriptures to Moses. Therefore, the Bible holds great authority for Christians.

brought about the means by which they could be restored and saved. The Old Testament contains many different types of literature – myth, history, songs, poetry, prophecies, laws and ethical teaching.

- Jews believed that the first five books, the Torah – Genesis, Exodus, Leviticus, Numbers and Deuteronomy – were written by Moses, so their authority is derived from their author. It was thought that God had sanctioned Moses because of the mighty actions that he performed (primarily gaining the miraculous release of the nation from slavery in Egypt) and spoke with him openly.

- The histories of Israel (e.g., Samuel, Kings, Chronicles) concentrated on its dramatic rise under King David and the fortunes of his descendants/successors. They send the clear message that those kings who kept God's laws achieved success, while those that were unfaithful did not. Again, it was clear that God had granted authority to King David. He was seen as the ideal ruler – strong, courageous, and a great warrior and commander, yet wise, compassionate and just. Above all, though he sinned (seriously at times), he remained committed to God throughout his life. Those writings that gave accounts of David's kingship in favourable terms drew on his authority and were included in the canon.

- From the eighth to the fourth century BCE, various individuals rose up and spoke out on social and political issues, claiming to speak with the authority of God. They were known as prophets. Many people today think of a 'prophet' as someone who gives insights into the future. Although there was an element of this in the writings of the Jewish prophets, they spoke primarily about situations in their own time and place. Often the prophets gave warnings or promises of future disaster or blessing based on the people's reaction to their message. Confusingly, not all of the prophets' utterances gave the same instructions from God; in fact, on many occasions, directly conflicting advice seemed to come from different prophets.

- Obviously, not all of the writings of the prophets were included in the Jewish canon. How were the authoritative writings chosen? There were two criteria: whether their messages agreed with the Torah and whether their predictions came true. For example, Jeremiah warned the Israelites that God was going to use the Babylonian Empire to destroy the nation because they had refused to follow the laws relating to social justice and treatment of the poor. At the time, his message was criticized, but, when the Babylonians actually did attack and destroy the nation, Jeremiah's words were retrospectively seen to be from God. His book was therefore included in the Bible.

Since the first Christians were Jews, it is unsurprising that the Old Testament held such great authority for them. The Jews believed it to be the Word of God, and it continued to be so for Jewish Christians. Gentile (i.e., non-Jewish) converts to Christianity also readily accepted it.

Taking it further

The authority of the Old Testament was strengthened for some early Jewish Christians when they found it had many prophetic references to Jesus. Most of these had long been accepted as pointing to the **Messiah**, but others were fresh interpretations of passages that had previously been understood differently. For example, Isaiah chapter 53 speaks of the suffering and rejection of the 'servant of God'. This did not fit traditional Jewish expectations of the Messiah and was understood by Jews to refer either to the prophet Isaiah or to the nation of Israel itself. Christians, however, found that it fitted as a prophetic description of the suffering and death of Jesus and used it to bolster the claim that the Jewish scriptures supported belief in Jesus as the Messiah. In a similar way, laws such as sacrificing animals for the forgiveness of sins were seen to symbolize Jesus' death.

Messiah is the title of the person the Jews believed God would send to save them from evil and oppression. Christians understood this title and person to be Jesus.

The Jewish Bible, then, remained authoritative for the first Christians, as it had been for Jews. There were problems, however; firstly, it was written hundreds of years before the time of Jesus, and so there were no explicit or direct references to him. Secondly, some of its teachings seemed to have a different emphasis than, if not actually conflict with, the teachings of Jesus. Since Jesus was the ultimate revelation from God, it was natural for Christians to want (or need?) some authoritative written records of his life. There were many stories of his life and works, including many eyewitness accounts, but, before long, all of the eyewitnesses, the original disciples among them, would be dead. This realization prompted the writing of the New Testament.

The New Testament

The Jewish scriptures held authority for Christians from the beginning. It was not long, however, before other writings also came to be seen as authoritative. In addition to the problems outlined above, there were at least two main reasons for this.

1   Although the first Christians were almost exclusively Jews, within a few years the majority were gentiles, who may have had little or no background knowledge or understanding of the key beliefs and traditions of Judaism.
2   The Jewish scriptures were quickly interpreted to show that Jesus was the expected Messiah. However, there was a great need for writings that referred clearly and specifically to *Christian* beliefs and practices in their own right.

The New Testament is made up of twenty-seven books, including the four Gospels (account of Jesus's life) and twenty-one letters. Several Christian writings were produced in a short space of time. It is highly likely that many accounts of the life of Christ were written in the century after his death – indeed, several, in addition to the four canonical Gospels, survive to this day. There would also have been no shortage of letters and treatises written by Christians advising others on matters of faith. Why is it that some were chosen to be part of the New Testament canon while others were not? The choice was by no means universal or immediate. Several different

A fresco from Trnava in Slovakia showing the four Gospel writers – or Evangelists – Matthew, Mark, Luke and John. Their accounts of the life of Jesus are held by Christians to be authoritative.

collections of writings were regarded as authoritative in the first two centuries of Christianity.

These differences should not be overstated. With a few notable exceptions, the vast majority of first- and second-century Christians recognized the **synoptic** Gospels of Matthew, Mark and Luke, and most also included John. The letters written by the apostle Paul were always considered to be important and were referred to by many Christians in several different countries.

The writings that were eventually selected to be part of what became known as the New Testament were chosen because they fulfilled certain criteria:

- they were widely regarded as historically trustworthy;
- they were written either by one of the original disciples or by one of their trusted companions (the contributions of Paul were an exception – he quickly gained similar status to the original disciples, and his writings were included on that basis. In fact, the Gospel of Luke and its sequel, the Acts of the Apostles, were admitted because Luke was a close companion of Paul).

Synoptic
means 'seen together' and is used of the Gospels of Matthew, Mark and Luke, which have many similar stories about Jesus and his teaching. John's Gospel is quite different from these three. The synoptic Gospels may have had some sources in common.

Progress towards the authoritative collection of writings that made up the New Testament was not smooth. There remained some disputes over a few individual books after the canon was generally approved. The authenticity and authority of Hebrews, Revelation and 2 Peter was decided only in the fourth century, and all three are now accepted. The Epistle of Barnabas (another close companion of Paul), the writings of Clement, and the Didachē (Teaching of the Twelve) were all counted as authoritative by large numbers of early Christians, but they are not now part of the Bible.

Ways of interpreting the Bible

To have a written source of authority is extremely important for Christians. On one level, a written source is immediately apparent to everyone who reads it. In practice, however, we have to remember that the Bible was written over a period of over 1,200 years by many different authors, who lived in different places and who had their own ideas about the events they were recording, and these influenced what and how they wrote. This also applies to readers of the Bible: every reader brings their own background, ideas, presuppositions and prejudices to the text. This explains why Christians disagree with each other about the meaning of biblical passages.

For example, some people believe that all Christian ministers/priests should be male and that gay marriage is a great **sin**, while others believe exactly the opposite – yet all appeal to the authority of the Bible to support their views. Broadly speaking, there are four approaches to interpreting the Bible that anyone studying it needs to be aware of. These are outlined below and summarized in table 1.2.

1 *Literalists* This group of Christians believe that the Holy Spirit inspired the human authors to write the exact words they did, and so the Bible contains the exact words of God. It is therefore completely without error, and the text must be read at 'face value' – i.e. every word must be taken literally. **Literalists** do not go as far as to interpret obvious metaphors (e.g., 'God is a rock', 'the Lord has stretched out his arm') as true. However, they would, for example, believe that what Jesus claims in Matthew 17:20 – 'If you have faith as small as a mustard seed, you can say to this mountain, "Move from here to there," and it will move' – can literally happen if the believer shows sufficient faith.

2 *Fundamentalists* These believe that the Bible is the *infallible* word of God – that is, there are no errors in the Bible. The Holy Spirit used human writers but inspired the exact words they wrote. Again, obvious metaphors are not taken literally. At GCSE level, the terms 'literalist' and '**fundamentalist**' may be used interchangeably. The only substantial difference between the two groups is that fundamentalists would allow for some degree of interpretation of the text. For example, they would not see the need to follow all 613 commandments in the Torah, even though the text insists on obedience. Neither would they think it compulsory to follow Jesus' command to the rich young man (Luke 18:22): 'Sell everything you have and give to the poor, and you will have treasure in heaven. Then come, follow me.'

Sin refers to something that is against the will of God.

A **literalist** is a Christian who takes the words in the Bible as literally true, because they are believed to be the actual words of God and that no interpretation is needed.

Infallible means 'incapable of error'.

A **fundamentalist** is a Christian who believes that many of the words in the Bible are literally true, though they may need some level of interpretation to make their meaning clear in the present day.

3   *Conservatives* Conservative Christians believe that the Bible is trustworthy and reliable. It can still be called the 'Word of God' because it was inspired by the Holy Spirit, who used human authors and their life experiences to write what they considered to be the truth about God and his actions in the world. Conservatives acknowledge that the many manuscripts of the Bible disagree about the exact text. However, they think that it is not the exact words but the message and general meaning of the text that are most important. For example, there are at least three different endings to Mark's Gospel, but Conservatives can understand each of them as having something to say to Christians today about the truth of Jesus' resurrection. They would take Jesus' statement 'They shall take up serpents; and if they drink any deadly thing, it shall not hurt them' (Mark 16:18) as *symbolically* rather than *literally* true. The same would be true when Jesus says, 'if your hand causes you to sin, cut it off and throw it away' (Matthew 5:30).

4   *Liberals* For **Liberals**, the Bible contains human reflections on the nature of God and his actions in the world. As such, it is an authoritative record for Christians to read, learn from and live their lives by. There is a range of opinions among Liberals as to the extent of God's role (if any) in the inspiration of the biblical writers. Some think that God had no role; others think that God guided and inspired the human authors in what they wrote, though not in the actual words they used. The most important things for a Liberal are the history, experiences and stories of ancient people, not the words of the text.

> A **liberal** is a Christian who believes that the Bible contains errors because it was written by human authors trying to reflect on their understanding of God's nature.

Table 1.2   Approaches to interpreting the Bible

Approaches to the Bible	Is it the Word of God?	Is it literal and accurate?
Literalist	Yes, the exact words of God	Yes, it is without errors of any kind
Fundamentalist	Yes, the exact words of God	Yes, but not everything should be taken at face value
Conservative	Yes, because God inspired the human authors	Symbolically true, not necessarily all literally true
Liberal	Human writings, inspired by God	Not necessarily accurate, but stories to interpret

Liberals understand that the biblical texts were composed over a long period of history by very different people who lived in disparate countries. These authors wrote about their beliefs concerning God's interaction with humans – about Abraham's faith and travels, Moses leading a people out of slavery into freedom, the prophets telling the Jews to obey God's laws, and many other things. These inspirational stories were not intended to be a historical record as people now would understand it. The authors used the literary forms of their day – myth, saga, legend, poetry and legal writing, as well as religious history. Liberals argue that we must interpret biblical stories in their original context so that Christians today may understand their meaning.

Outdated beliefs and cultural bias need to be dismissed so that the significance of God's actions through history may be properly understood.

For instance, Liberals see many biblical stories as having symbolic meaning. Genesis 1 outlines that the world was created in six days, with man and woman created on the sixth day. It does not provide a scientific account of how the universe began, but it does express religious and theological ideas about why God created the world. In a similar way, Jesus' miracles may be seen as exaggerated accounts of actual events. The feeding of the 5,000, for example, may be understood as the people's reaction to Jesus sharing some food with those close by and the rest of the crowd following his example. The exaggeration of the 'miracle' may have happened rather in the manner of 'Chinese whispers'. The message for Christians today might be that sharing resources is a good thing to do.

> **Task**
>
> Explain why different Christians disagree about the meaning of biblical passages.

Jesus

Jesus of Nazareth was a Jew who lived a little over 2,000 years ago in the land of Israel (called 'Palestine' at the time). At the age of thirty or so, he began to preach about the imminent coming of the Kingdom of God.

Many people reported that they witnessed miracles performed by Jesus, including individuals being healed and even being raised from the dead. Jesus gained a large number of followers who believed (NB on the basis of prophecies in the Jewish scriptures) that he was the Messiah. The four Gospels record aspects of his life, and there are references to several occasions when he experienced God speaking to him. Christians believe that Jesus understood the purpose of his life was to achieve salvation for the human race through his own death. The Roman authorities brought this about when they crucified Jesus on a charge of sedition.

Shortly after his death, there were widespread reports of Jesus being seen by his disciples. People remembered that he had predicted his death and resurrection on several occasions. His first followers were all Jews, but soon a growing number of gentiles began to join what became known as the Christian Church.

The person of Jesus is absolutely central to Christianity and, as its founder, is its most important source of authority. This authority is founded on several key ideas.

Monotheism is the belief that there is only one God. Both Christianity and Islam are monotheistic religions.

- Christians soon began to worship Jesus, pray to him, and refer to him as 'the Lord' (a title previously strictly reserved only for God himself). He was quickly recognized not only as a messenger from God but as the Son of God, or even God himself in human form. This idea caused a lot of problems for his earliest Jewish followers, as it seemed to be contrary to their strict **monotheistic** beliefs. It is very likely that his original disciples thought of Jesus as a human being, possibly the Messiah, who was sent by God. The earliest of the four Gospels (Mark) does not refer to Jesus as 'God', though the latest Gospel (John) has this as its most important theme.

- Jesus is believed to have lived a perfect, sinless life. Though he was tempted to sin, he always resisted and is therefore seen as a perfect moral example. The book of Hebrews (4:15) says 'he was tempted in every way as we are, and yet was without sin.'

- In Jesus' life, death and resurrection, Christians understand the saving actions of God in human history. God himself has bestowed ultimate authority on his Son, Jesus. For example, at Jesus' transfiguration (Matthew 17:1–9; Mark 9:2–8; Luke 9:22–34), a voice came from heaven, saying, 'This is my Son in whom I am well pleased. Listen to him.' The most important sign of Jesus' authority is the resurrection. Christians believe that he was brought back to life by God and will never die again. If this is correct, then Jesus must be uniquely special and therefore trustworthy. He is therefore the only person who may talk authoritatively on life after death and how to live in order to overcome death.

- The miracles that Jesus apparently performed endowed him with lasting influence: if he has the power to heal the sick, raise the dead, calm the wind and waves, etc., then he must be uniquely special and important. His extraordinary actions convince people of his authority.

> A **doctrine** is an official belief of a religion – for example, the Trinity in Christianity or the Five Pillars in Islam.

> **Theology** is the study of God and his actions in the world.

Taking it further

For Christians, the idea that Jesus is the ultimate authority is central. Christian faith is focused on him: the events of his life, death and resurrection are the foundation of Christianity – without them, Christianity would not exist. However, this is a very difficult idea to understand. Jesus of Nazareth was a historical figure, so there ought to be some reliable evidence concerning what happened during his life, what kind of person he was and what he really said and did.

However, since the early centuries of the Church, **doctrines** *about* Jesus were developed, and these have often taken priority in Christian thought, even though they bear little relation to the historical events of his life. For example, there were great debates in the early Church regarding the divinity of Jesus, his real humanity, the precise ways in which he could be both human and divine, his relationships to God the Father and to the Holy Spirit, and so on. The theologians who developed these doctrines did not question the reliability and accuracy of the historical records (primarily the Gospels).

This whole issue came to the forefront of Christian **theology** in the mid-nineteenth century. Liberal theologians and biblical scholars began to cast doubt on the historical reliability of certain aspects of the biblical accounts of Jesus' life, and they attempted to identify the real person in what became known as 'the Quest of the Historical Jesus'. Many people expressed the idea that the historical events of his life were not that important anyway, and what mattered was personal faith in the resurrected Jesus and the difference this faith makes to the individual's experience of life. This was known as the 'Jesus of history vs. Christ of faith' debate.

The problem in using Jesus as the supreme source of authority is that we cannot be certain about what he said or what he did. The authors of the Gospels had their own beliefs about his significance, and they used the stories they had to put their beliefs in writing. For instance, Mark saw Jesus as the Messiah, a human figure sent by God to save people from sin and death. John, on the other hand, saw Jesus as God Incarnate in human form, who existed from the beginning of the universe, and whose miracles were 'signs' of who he was. It therefore seems that Christians must realize that, although Jesus can still be seen as the most important source of authority, we cannot have a clear picture of the historical figure. We understand him only as seen through the eyes of the many early theologians of the Church who philosophized about his significance.

Task

Do you think that accurate records of Jesus' life, death and resurrection are essential for faith? Give reasons for your answer.

The Apostles

Apostles is the collective name given to the original 12 disciples of Jesus (minus Judas Iscariot) who became the leaders of the Christian Church.

The **Apostles** (i.e., Jesus' twelve disciples, minus Judas Iscariot) were from the very beginning of Christianity endowed with great authority. As Jesus' closest companions during his life, they inherited their authority directly from him. Jesus had specifically chosen them to be his key disciples and had taught them for the three years or so of his public ministry. On several occasions, the Gospels record him specifically granting authority to the Twelve. For example, Matthew 10:1: 'Jesus summoned His twelve disciples and gave them authority over unclean spirits, to cast them out, and to heal every kind of disease and every kind of sickness.'

The word 'apostle' literally means 'messenger', and all of the first Apostles undertook some missionary work. The role of an apostle in the early Church, however, consisted of much more than going out to gain converts to the new faith: they were seen as specially appointed leaders responsible for the founding, establishment, growth and maturity of the Church.

In addition to the original disciples, there were others in the early Church called apostles. James, Jesus' brother, became the leader of the Church in Jerusalem. Paul and his friend Barnabas also bore this title. In his letters, Paul refers to several others as apostles. It seems that the authority of an apostle, particularly the members of the original group, was one that was conferred upon them. This authority could then be passed on to others, but it should always ultimately be derived from Jesus himself. The Apostles used their authority to shape the teachings of the Church, such as stating that non-Jewish converts to Christianity did not have to be circumcised (which was part of Jewish Law from the Old Testament).

Task

Explain why it might have been important for the early Christians to give authority to those who had some clear connection with Jesus.

Individual religious experience as a source of authority

There are several different types of **religious experience**, each of which can be seen as a source of authority for Christians. These include *conversions* (e.g., St Augustine, Samuel Wesley, Nicky Cruz), *mystical experiences* (e.g., St Teresa of Avila, St Bonaventure, St John of the Cross), *revelations* (e.g., Moses, John the Apostle, Martin Luther), and *visions* (Isaiah, Ezekiel, Mother Julian of Norwich). You can find out more about religious experiences in chapter 4, pp. 67–80.

> **Task**
>
> Find some information about each of these types of religious experiences. Choose one of the examples of those who have had that experience to see how he or she was affected by it.

The authority of such an experience rests in how far it convinces both the individual who has undergone it and others of its substance. If the experience is real and not imagined, and if it really comes from God, then it certainly carries great weight as a guide to faith and practice. If the experience is not real, then it carries no religious authority at all. If the experience is real but has come only from the emotional state of the person, then similarly it has no real religious force.

For people who actually have a religious experience, such an event is hugely important. They are convinced that the experience was real and, usually, that it was from God. In some cases, the person can be overcome by the experience itself but confused about its origin. This is especially so if the experience or its effects conflict with the individual's previous beliefs or the teaching of other authorities. A famous example is St Teresa of Avila (1515–1582), who had many overwhelming mystical experiences but became very worried that she might be deluding herself, and that they were the result of mental illness or psychological disturbance. She allowed herself to be guided by the authority of her superiors in the convent, who investigated the occurrences and agreed that they were genuinely from God.

Genuine religious experiences have a range of effects on a person's life:

- they can confirm or convince the person of the reality of God
- they can produce or enlarge a sense of value or worth in life
- they can inspire a sense of morality, characterized by love
- they can give a greater depth of experience, characterized by peace.

> **Task**
>
> There are many examples of religious experiences, but one of the most interesting, and one which was quite recent, occurred at Medjugorje in Bosnia-Herzegovina in the 1980s. Six children had mystical experiences of the Virgin Mary, who gave them messages of peace for the world. Find out about the children and produce a report on who they were, what they experienced, how long the messages lasted for, and what reactions they caused.

A **religious experience** is when an individual or group believes that they have received a special message from God, typically by having a vision, conversion or mystical experience.

A **vision** is a form of religious experience in which the person 'sees' God or another holy figure.

The **Principle of Testimony** is Swinburne's idea that what people say is probably genuine.

The **Principle of Credulity** is Swinburne's idea that how things seem to be is a good guide to how they are.

The word **tradition** actually means *handing down* something to someone else. A capital 'T' is used for sacred Tradition to distinguish it from traditions that are just customs or habits.

In deciding whether someone's religious experience is authoritative for other Christians, a key question is how to measure if they are genuine. Christian scholars tend to use what are called the '**Principle of Testimony**' and the '**Principle of Credulity**', which were formulated by the English theologian Richard Swinburne. He said that we need to think about

1 the likelihood that these experiences are real to the person who experiences them (i.e., that they are not hoaxes)
2 the likelihood that these experiences have their origin in God (i.e., that the person is not mistaken about the nature of their experience).

If both of these principles are confirmed, then the person's religious experience should be thought of as genuine. If neither, or only one, is confirmed, then it is not a genuine religious experience.

Tradition as a source of authority

Tradition is an important source of authority for many Christians, especially Roman Catholics. For many people, the past has enormous value. The fact that something has been done for hundreds or thousands of years gives it a strong sense of authority. If many people in the past have felt that a particular belief or practice is correct, then it seems arrogant for us to reject it without some overriding authority. Religion is an aspect of human existence that particularly values continuity, stability and the wisdom of the past. It is not that change and development are not recognized or valued in themselves but, rather, that change and development should take place within the context of an accepted body of belief and practice that can be used to measure the value or quality of new ideas. In the context of busy twenty-first-century lifestyles, with constantly changing values, severe social problems, rising crime, family break-ups, depression and anxiety, many people want a return to 'traditional values'.

Christianity has been a powerful force for positive change in societies, but often by way of upholding traditional values such as justice in situations where they have been neglected. For example, the movement to abolish slavery in Britain was led by William Wilberforce on the basis of biblical ideas about equality and justice. His inspiration was the slave trader John Newton, who was converted to Christianity (the composer of the hymn 'Amazing Grace').

'**Tradition**', as a theological concept, has been associated mostly with the Roman Catholic Church. Catholics understand tradition as descending ultimately from Jesus Christ. For them, it is a living gift that Christ gave to the Apostles and has been handed down from generation to generation, and it is how the Holy Spirit makes the risen Jesus present among Christians today.

So then, brethren, stand firm and hold to the traditions which you were taught by us, either by word of mouth or by letter. (2 Thessalonians 2:15)

For I received from the Lord what I also handed on to you . . . (1 Corinthians 11:23)

Task

Look up the following references in the Bible and see what they have to say about the source of tradition: 1 Corinthians 15:3; 2 Timothy 1:11–14; 2:1–2; Jude 1:3.

Taking it further

Roman Catholics believe that the Apostles were commissioned to pass on the authentic Tradition, which is therefore firmly rooted and legitimized. The Apostles dedicated their lives to the mission of passing on the message of Jesus and then appointed other faithful Christians to succeed them and carry on the work.

The Roman Catholic Church has affirmed this idea. The document *Dei Verbum* ('On Divine Revelation') was written after the Second Vatican Council (which took place between 1962 and 1965) and contains definitive teaching on the meaning of Tradition for all Catholics. It includes the following statements, showing that Tradition comes from Christ and was handed down by the Apostles:

> In His gracious goodness, God has seen to it that what He had revealed for the salvation of all nations would abide perpetually in its full integrity and be handed on to all generations. Therefore Christ the Lord in whom the full revelation of the supreme God is brought to completion . . . commissioned the Apostles to preach to all men that Gospel which is the source of all saving truth and moral teaching, and to impart to them heavenly gifts. (*Dei Verbum*, 7)
>
> This commission was faithfully fulfilled by the Apostles who, by their oral preaching, by example, and by observances handed on what they had received from the lips of Christ, from living with Him, and from what He did, or what they had learned through the prompting of the Holy Spirit. The commission was fulfilled, too, by those Apostles and apostolic men who under the inspiration of the same Holy Spirit committed the message of salvation to writing. (*Dei Verbum*, 7)

Religious leaders as sources of authority

The obvious examples of religious leaders as sources of authority are Jesus, the Apostles and other biblical characters. As we have talked about some of them already, however, we will mention briefly some other authoritative religious leaders in this section, focusing on Roman Catholicism.

Throughout Christian history, there have been influential and authoritative individuals who have led the Church to develop new ideas, doctrines and practices and to explain these to both Christians and non-Christians. Individuals such as Irenaeus, Tertullian, Origen, Clement of Alexandria, Justin Martyr, Jerome and Augustine of Hippo all had such authority, as did many saints and scholars of later times. The most significant Christian leader, however, has been the Pope. The papacy, of course, is an office occupied by one person at a time. The current Pope, who was elected on 13 March 2013, is Pope Francis, the 266th individual to serve in this position.

The institution of the papacy in Catholic Christianity is traced back to Jesus, who appointed Peter and his successors as shepherds of the Christian flock. At the end of

Pope Francis is the head of the Roman Catholic Church. Roman Catholics believe that he is a figure of authority because he is the successor of St Peter.

Papal infallibility is a doctrine in the Roman Catholic Church which says that, when the Pope speaks '*ex cathedra*', whatever he says has God's authority and becomes Christian doctrine.

Dogma refers to key principles of faith, such as transubstantiation for Roman Catholic Christians or belief in angels and the day of destiny for Muslims.

John's Gospel (21:15–17), Jesus gives Peter the authority to lead the followers of Jesus with the words 'feed my sheep'. The Pope shows his authority through his teaching and preaching role. He has a major influence on individual Christians when he preaches the message of God's love to non-Christians and shows compassion and love for believers as he travels widely around the world meeting fellow Christians, encouraging them in their beliefs and faith. At the First Vatican Council, in 1869–70, the Pope's authority was declared to be 'infallible'. **Papal infallibility** is a **dogma** that states that, because of the promise of Jesus to Peter, the leader of the Apostles (Matthew 16:18), the Pope is preserved from the possibility of error.

Taking it further

For Catholics, the Pope's foremost role is that of the supreme pastor. This means that he demonstrates the same love and concern for every individual Christian as Jesus did. The Pope should get to know ordinary people, understand how they live and share their sufferings and joys.

Another papal role is to unify the people of God. Christianity has spread throughout the world so is an international religion. This creates many demands on its leader, who has to use his authority to balance the worldwide nature of the Church with the power and needs of local churches. The Pope, through many archbishops, bishops and others, has to guide and inspire Catholics as they live their daily lives and in confronting difficulties with the faith around the world – issues such as the use of contraception or women priests. The Pope also has to build relationships with other Christian denominations and their leaders.

One of the many titles of the Pope is 'successor of St Peter, Prince of the Apostles'. This authority was confirmed in the statement from the Second Vatican Council: 'The Roman Pontiff, as the successor of Peter, is the perpetual and visible source and foundation of the unity both of the bishops and of the whole body of the faithful' (*Lumen Gentium*, 23). The doctrine of papal infallibility states: 'when, in the exercise of his office as shepherd and teacher of all Christians, in virtue of his supreme apostolic authority, he defines a doctrine concerning faith or morals to be held by the whole Church' (*First Dogmatic Constitution on the Church*, chapter 4, 9).

In Catholic theology, there are several areas in which the Pope might speak 'infallibly': on revelation, scripture, Tradition and the magisterium (the teaching role of the Church). If he were to speak 'infallibly', it is called speaking **ex cathedra** (i.e., 'from the chair' that is the symbol of his authority). What he said would have to conform to already established beliefs understood as being derived from scripture and tradition. *Ex cathedra* statements are considered to have apostolic and divine authority. This power was declared in 1870 and has been used only extremely rarely. The best-known example was when, in 1950, Pope Pius XII defined the doctrine of the Assumption of Mary as an article of faith.

Tasks

Find out more about the idea of papal infallibility and how it is linked with the Pope's authority.

Find out how the authority of the Pope has come into conflict with the authority of secular leaders. You might start with some of those that took place in the medieval period, such as Henry VIII's divorce from Catherine of Aragon.

Do you think it is correct for one individual to have this much power? Give your reasons.

Ex cathedra statements are considered to have apostolic and divine authority. Only the Pope may make this kind of statement.

Natural law as a source of authority

In Romans 1:20, the Apostle Paul argued that God's law may be seen in the world: 'Ever since the creation of the world, his invisible nature, namely his eternal power and deity, has been clearly perceived in the things that have been made.' Christian theologians, particularly St Thomas Aquinas in the thirteenth century, used this statement to develop a belief that, because God has made his moral law clear in the world, humans can have no excuse for disobeying it. God provided humans with the power of reason so that they would be able to discern God's law in nature. Aquinas thought there were four kinds of law:

- eternal law – God's will and wisdom
- divine law – where the eternal law is revealed (shown) in the Bible and the Church's teachings
- **natural law** – where God's wisdom is shown

Natural law refers to the idea that God, when he created the universe, implanted certain fundamental laws that both nature and humans should obey.

- human law – which is derived from natural law. Human laws are seen to be an extension of divine and natural law.

For Catholics today, natural law is still an important source of authority, particularly when it comes to moral issues. For instance, when, in the Old Testament, Cain killed his brother Abel (both sons of Adam and Eve), even though the Ten Commandments (including 'Thou shall not kill') had not yet been written, Cain was guilty of sin because he would have instinctively known it was wrong to kill. The same goes for serious crimes committed by people who may not have read or heard of the Bible – the idea is that all humans instinctively know God's law in nature, including the law that it is wrong to kill.

One of the strengths of natural law is that it appeals to people's sense that morality is more than just opinions about what is right and what is wrong. It upholds the idea that some things are of intrinsic value. This means that they apply to everyone, not just to some people. Another strength is that, because these moral laws come from God, they are absolute and must always be obeyed. Moral decisions about abortion, for example, do not depend upon the circumstances at the time but are always the same, regardless of who is involved or what their circumstances are. As we shall see in later chapters, natural law has a very important voice in the discussion of Catholic views on moral issues.

Conscience as a source of authority

Conscience is a faculty that helps humans to reflect on their actions; it is seen as a guardian of a believer's moral health.

Individual **conscience** is an important source of authority for many Christians, particularly Roman Catholics. Conscience was defined by Bishop Butler (1692–1752) as 'a principle of reflection in men, by which they distinguish between and disapprove their own actions'. According to the Catechism of the Catholic Church,

> Deep within his conscience man discovers a law which he has not laid upon himself but he must obey. Its voice, ever calling him to love and to do what is good and to avoid evil, sounds in his heart at the right moment. . . . For man has in his heart a law inscribed by God. . . . His conscience is man's most secret core and his sanctuary. There he is alone with God whose voice echoes in his depths. (Part III, Section 1, Chapter 1, Article 6)

From these statements, therefore, we can see that conscience plays a very important part in how Christians should make moral decisions. Individuals may have the right to 'object' to a law on the basis of their individual conscience. A medical doctor, for instance, may object for conscientious reasons to performing an abortion because she thinks it is contrary to her Christian beliefs.

The importance of conscience for Christians is strengthened because it is discussed in the Bible. The New Testament sees the conscience as the guardian of a believer's moral health. Conscience is a God-given capacity to help humans decide whether they have acted according to God's laws (1 Corinthians 4:4; Romans 2:14–15). It is seen as a 'witness' to something and can be 'good' or 'clear' (Romans 2:15; 9:1; 2 Corinthians 1:12; 4:2; 5:11). Conscience is understood as a witness because it is not an independent authority and does not make judgements by itself. A witness in court does not create evidence but has to report or respond to evidence that already exists. In this sense, the conscience does not dictate the content of what is right or wrong; it reacts to what is right or wrong. This is why a person can feel guilty about having undertaken a particular action, because they know they have chosen to do the 'wrong' rather than the 'right' thing. Conscience, therefore, can be 'weak' or 'strong' (1 Corinthians 8:12; 10).

Some people think that using conscience as a moral guide can lead to errors of judgement. The philosophers Thomas Hobbes and David Hume rejected conscience as being too subjective – different people can have very different opinions on what is right and wrong. The psychologist Sigmund Freud thought that the guilt that people feel comes not from God-given conscience but is the unhealthy product of negative family relationships in childhood. However, most Christians agree that conscience is a uniquely human characteristic and that it becomes more effective and helpful with experience and through God's grace.

> **The Qur'an**
> is the Muslim holy book, believed to have been revealed to the Prophet Muhammad. It consists of 114 surahs (chapters), each of which is sub-divided into ayats (verses).

Sources of authority in Islam

Table 1.3 shows the sources of authority in Islam to be discussed in this section.

Table 1.3 Sources of authority in Islam	
The Qur'an	The Holy Book of Islam, containing the speech of Allah
Sunnah and ahadith	The sayings and actions of the Prophet Muhammad
Religious experiences	In Sufism, mystical experiences bring believers into contact with Allah
Fiqh	The body of rules and laws based on understandings of Islamic principles

The Qur'an

ISLAM

In the world today there are over 1 billion Muslims, who regard the **Qur'an** as Allah's last revelation and a supreme source of authority. Many think of it as the direct speech of Allah. **Surah** 2, *al-Baqarah* (The Cow), says: 'This is the Book. In it is guidance without doubt for those who fear God.' The word 'qur'an' is used about seventy times in the book and has several differing meanings, but the core meaning is 'the recitation'.

Muslims believe that the Qur'an was revealed by Allah to the Prophet Muhammad through the angel Gabriel (Jibril). This took place gradually over a period of about twenty-three years, beginning on 22 December 609 CE, when Muhammad was forty, and concluding in 632 CE, the year that he died. Every verse of the Qur'an was spoken by the Angel Jibril to Muhammad, and he was given the ability to write it down, even though he had not previously learned to write. Muslims regard the Qur'an as the pinnacle of the revelations of Allah to the prophets, starting with Adam and ending with Muhammad – proof to many that Muhammad was divinely inspired. Some traditions

> A **surah**
> is a major division (or chapter) in the Qur'an. There are 114 surahs.

The Qur'an is the Muslim holy book. Muslims believe it is the Word of God revealed to the Prophet Muhammad by the angel Jibril.

in Islam say that, when the Prophet received the messages from Jibril, he recited them word for word and his companions wrote them down immediately afterwards.

For many Muslims, the Qur'an is more than a sacred book: it is the speech or actual words of Allah. Other religions have their sacred texts, but only Islam has the speech of Allah. The Qur'an came to be regarded as 'uncreated', and therefore it exists alongside Allah. This idea is similar to the way that Christians believe Christ is coexistent with God. Because of this status, no Muslim should hold a copy of the Qur'an unless he or she is in a state of ritual purity. The way the Arabic is pronounced is just as important as the meaning of the words. The style of language used, which is very elegant, is thought to be finer than any poetic or other literature written in Arabic since. In fact, Surah 10:37–8 sets out a challenge to anyone who thinks they can produce even one chapter that achieves the same level of elegance as the Qur'an:

> And it was not [possible] for this Qur'an to be produced by other than Allah . . .. Or do they say [about the Prophet], 'He invented it?' Say, 'Then bring forth a surah like it and call upon [for assistance] whomever you can besides Allah, if you should be truthful.'

Another reason that Muslims believe that the Qur'an is supremely authoritative is that Allah has protected it from change or corruption, and it contains the exact words of Allah. Other holy books are mentioned in the Qur'an – Tawrat, Zabur and Injil – but these have lost their original wording and have been altered and edited over the years, so they are neither accurate nor authoritative. Further, Muslims read and recite the Qur'an in the original Arabic, not in translation, which is believed to preserve its authenticity and means that they may be certain that their knowledge of Allah in the Qur'an is correct. Although the book has been translated into many of the world's languages, some Muslim scholars believe this may bring errors into the sacred text.

Studying the Qur'an encourages Muslims to lead a life that reflects the message of peace it contains; it offers support to people in times of need or hardship and can bring inner peace to those who reflect on its divine message. These points support the view that the Qur'an is true to the claim it makes of itself, that it is 'a straight path in which there is no doubt'. Its verses may be unchanging, but they are capable of being interpreted in a variety of contexts and of being explored and relevant as people and societies change.

The Sunnah and ahadith as sources of authority

The word 'sunna' in Arabic means 'a clear and well-worn path'. '**Sunnah**' refers to the sayings and deeds of the Prophet Muhammad and his practices to be followed by later Muslims. Given that Muhammad had been specially chosen by Allah to receive the Qur'an, it was natural for people to want to understand his teachings.

These teachings help Muslims today to live their lives according to Islamic principles in a world that is constantly changing, as the Sunnah deals with issues that are not specifically mentioned in the Qur'an. It is particularly important because it records the Prophet's teachings about family life, friends and government. Examples include instructions to speak softly and politely, to visit a Muslim when he or she is sick, and not to complain about food you don't like. The Sunnah is second only to the Qur'an as the source of Islamic law.

An individual saying of the Prophet Muhammad is called a '**hadith**' (plural 'ahadith'). Originally, Muslim scholars who recorded everything they could concerning the life and teaching of Muhammad made a distinction between the Sunnah and the ahadith. The Sunnah was more akin to biographical information about the Prophet, while his sayings and teachings were contained in the ahadith. Over time, this distinction was lost, particularly as the ahadith became more and more popular and well known.

There are two kinds of ahadith – sacred (Qudsi) and prophetic. The prophetic ahadith are the wise sayings of the Prophet Muhammad, and they show him as a kind and compassionate man, full of practical wisdom. Muslim scholars claim that the sacred ahadith go back to Allah himself and provide traditions and messages that were not included in the Qur'an. This is why these ahadith are treated with a great deal of respect and hold huge authority for Muslims today. The Qudsi ahadith are studied constantly by scholars and are used to provide guidance for modern Muslims on many matters. For instance, Qudsi hadith 9 states that 'the first of his actions for which a servant of Allah will be held accountable on the Day of Resurrection will be his prayers.'

A very important aspect of the ahadith is their authenticity. Authentic ahadith are traced back through 'chains' of transmission, called the '***isnad***', to an individual who was close to the Prophet. Such a chain is similar to an email or text trail, showing a

The Arabic word **Sunnah** refers to the things the Prophet Muhammad said and did and how Muslims have put these into practice.

A **hadith** is an individual saying of the Prophet Muhammad. The plural form of this is **ahadith**.

Isnad is a 'chain' of comments on a hadith from several Muslim scholars.

conversation going back to the original email or text. Most ahadith contain a chain of credentials that demonstrate their reliability. Many chains can be traced back all the way to Aisha, the youngest wife of the Prophet Muhammad. Many scholars have spent a lifetime checking ahadith and sifting the genuine from the false. This task is considered to be a sacred duty. The principles used are:

- having a reliable 'chain' of transmission
- being consistent with the revelation in the Qur'an.

Any hadith that does not accord with both of these principles is discarded.

Taking it further

Of the hundreds of thousands of ahadith counted in the early centuries after the death of the Prophet Muhammad (one estimate of their number three hundred years later was 600,000), only about 1 per cent were accepted as genuine. Ahadith are classified as '*al-sahih*' (sound), '*al-hasan*' (adequate) or '*al-dai'if*' (weak). These are further subdivided into more than fifty categories (see www.al-islam.org/al-tawhid/vol1-n12–3/outlines-development-science-hadith-dr-mustafa-awliyai/part-3#kinds-hadith). Weak ahadith cannot be used in matters of law but can be helpful in spiritual and ethical discussions. **Sunni** Muslims today use six collections of ahadith:

Sunni Islam is the largest branch of Islam, with about 90% of Muslims worldwide.

- Sahih Muslim
- Sunan abu Dawud
- Sunan ibn Majah
- Sahih al-Bukhari
- Jami' at-Tirmidhe
- Sunan an-Nasa'i.

Shi'a Islam is a branch of Islam made up of about 10% of Muslims worldwide, most of whom live in Iran and Iraq.

These collections form the basis of Shari'a (Islamic) law. **Shi'a** Muslims use a different collection of ahadith, which are traced back to Ali, the early follower of the Prophet Muhammad.

Religious experience as a source of authority

As in Christianity, religious experience is an important source of authority in Islam. The main strand of religious experience (other than the revelations of the Prophet Muhammad and the Hajj – the pilgrimage to Mecca) that is important to consider is **Sufism**.

Sufism is a branch of Islam that focuses on mystical experience and personal relationship with God.

Sunni and Shi'a Muslims make up the two major branches of Islam. Apart from these is a third group – Sufis. Sufism is the overtly spiritual aspect of Islam. Sufis are not content to know about and perform the beliefs and practices of their religion; they want to experience its truth individually in a spiritual way. Another name for Sufism is '*Ihsan*', or 'sincerity', and the Sufis are sincere in their quest to feel as close to Allah as

Whirling Dervishes are Sufi Muslims who seek mystical experience of God through rituals and practices such as the whirling shown here, which gives them their name.

possible in a spiritual way, not just in an intellectual way. As Mona Siddiqui (in *How to Read the Quran*, p. 59) writes: 'For the Muslim mystics known as Sufis, external rituals are symbolic of an inner journey toward God, the ultimate and only reality.'

Sufis are mystics – people who have experienced Allah in such a personal way that they have been overcome by the experience, which brings about a change of lifestyle and outlook on life. It may be that this kind of episode happens only once in a person's life, or it may happen more frequently. Some individuals develop rituals and practices to attempt to induce a mystical state. One such group in Islam is the Sufi Whirling Dervishes.

Their mystical experience of Allah makes many Sufis want to give up the desire for worldly wealth and a luxurious life. They model themselves particularly on the first four caliphs, who were men of simple tastes and were very close to Allah. Sufis aim for a simple lifestyle, focusing on searching for spiritual truth to be found inside the person, not in material goods. They attempt to achieve this state by practices that overcome the appetites of the body and so realize a direct spiritual connection with Allah. In this state, they become so united with Allah that they lose their own consciousness and become part of Allah's consciousness.

Taking it further

Sufis follow a 'path' (*tariqah*), which is a method of achieving union with Allah. Each *tariqah* is known as an 'order', all of which are thought to date from the time of the Prophet Muhammad. Some orders practise silent meditation, others chanting or rhythmic dancing. The best-known Sufi order is the Mevlevi Order, commonly known as the Whirling Dervishes, who are based at the city of Konya in Turkey and were founded in the thirteenth century by Jalal ud-din Rumi (usually known just as Rumi). Rumi became the most famous and influential mystical poet in Islam, and his work talks of the spiritual journey of man's ascent through the mind and human love to the perfection of life with Allah.

Task

Read the following excerpts from Rumi's poetry and write a paragraph on how they encapsulate his life's aim.

There are many roads to the Ka'bah [the building at the centre of Islam's most sacred mosque in Mecca] . . . but lovers know that the true Holy Mosque is Union with Allah.

When the soul is attuned to Allah, every action becomes music. When the soul dances, every movement of life becomes a miracle.

Before the dancers perform, there is a recitation from the Qur'an. Another recitation follows the end of the dance, which shows that the dance is sacred. It is accompanied by music – a discontinuity from normal Muslim teaching, as music is not allowed in worship. There are twelve musicians and twelve dancers, who spin round and round while moving across the room, holding one hand raised towards heaven and pointing the other down to the earth. This symbolizes the idea that the dervishes are a conduit between God and humans, heaven and earth. Because they are performing a religious rite, their movements are ordered and controlled. The Sufi dervishes are held in very high esteem in the Muslim world and are considered to be a source of inspiration and authority in spiritual matters.

Fiqh as a source of authority

Fiqh
refers to God-given knowledge and understanding to help Muslims live their lives. It also refers to Muslim principles of law.

'**Fiqh**' is an important element in understanding how Muslims live their lives and is usually translated as 'jurisprudence', a word normally confined to legal circles, as it is concerned with the principles of law. In Islam it is understood, in a wider sense, as knowledge and understanding, particularly as it relates to how Muslims live their daily lives, as it also has to do with the way that such knowledge is put into practice. Fiqh is derived ultimately from the Qur'an and from the ahadith, the records of the sayings and example of the Prophet Muhammad. The system of Islamic law is called Shari'a. Fiqh, therefore, provides the principles behind Islamic law as well as guidelines for putting it into practice.

Fiqh divides human behaviour into five categories.

1 **Fard** are things that are compulsory and non-negotiable, such as daily prayer and fasting during Ramadan. These are duties that, if performed, will be rewarded; if they are not, the individual will be punished.

2 **Mandub** are things that are recommended but not compulsory, such as forgiving someone or doing a kind deed. These will be rewarded, but their omission does not lead to punishment.

3 **Mubah** are actions that are decided by the individual's conscience and are permissible because there is no religious objection to them. An example of this is **halal**, which is neither forbidden nor recommended. This word is most often encountered in the context of food and drink, but it can refer to all matters of daily life.

4 **Makruh** is anything that is inappropriate, distasteful or offensive. Such actions are not forbidden but are disapproved of. Examples would include divorce or smoking.

5 **Haram** are things that Muslims should never do and which attract punishment. Examples are gambling, homosexuality and drinking alcohol.

Haram
describes what is forbidden in Islam.

These five categories help Muslims in their daily behaviour. Most decisions required fall into the Mubah category, which is religiously neutral, and individuals have to be guided by their conscience in many instances. Because these categories are embedded in the laws of some Islamic states, any person who does something that is forbidden (haram), will be punished according to that country's law and treated as a criminal.

An important issue in relation to Shari'a law as a source of authority is how and by whom it is administered. Shari'a law operates as the legal system of some Muslim countries, such as Saudi Arabia, Iraq and Djibouti. In some places the laws are very strictly observed, and many examples have caused much controversy, particularly in Western European countries and North America. In Saudi Arabia, for instance, Shari'a law is the only legal code and the most important source of authority in that country, because the Prophet Muhammad was born there and Islam began there. Laws are strictly enforced according to statements in the Qur'an and the sayings and practice of the Prophet. It is well publicized in the Western world that thieves are publicly flogged or have a hand or foot amputated. These laws are relevant not just to Muslims but to all citizens and inhabitants, regardless of their nationality, religious beliefs or social status. Shari'a law is a source of authority for all people in Saudi Arabia.

There has been recent controversy about whether Shari'a courts are active in Britain and, if so, whether they are consistent with British law. There are fears, for instance, about Muslim women being discriminated against when family disputes are settled according to Shari'a law. One estimate is that there are more than eighty Shari'a courts in operation across Britain, often attached to mosques. While these are not courts of law, they act as 'councils' that make decisions on religious rather than legal matters, and they cannot make binding decisions that are contrary to British law.

A shari'a council at Birmingham Central Mosque. Shari'a councils, trained in Islamic law and teaching, are figures of authority on legal matters such as divorce.

Shari'a councils deal mostly with issues surrounding family life, such as religious divorce. It is quite clear that they do not make legal rulings about divorce, so, if a council declares that a couple is no longer married, this is only in a religious sense, not a legal sense. Under the law, the couple would still be legally married; if they want to divorce legally, they would still have to go through the same process as any other (non-Muslim) couple seeking a divorce. The Shari'a councils, then, are a recognized source of authority in Islam in Britain, but they cannot make decisions that have legal status or that are contrary to British law.

TICK THE TOPICS

Now you should tick all the relevant boxes for what you have learned in this chapter:

Sections	Topics	Tick
Religious text: Christianity	Bible	
Ways of interpreting the Bible	Literalist	
	Fundamentalist	
	Conservative	
	Liberal	
Sources of authority: Christianity	Jesus and the Apostles	
	Tradition	
	Religious leaders	
	Religious experience	
	Natural law	
	Conscience	
Religious text: Islam	Qur'an	
Sources of authority: Islam	Sunnah and ahadith	
	Religious experience	
	Fiqh	

2 The Existence of God

CONTENTS

In this chapter, you will study some of the most famous and important **arguments** for the existence of God. These are arguments that use reason and logic to try to show that it is reasonable to believe in God. However, since faith is such a personal thing for religious believers, it can be difficult to analyse.

Table 2.1 gives a very brief summary of each of the arguments for God's existence to be considered in this chapter.

Table 2.1 Arguments for God's existence	
Design argument	When we look at the world, we see order, complexity and purpose. This points to God's existence.
Cosmological argument	The very existence of the universe and how things happen in the world require a being such as God to provide a complete explanation.
Religious experience	Many religious people have unusual experiences (such as visions) that they claim come from God.
Miracles	Impossible things seem to happen to people. This may point to God's existence.

The design argument (or the teleological argument)

The design **argument** is probably the most common and best-known argument for the existence of God. It is very ancient – the first known version came from the ancient Greek philosopher Anaxagoras (c. 500 BCE), who argued that there was an 'intelligence' or 'mind' (*nous*) that gave the universe its natural order. Plato's teacher, Socrates, was probably the first philosopher to put forward a formal argument from design for the existence of the gods (he was a **polytheist** of course).

In a discussion with Protarchus, Socrates talks about the apparent order throughout nature, using as an example the way the parts of the human body seem to be adapted to each other, such as how the eyelids protect the eyeballs. According to Socrates, this could not have happened by chance, so must show wise planning in the universe by a loving creator.

> An **argument** is a reasoning process that gives carefully stated evidence leading to a conclusion that can be agreed or disagreed with.

> A **polytheist** is someone who believes in and may worship many gods.

Taking it further

Plato develops a design argument in his famous work *The Republic* (Book X) and in the *Timaeus,* where he argues that a cosmic creator, whom he calls the 'Demiurge', had supreme intelligence to design the world. The Demiurge did not have the power to create anything out of nothing (*ex nihilo*) but used the already existing material in the universe to create an orderly and beautiful world. Later, Plato's pupil Aristotle developed the idea of a creator of the entire cosmos, which, in his book *Metaphysics,* he referred to as the 'Prime Mover'. The idea of the Prime Mover becomes very important later in Christian philosophy, when St Thomas Aquinas uses it to refer to how God created the universe. Aristotle argued that the whole of nature displays an inherent purpose and direction. Aquinas' arguments will be discussed below (see pp. 29–31). In the first century BCE, the Roman writer Cicero also formulated a design argument. In his work *De natura deorum* (*On the Nature of the Gods*), he maintained that there is a divine power to be found in the principle of reason that pervades the whole universe:

> When you see a sundial or a water-clock, you see that it tells the time by design and not by chance. How then can you imagine that the universe as a whole is devoid of purpose and intelligence, when it embraces everything, including these artifacts themselves and their artificers? (*De natura deorum,* ii. 34)

Design arguments for God's existence have existed since the beginning of Christianity. St Paul says, in Romans 1:18–20:

> The wrath of God is being revealed from heaven against all the godlessness and wickedness of people, who suppress the truth by their wickedness, **19** since what may be known about God is plain to them, because God has made it plain to them. **20** For since the creation of the world God's invisible qualities – his eternal power and divine nature – have been clearly seen, being understood from what has been made, so that people are without excuse.

Paul is saying here that God's power and nature make it obvious that the universe has been created so that even godless and evil people should be able to see that it has been designed.

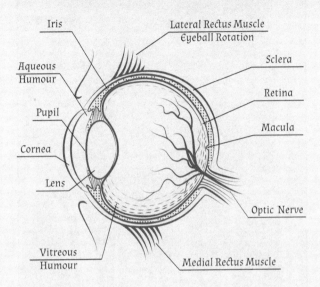

HUMAN EYE STRUCTURE

To many, the complexity of human organs such as the eye suggests that they must have been designed by a creator and could not have appeared by chance.

The early Christian writer Minucius Felix (late second century CE) used an analogy to argue for the existence of God:

> Supposing you went into a house and found everything neat, orderly and well-kept, surely you would assume it had a master, and one much better than the good things, his belongings; so in this house of the universe, when throughout heaven and earth you see the marks of foresight, order and law, may you not assume that the lord and author of the universe is fairer than the stars themselves or than any portions of the entire world?

And another influential early Christian thinker, St Augustine (354–430 CE), put forward the view that the world's 'well-ordered changes and movements', together with 'the beautiful appearance of all visible things', provided strong evidence that it it could only have been created by (the Christian) God.

Christian design arguments

The term *a posteriori* refers to a kind of argument based on evidence and experience.

St Thomas Aquinas (c. 1225–1274) was one of the greatest theologians and philosophers. His many writings influenced Christian thought and practice for many centuries, and his system of theology was so influential that it became known as 'Thomism'. He was made a saint in 1323. Aquinas developed five **a posteriori** arguments for the existence of God, known as 'the Five Ways' (*quinque viae*).

St Thomas Aquinas (1225–1274) was an Italian friar and philosopher whose work has been very influential in Roman Catholic theology in particular.

For Aquinas, the existence of God was not self-evident; it needed to be demonstrated, which he attempted to do by using reason and logic. The fifth of his 'ways' is a design argument. He says that the natural world shows evidence of purpose and order, and from this observation he infers that there must be an intelligent being who orders and creates a purpose for the universe. This, for Aquinas, must be God. Things do not simply exist randomly; instead they act for some reason or purpose (their *telos*). Aquinas does not provide any examples here, but he would have thought of plants growing in the correct conditions and the way that the seasons of the year operate. He sets out the argument in the following way.

1   The fifth way is taken from the way the world operates.
2   We see that natural bodies (e.g., trees) act for an end (to provide fruit or fuel), and this is evident because they usually act in the same way so as to obtain the best result.
3   So it is clear that they achieve their purpose not randomly but by design.

4 Now whatever lacks knowledge cannot move towards an end or purpose unless it is directed by some being which has knowledge and intelligence.

5 For example, an arrow cannot fly towards its target by itself; it must be fired by the archer.

6 Therefore, some intelligent being exists by whom all natural things are directed to their end, and we call this being God.

So we can see that Aquinas talks of two things in nature that point to the world being designed. The first is order ('Things usually act in the same way'); the second is that the order in the world seems to be beneficial. For Aquinas, the ordinary processes of the world, which are regular and orderly and bring about a beneficial result, seem to point to the existence of an intelligent designer. Beneficial order cannot occur by chance. This intelligent designer is what everyone calls God.

Tasks

The eighteenth-century philosopher Immanuel Kant said of the design argument: 'This proof always deserves to be mentioned with respect. It is the oldest, the clearest and the most accordant with the common reason of mankind.'

1 Make your own summary of Aquinas' argument. You might want to do it as a diagram or flow chart.

2 Do you agree with Kant's statement? Give your reasons.

Natural theology was the attempt by Christian scholars to find evidence of God's existence by looking at the natural world.

William Paley (1743–1805) was an English theologian and priest in the Anglican Church and served as archdeacon of Carlisle Cathedral from 1782 until his death. He wrote several books in defence of Christianity, the best known of which is *Natural Theology or Evidences of the Existence and Attributes of the Deity*, published in 1802. Paley assumes that it is the Christian God who designed the world – so his argument is an attempt to prove not only the existence of God but the existence of the Christian God – i.e., an all-knowing, all-powerful, all-good Being. Paley's readers would also have assumed these ideas of God. *Natural Theology* was a very popular and widely read book that is still used by Christians today in the debate about evolution and God's existence. Charles Darwin read it and for some time was convinced of the arguments Paley put forward.

In the eighteenth and nineteenth centuries, a popular way to argue for the existence of God was by using analogies. An analogy is a comparison between one thing and another, typically for the purpose of explanation – we would say one thing 'is like' something else, in order to clarify what that 'one thing' was. For example, if we wanted to explain what a unicorn was, we might say it is like a white horse with a horn on its head. The object of using analogies in arguing for God's existence was to show a

Design suggests that something shows order, complexity and purpose, as opposed to random existence.

resemblance between the production of things in nature and the production of things by humans. If this could be demonstrated, then, by the principle that similar effects imply similar causes, one might argue that the causes of those effects resembled one another.

Paley used the method of analogy to good effect in his version of the **design** argument by putting forward an analogy of a watchmaker. It is worth saying that Paley was not the first to use this analogy. It was used long before his time by the Roman Stoic philosopher Cicero (107–44 BCE), as well as later by the English philosopher Robert Hooke (1635–1703) and the French philosopher Voltaire (1694–1778).

Paley presented his version of the design argument in chapter 3 of his *Natural Theology*:

> In crossing a heath, suppose I pitched my foot against a stone, and were asked how the stone came to be there. I might possibly answer that, for anything I knew to the contrary, it had lain there forever; nor would it, perhaps, be very easy to show the absurdity of this answer. But suppose I found a watch upon the ground, and it should be inquired how the watch happened to be in that place, I should hardly think of the answer which I had before given – that, for anything I knew, the watch might always have been there. Yet why should not this answer serve for the watch as well as for the stone that happened to be lying on the ground? Why is it not as admissible in the second case as in the first? For this reason . . . that when we come to inspect the watch, we perceive . . . that its several parts are framed and put together for a purpose . . ..

Paley makes the point that a watch is a precise and intricate mechanism. It has parts that function together in a clearly defined way to perform a specific task – to tell the time. It would be highly unlikely that this complex mechanism should come about by chance or random factors: it is too complex and well designed. Paley continues by saying that the watch, precisely because it is complex and obviously purposeful, cannot have come about by chance. Some other explanation must be found, and he suggests that the only acceptable answer is that a watchmaker, an intelligent designer, must have made the watch. Only this interpretation explains the order, complexity and purpose of the watch.

Paley gives many other examples of complex and purposive mechanisms, including the human eye. The eye is certainly not an inanimate random lump of matter like the stone but, like the watch, is a complex and highly efficient mechanism at performing a function. In many ways, the human eye and the watch share the same characteristics. So, for Paley, the eye must have been designed in just the same way as the watch.

Paley takes this idea further; all the evidence from looking at things in nature (and most of Paley's book gives many examples from the natural world) points to the idea that there is a great deal of fine tuning in the world that helps to preserve life. There is the correct amount of water, the correct amount of heat, the right balance of gases, the ozone layer that protects humans from the sun's harmful radiation while allowing essential light energy through. Paley argued that it would be ridiculous to think that all this could be a product of chance factors or to suggest that all the order and complexity could just be due to some freak cosmic accident.

If it is accepted that these features of the universe are clear evidence of design and purpose, it must follow logically that anything that has a purpose must have an intelligent designer. For Paley, the only reasonable explanation for the complexity and order in the world is that the intelligent designer is God.

Summary of Paley's design argument

- The universe is made up of countless parts that function together in an ordered way.
- They work together to achieve a purpose.
- A universe so ordered and so complex could not come about by chance.
- Order, complexity and purpose are the products of design.
- There must have been a designer and creator of the universe.
- This designer and creator is God.

Task

Draw a diagram to explain Paley's analogy. Do you agree with the analogy? Give your reasons.

ISLAM

Islamic design arguments

The design or teleological argument for God's existence has been written about and discussed in Islam. Muslim scholars believe that the Qur'an offers guidance on the kind of evidence to use in the attempt to demonstrate God's existence. Surah 2:164, for instance, says:

> In the creation of the heavens and the earth; in the alternation of night and day; in the ships that sail the seas with goods for people; in the water which God sends down from the sky to give life to the earth when it has been barren, scattering all kinds of creatures over it; in the changing of the winds and clouds that run their appointed courses between the sky and earth: there are signs in all these for those who use their minds.

Several of the most famous and influential Muslim scholars have produced design arguments. Among these are Al-Ghazali (1058–1111), Ibn Rushd, often called Averroes (d. 1198 CE), and Fakhr al-Din al-Razi (1149–1209). Al-Razi wrote the following:

> Whoever contemplates the various parts of the higher and lower worlds will find that this world is constructed in the most advantageous and best manner, and the most superlative and perfect order. The mind unambiguously testifies that this state of affairs cannot be except by the governance of a wise and knowledgeable being.
> ('Matalib al- Aliya' 1, quoted in *The Cambridge Companion to Classical Islamic Theology*, p. 202)

Providence
is the idea that God provides for and takes care of humans.

In this passage, al-Razi distinguishes between two kinds of evidence of design in the world. The first is evidence of God's **providence**, or the advantages God has given to human beings – such as the way the world is constructed for the benefit of humans. The second type points to the signs of 'perfect order' in the universe. Both of these indicate a God who has supreme wisdom and power.

The signs of 'perfect order' can be found in both the 'lower world' and the 'higher world'. In the lower world – the human world – such entities as the human body, the human psyche, animals, plants, minerals and the elements show evidence of God's

A bee pollinates a plum blossom. The bee gets pollen and nectar, and the plum tree gets its flowers fertilized. The result provides fruit, which is food for creatures such as birds and, indeed, humans, showing how God's creation is ordered to provide harmoniously for living things.

perfect order. Each of these, says al-Razi, gives many examples of the complexity of creation. For example, the human body is studied in anatomy, plants in botany, and so on for each of the areas from the lower world. In the 'higher world', al-Razi includes the nature of the celestial spheres and the planets, their complex motions, and the way in which they influence the lower world that is beneficial for humans and other animals. He also discusses the ways in which daily, monthly and annual cycles of nature all depend upon the motions of the celestial bodies and the marvels that can be seen in the motion of the sun and the stars. Al-Razi's *Great Commentary* on the Qur'an gives many examples of how the evidence of God's design may be discerned by humans.

Criticisms of the design argument

There are several important criticisms of the design argument. Essentially, they fall into two areas: **philosophy** and science.

Criticisms from philosophy

The most important critic from philosophy was the Scottish philosopher **David Hume** (1711–1776). Hume's first criticism is based on the principle that, when we argue that one thing is like another, we do so on the basis of the available evidence and our experience. We have experience that watchmakers design watches. We do not have

Philosophy means the love of wisdom, involving argument concerning reality, persons, ethics and religion, among many other things.

experience that world-makers make worlds. Hume says that we cannot compare a watch with the world. We already know, from our experience, that a watch has been designed – we see many examples of watches, and we may know how they are made and about the skill required to make them. We can compare one watch with another. We cannot say the same about the world because we do not and cannot have any experience of seeing a world being made. There is only one world, and so we cannot compare it with another one to determine whether it is designed. The analogy of watch → watchmaker and world → world-maker is flawed and cannot prove the existence of God.

Hume's second philosophical criticism asks the question of why the design argument should conclude that there is only *one* God. There is no logical reason why there must be only one God who has designed the world. It is just as likely that a whole team of gods made the universe. Perhaps different gods took responsibility for different parts of the universe. Or perhaps an apprentice god practised his world-making skills and created the universe. Making the leap from the existence of the universe and the assumption that it has been designed does not lead to *one* God.

Hume further suggests that the world-maker may not have been perfect. When we look at the 'created' world, we see many imperfections – earthquakes, tsunamis, wars, diseases, murders, terrorism, to name only a few. It is not necessarily in perfect order, as Aquinas or al-Razi suggest. These imperfections do not lead us to think that an omnipotent, omniscient and benevolent God was responsible for the 'creation' of the universe.

Taking it further

Interestingly, Hume wrote about the weaknesses of the design argument twenty-three years before Paley produced his version. Many people have asked the question: Why did Paley not take Hume's criticisms into account? The answer is probably that Hume was quite unpopular in Britain until late in his life and his works were not widely read – indeed, some of his books were not published until after his death. His philosophical arguments were accepted only very gradually because few people read his books until the nineteenth century. Although Paley knew of Hume and his views, it seems that he was unaware of the latter's specific work on the design argument.

Anthropomorphism is a way of giving God human characteristics, such as having a body, being able to speak, and so on.

Another philosophical criticism of Paley's argument is that it leads to **anthropomorphism**. If there is a strong point in the design argument, it is the analogy between the universe and a mechanism. To be consistent, we would then have to think of the world-maker as resembling a human designer in some ways. This would lead us to ask whether God has a body or a gender, whether God is limited or mortal like humans. How far can we take this analogy? If these questions lead us to deny that there is a close resemblance between the world-maker and a human designer, then the strength of the analogy on which the argument hinges breaks down and the whole argument loses any force it might have.

Criticisms from science

The biologist and explorer **Charles Darwin** (1809–1882) is well known as the scientist who popularized the idea of **evolution**. He was not the first scientist to discover the evidence for evolution, but it is his groundbreaking book *The Origin of Species* that became an instant best-seller. As Richard Dawkins wrote, on the first page of *The Selfish Gene*, 'all attempts to understand humanity before 1859 are useless' (this was the original date of publication of *The Origin of Species*). In this book, Darwin provides an exhaustive theoretical explanation for how evolution works. Darwin had travelled to far-flung parts of the world to study animals in their natural environment, where he discovered that similarities between species might be explained by a common heredity – i.e., that they share a common ancestor. He called this phenomenon 'adaptation'.

When any species of animal reproduces, it passes on the DNA information contained within its genes to the next generation. Quite frequently, however, there are small variations in this genetic message so that the offspring differ slightly from their parents. For the most part these variations are irrelevant or a disadvantage, but occasionally they will give an animal a small advantage in its environment. For example, where the main source of food is leaves on trees, an animal born with a longer neck than other members of its species will have access to food the others cannot reach. This animal has 'adapted' to its environment and will pass on this genetic 'improvement' to the next generation. This is what Darwin calls '**natural selection**' or the 'survival of the fittest'.

> **Evolution**
> is the principle that living organisms change and develop over time so that only the fittest survive.

> **Natural selection**
> is Darwin's idea that animals and plants which are best adapted to their natural environment will survive and pass on their 'improvement' to the next generation.

> We will be looking in more detail at Darwin's theory of evolution in chapter 6, pp. 116–19.

Darwin's theory of evolution has radical implications for the design argument. **Richard Dawkins** (b. 1941) is a neo-Darwinist biologist who has written extensively on the conflict between science and religion. He agrees with those philosophers and theologians who see that the world is full of complexity and that this needs to be explained. However, for Dawkins, natural selection explains decisively why species appear to be suited to particular habitats. Natural selection is not, for Dawkins, an intelligent designer but is selective in the sense that, if a species does not adapt to changes in its environment, it will not survive. Evolution is a race where we see only the winners, and this is why it looks as if they have been designed for the race. It is not the result of real or actual design but just our imagination and mistaken perceptions.

For Dawkins, the appearance of design in the universe is an illusion. There is no God masterminding the process, only 'the blind, unconscious automatic process which Darwin discovered'. Darwin's discoveries make God redundant. For Dawkins, the design argument comes a poor second to natural selection, because natural selection is self-contained and self-explanatory.

Several philosophers and theologians take the view that science and the design argument are not contradictory and can be held together. These theologians have developed a new version of the design argument, called the **Anthropic Principle**, which states that everything in the universe was made specifically in order that humans could flourish. One of these theologians was **F. R. Tennant** (1866–1957), in his book *Philosophical Theology* (1928). Tennant argued that natural selection is entirely in agreement with God's purpose in creating the universe. Evolution is the means by which God created the universe, and God designed it to favour human life.

The **Anthropic Principle** is the idea that the universe was designed by God in order that humans could thrive in it.

This view of the Anthropic Principle has been developed further by scholars such as **John Polkinghorne** (b. 1930), a former nuclear physicist who became an Anglican priest and professor of theology. In *Beyond Science* (1966), Polkinghorne says that a universe that has produced life is a remarkable fact and that this calls for an explanation. The complexity and number of conditions necessary for the emergence of intelligent life cannot have happened by chance. Instead, he offers a theistic explanation:

> I believe . . . anthropic considerations are . . . part of a cumulative case for theism. I believe that in the delicate fine tuning of physical law, which has made the evolution of conscious beings possible, we receive a valuable, if indirect, hint from science that there is a divine meaning and purpose behind cosmic theory.

Polkinghorne is therefore saying that we can use scientific evidence to argue for a religious view of the origin of the universe. He bases this on the observation that the beauty of the natural laws of the universe suggests that it could not have come about by chance, so must have been designed. In his view, God is the 'total explanation for the design of the universe'.

Taking it further

Darwin thought that belief in natural selection and belief in God could be held together; in his view, they were not opposed to each other. In a letter to Asa Gray [1860], he said:

> With respect to the theological view of the question; this is always painful to me. I am bewildered. I had no intention to write atheistically. But I own that I cannot see as plainly as others do, and as I should wish to do, evidence of design and beneficence on all sides of us. There seems to me too much misery in the world. I cannot persuade myself that a beneficent and omnipotent God would have designedly created the Ichneumonidae with the express intention of their feeding within the living bodies of caterpillars, or that a cat should play with mice. . . . On the other hand, I cannot anyhow be contented to view this wonderful universe, and especially the nature of man, and to conclude that everything is the result of brute force. I am inclined to look on everything as resulting from designed laws, with the details, whether good or bad, left to the working out of what we may call chance.

> **Task**
>
> How would you respond to the following statement?
>
> 'Some people think that evolution by natural selection leads us immediately to abandon the design argument and a religious view of nature. Darwin was a religious man and evolution did not destroy his faith in God.'
>
> Give reasons for your answer.

> **Task**
>
> In chapter 3, we will be looking at the main characteristics of God's nature. In both Christianity and Islam, one of the core features of God's nature is benevolence – that is, God's goodness. For many religious believers, the theory of evolution, with its random mutations and developments, causes a serious problem to continued belief in a benevolent creator God.
>
> Read the following paragraph and give your response to the criticism it makes about the nature of God.
>
> I can't understand why a benevolent and loving God would create such a seemingly random and brutal process as natural selection. It is blind and utterly indifferent to suffering. Probably 98 per cent of all the species of animal that have ever existed on this planet have become extinct. This seems to me to be too incredibly wasteful for it to be the product of a loving creator. It also seems to me that the means by which some animals adapt to survive are incredibly cruel by our standards. Here is one example that horrified Darwin and admitted that it troubled his faith in God. There is a species of wasp that will paralyse its victims with its sting and then lay its eggs in its flesh. After a short time the eggs will hatch and the wasp larvae will begin to eat the still living host. To be sure this is a useful evolutionary adaptation, as the wasp larvae will get an advantageous start to their lives. But I cannot see how a benevolent God could create a process that actually contained so much suffering.

Cosmological arguments

Cosmological
means 'to do with the world' and is the name given to a group of arguments for God's existence based on cause and motion.

A **cosmological** argument is one that looks at the world (from the Greek word 'cosmos', meaning 'world'), searching for evidence that God exists. It does this by looking for evidence in the universe as a whole of alleged facts about causation, motion or change on a very general level and attributes these to God.

Islamic cosmological arguments

Kalam
is a Muslim argument that claims that God may be known by the application of human reasoning, not just by direct revelation from God.

In Islam, there is a long and distinguished tradition of arguing for God's existence by using cosmological arguments which pre-dates its Christian use. The best known of these arguments is the version by Al-Ghazali and is usually called the **Kalam** Argument.

The Kalam school of Islamic theology was founded in the tenth century by al-Ashari (878–941). The word '*kalam*' means 'discourse' or 'argument', suggesting that God could be known though the application of human reasoning, not just through revelation directly from God. The philosophy behind this moderate school was strongly

ISLAM

based on the works of **Aristotle** (c. 384–322 BCE) and was originally written in Greek, but it was rediscovered by Muslim scholars and translated into Arabic at a time when they were unknown to Western philosophers. It became known to Western scholars only at the end of the twelfth century, and this was largely through the use that St Thomas Aquinas made of them in debating with the Kalam school of Islam.

> **Task**
>
> Research the Islamic scholar **Al-Kindi** (c. 801–873 CE) and note his version of the Kalam argument. What differences, if any, can you find between his version and that of Al-Ghazali below?

Al-Ghazali was worried that Muslim philosophers were being negatively influenced by the philosophy of Plato and Aristotle, to the extent that they were denying God's creation of the universe. They argued that, because the world had 'flowed' out of the body of God, there was no point at which the universe began. Al-Ghazali wrote *The Incoherence of the Philosophers* in order to counteract this un-Islamic view. For him, the idea that the universe had no beginning was logically and practically absurd. The universe, he said, must have a beginning, because nothing can come into existence without there being a cause; there must have been a beginning of the universe, and this must have been caused by the transcendent creator of the universe, God.

Al-Ghazali's very simple argument may be described as follows.

- Whatever begins to exist has a cause.
- The universe began to exist.
- Therefore, the universe had an initial cause.

This argument is based on a widely held – perhaps universally held – idea that everything has a cause, so that nothing can come from nothing. For instance, if you feel unwell and need to go to your GP, the doctor will ask you what your symptoms are and will assume that something has caused you to be unwell. No doctor will say that illness 'just happens' without something to cause it.

> **Task**
>
> Work out the cause of each of the following and note if any of the examples could have occurred without a cause.
>
> - It starts to snow outside.
> - A car engine starts.
> - You sneeze.
> - A coastal town suffers severe flooding.
> - Many people die when a gunman attacks a theatre performance.
> - An explosion occurs in someone's house.
> - A baby is born but dies within minutes.
> - A volcano erupts, causing devastation across a wide area and forces hundreds of people out of their houses.

Christian cosmological arguments

St Thomas Aquinas

The first version of a cosmological argument in Christianity was probably that of St Bonaventure (1221–1274), but the most famous version was produced by Aquinas, which has continued to be discussed and developed by subsequent philosophers and theologians up to the present day. One of the specific reasons why Aquinas used the cosmological argument was to provide guidance for Christian priests whose parishioners were being tempted away from Christianity towards Islam.

Aquinas developed five separate but linked arguments for the existence of God. These are known as the **'Five Ways'** to 'demonstrate' God's existence. Three of the Five Ways are cosmological arguments.

The first way is the argument from motion or change and may be summarized as follows.

- The universe exists.
- In the world, things are in motion or change.
- Whatever is in motion/change must have been put into motion/change by something else.
- This chain of motion/change cannot go back into infinity.
- Therefore there must have been a first or Prime Mover/Changer which is itself unmoved/unchanged by anything before it.
- This Prime or Unmoved Mover/Changer is God.

Let us take a simple example to explain what Aquinas means here. A tennis ball flies in through the window and knocks a glass off the table, smashing it. The glass

The **Five Ways** is the name given to five arguments for the existence of God by St Thomas Aquinas.

CHRISTIANITY
ROMAN
CATHOLICISM

For a chain of dominoes to fall, something must knock the first domino over. The source can be traced back along the dominoes to the original cause or first mover. Cosmological arguments trace back in a similar way to the original cause and first mover of the universe – God.

was moved (or knocked) by the tennis ball. The ball was moved (hit) by a tennis racquet, and the racquet was moved (swung) by an arm, which was moved by the person holding the tennis racquet, and so on. The chain of motion goes further and further back – but the chain of motion cannot go back forever. There is something that starts the motion, and, for Aquinas, this is God.

Taking it further

It may not be an earth-shattering start to claim that the universe exists, but Aquinas wants these arguments to answer the question of why there is a universe at all, so he has to begin with the statement that the universe does in fact exist. When Aquinas talks of 'motion', he means this in a very general sense; he means change of any kind, from one state to another. He uses the example of wood and how fire makes it hot. The fire changes the wood from its initial (cold) state into a different (hot) state. In his terms, the wood has the *potential* to become hot and the fire makes this potential *actual*. This is an idea Aquinas takes from Aristotelian philosophy. He does not believe in an infinite series of things being moved and says that, if there were an infinity of things being moved, there would be no beginning, no first movement, but that would mean that there could not be any subsequent movement and no movement now. It is clear that things are in motion now as we can see these all the time; therefore there must be an exception to this chain of moved things, and this must mean that there is an original, unmoved mover. Aquinas calls this God.

The second way is very similar to the first but focuses on cause and effect. It may be summarized as follows.

- The universe exists.
- Things are caused to come into being.
- Nothing can be the cause of itself.
- There cannot be an infinite chain of causes and effects.
- Therefore, there must have been a First Cause which is not caused to come into existence by anything before it.
- This First Cause is God.

Again, let us take an example. If I want to watch a TV programme, I must first turn on the TV. Before I can do that, the electricity must be working. For that to happen,

Taking it further

Aquinas here replaces motion or change with cause and effect. If something caused itself to exist, that would mean that it was its own cause, or that it existed before it existed. This is illogical and therefore not acceptable as an argument. Aquinas therefore rejects an infinite series of causes and effects and argues that there must be a first cause which was itself uncaused by anything before it. He understands this First Cause to be God.

I must have paid my bill, and so on. There is a connecting chain of cause and effect. Aquinas says, though, that this cannot go on into infinity. There must be a first cause which is not part of the chain. This is God.

The third way focuses on **necessity** and **contingency** and may be summarized as follows.

- Everything that exists came into existence, so has contingent existence.
- If everything that exists was contingent, there would have been a time when nothing existed.
- If there was a time when nothing existed, there could be nothing now.
- Things do exist now.
- Therefore there must have been something that was not contingent – i.e., had necessary existence.
- This necessary thing is God.

Let us take the simple example of families. You have (or had) parents, they had parents (your grandparents), who had parents, and so on back into the past. Each new generation is dependent on the previous one (i.e., you would not be here if it were not for your parents), but Aquinas says that this cannot go back into infinity. There must have been a first 'parent' to start everything off. For Aquinas, this was God.

> **Necessity** is a logical term used in some arguments for God's existence to conclude that God *must* exist – that he cannot *not* exist.

> **Contingency** is a logical term used in some arguments for the existence of God to conclude that everything there is, except God, came into existence and will cease to exist at some point.

Taking it further

According to Aquinas, everything that exists has 'existence'; it 'is'. Everything in the world that 'is' has come into existence; it did not always exist, and therefore it has 'contingent' existence. Anything we can think of has contingent existence – i.e., at some point it came into existence, and at some point it will cease to exist. To take just one example, at some point you came into existence (were born), and at some point you will cease to exist (you will die). Aquinas argues that, if everything in the universe were contingent, there would be a time when nothing existed. If this were true, however, then nothing could exist now. Things do exist now, so there must be something which is not contingent but has necessary existence, and this is God.

Leibniz's cosmological argument

The German philosopher **Gottfried Wilhelm Leibniz** (1646–1716) put forward a version of the cosmological argument which attempted to avoid one of the problems for which Aquinas was criticized – that of an infinite regress (see below). He asserts that everything in the universe has a 'sufficient reason' for its existence – that is, there is an explanation for why things are as they are. In this book *Theodicy* (1710), Leibniz argued as follows.

- Suppose you have a rare book on mathematics, the contents of which have been copied from one generation to the next through many generations.
- If you ask 'What is the explanation for this book?', the answer might be that it has been copied from a previous one, and that was copied from an earlier one still.
- You would not be satisfied with this answer, because you would want a full and

final explanation for the existence of the book – its ultimate cause. You would want to know why the original author decided to write the book.

- Leibniz calls this idea the '**Principle of Sufficient Reason**'.
- Everything has a sufficient reason for its existence, an ultimate explanation that is external to itself. As the universe cannot explain why it exists, there must be some other 'sufficient reason' for its existence.
- For Leibniz, the sufficient reason for the universe is God.

The **Principle of Sufficient Reason** is Leibniz's idea that everything has a reason for why it is what it is.

> **Task**
>
> If you feel brave, have a look at Richard Swinburne's version of the cosmological argument. Be warned: this is an advanced argument, and you may find it difficult to understand! Ask your teacher where you can find it, or enter 'Swinburne's version of the cosmological argument' into a search engine.

Criticisms of cosmological arguments

Many religious believers have accepted the cosmological argument and found it helpful for their belief in God. Others, however, have found it inadequate as a proof for the existence of God. The Scottish philosopher David Hume produced a devastating analysis of the argument in his *Dialogues Concerning Natural Religion*, which was published after his death. It is written as a dialogue or conversation on the nature of God between three characters. The main criticisms made by Hume (through the characters) are as follows.

Infinite regress refers to the idea that there is an unending chain of causes and effects, so that there was no beginning and will be no end.

1 *Infinite regress* Hume criticizes the idea that there cannot be an **infinite regress** of causes or motion. This is an attack on one of the fundamental parts of Aquinas' argument that there is a Prime Mover. Hume asks the question: Why can't there be an infinite chain of cause and effect? He says that it is perfectly possible for us to think of something that comes into existence from nothing without anything to cause it to do so. Hume does not claim that this has actually happened – only that it is possible to think that it could happen. As far as we can tell, the universe may have come into existence without any cause. If it is possible for Aquinas to argue that God could have existed without anything to cause his existence, then, logically, it is possible that the same is true of the universe. This means that matter could be eternal in just the same way as God is eternal and therefore needs no explanation for its existence.

Fallacy refers to an error in logic or a mistake made in an argument.

2 *The fallacy of composition* A '**fallacy**' is an argument that has a fault in it. Hume argues that, just because we know the causes of some individual things in the universe, it does not mean that the universe as a whole has a cause. The atheist philosopher **Bertrand Russell**, in a famous radio debate in 1948 with the Jesuit theologian **Frederick Copleston**, used the example of saying that every human being has a mother, but this does not mean that there is a mother for the human race. In his *A Treatise of Human Nature*, Book 1: *Of the Understanding*, Part 3: *Of Knowledge of Probability*, Hume gave the following example to illustrate his point, showing that it is necessary for a husband to have a wife, but it is not necessary for every man to be married:

> But this does not prove, that every being must be preceded by a cause; no more than it follows, because every husband must have a wife, that therefore every man must be marry'd. The true state of the question is, whether every object, which begins to exist, must owe its existence to a cause: and this I assert neither to be intuitively nor demonstratively certain . . .

Hume's point is that we know about causes within the universe, but this does not give us any right to conclude that there is a cause of the universe as a whole.

3 *Like causes resemble like effects* Hume says that all we can conclude from finite effects are finite causes, not an infinite one. All we can hope for and all that is reasonable to expect is that we can find some of the causes for a particular occurrence; we cannot expect to find every single cause. If this is true, the cause of a finite effect will be a finite one. It makes no sense at all to attribute every cause to God when it is God's existence that we are trying to prove! For instance, if you do something at school that is against the school rules, you might not be able to explain *all* the reasons why you did it. You might be able to explain some of them. If some of your friends also broke the same rules, they might have different reasons from yours, but the outcome for all of you might still be the same – a punishment of some sort. It does not mean that there is a *single overarching reason* for what happened. Hume is saying here that it is impossible to try to give a single explanation for the existence of the entire universe. There could be millions of reasons why it came into being. Saying that it was God explains nothing.

4 *Empirical to non-empirical evidence* One of the most serious criticisms comes from the Prussian philosopher **Immanuel Kant** (1724–1804) (Prussia was an independent state in Kant's day, but it is now part of northern Germany). Kant states that the argument is fundamentally flawed in that it moves from **empirical** evidence (our observations of what and how things happen in the actual world) to non-empirical projection (that there is a God). This is a logical error, because the conclusion that God exists is outside the sphere of our knowledge and experience of the world. The argument makes a false link between empirical and non-empirical evidence. This is rather like saying that, because children receive presents on Christmas Day (empirical evidence), then Father Christmas must exist (non-empirical projection). Kant here delivers a compelling criticism of the cosmological argument.

Empirical
means based on observations of what happens, and how, in the world around us.

The argument from religious experience

Religious experience is a very important aspect of the nature of any religion. We will be studying the types and authority of religious experience in more depth in chapter 4. Here we will be looking at it briefly as an argument given for the existence of God.

A religious experience is usually an experience that is out of the ordinary, that is different in some way and perhaps cannot be explained in normal terms. A person might 'see' a vision of God or a holy person or have a **conversion** from one set of beliefs to a different set of beliefs, typically from being atheist to believing in God. People who have these experiences often have difficulty in explaining them to others.

A **conversion** is a form of religious experience that causes a person to change radically, typically from being atheist to being religious.

In Christianity, for instance, the religious experiences of Jesus, his disciples or St Paul, or those recorded in the book of Revelation, give the impression that such occurrences are central to religious faith. In the Old Testament, Abraham, Moses and the prophets all had religious experiences. For instance, Abraham and Moses had visions of God where they were given tasks to undertake. Abraham was told to move from the Land of Ur to Canaan and was given promises by God, while Moses received a special message from God – the Ten Commandments. In Islam, the Prophet Muhammad had the Qur'an revealed to him over a long period of time, and other Muslims have had religious experiences.

There are many differing types of religious experience. The English philosopher **Richard Swinburne** (b. 1934) defined five different types, two of which are 'public' and three of which are 'private'. By 'public', Swinburne meant that they could be experienced by anyone who was present at the time, and by 'private' he meant that they could be experienced only by the person who had them.

- **Public 1:** Someone experiences God in a public place or object. Other people could explain this kind of religious experience in other ways. For example, someone might be walking along a lonely beach and see the glory of God's creation in the sunset. Someone else, walking along the same beach at the same time, might see only a lovely sunset.
- **Public 2:** Someone might experience a very unusual event that seems to break a natural law. The sun standing still or someone walking on water or appearing in a locked room would be examples of this kind of experience. A religious person would understand these events to be evidence of God, while an atheist might see them as inexplicable occurrences but not anything to do with God.
- **Private 1:** This would be an experience that an individual can describe by using ordinary language. Abraham's call by God to leave his home country and travel to Canaan or the appearance of the angel Gabriel to the Prophet Muhammad would be good examples.
- **Private 2:** This is an experience that seems very real to the person who has it but, because of its nature and intensity, cannot be described in normal language.
- **Private 3:** In this type, there is no actual experience, but an individual may feel that God is active in their life and looking after them.

Swinburne argues, in *The Existence of God* (1982), that there are two central principles that, because they are fundamental to rationality, give religious experiences validity as evidence of God's existence. These principles are the **Principle of Credulity** and the **Principle of Testimony**. Swinburne explains the Principle of Credulity as follows:

> How things seem to be is a good guide to how things are. From this it would follow that in the absence of special considerations, all religious experiences are to be taken by their subjects to be substantial grounds for the belief in the existence of their apparent object – God, or Mary, or Ultimate Reality, or Poseidon. (p. 270)

This principle appeals to common sense. When we see something, it is normally likely that we have actually seen what we think we have seen. We normally trust our senses

Some people who are cured of illnesses such as cancer may see their healing as the work of God. They might experience God's presence in difficult times and in the care they receive.

Task

Try to think of examples of each type of religious experience. Some have been given for you. Put your results in a grid like this.

Type	Example	Religious explanation	Non-religious explanation
Public 1	Feeling exhilarated after climbing to the top of a mountain		
Public 2			
Private 1	Having a lucid dream where you are given insight into a forthcoming event		
Private 2			
Private 3			

unless there are very good reasons not to do so. Swinburne explains the Principle of Testimony as follows:

> In the absence of special considerations the experiences of others are (probably) as they report them . . .. In general there are no special considerations for doubting what subjects report about their religious experiences. (p. 272)

Swinburne claims that most people naturally tell the truth unless there are 'special considerations' that lead them not to. Those who claim to have religious experiences are therefore probably telling the truth about them.

> **Task**
>
> If someone who was known to be a liar or a mentally disturbed person claimed to have had a religious experience, would you believe him or her? What if the same people claimed to have seen a car driving itself – would you believe them? Give reasons for your answer.

A number of challenges may be raised against accounts of religious experiences. We will look briefly at five.

1   If religious experiences are genuine, why do so few religious people have them?
2   Many religious experiences are 'private' for the individual who has them. Why, if they are genuine, are more not made public? Surely God would want to reveal his message or provide hope or guidance for as many believers as possible?
3   The psychologist **Sigmund Freud** (1856–1936) said that religious experiences are just wishful thinking. The human mind creates an illusion as a way of dealing with the outside world. For Freud, religion and, specifically, religious experiences are evidence of a 'neurotic illness' that can be explained as a kind of security blanket. Religious people need a divine figure to help them deal with the fact that they are alone in the world.
4   It is seen as a weak point that people who claim to have had a religious experience encounter only manifestations of their own religion, so a Christian will see Jesus or Mary, while a Hindu will see Krishna or another Hindu god. This means that each person will give a different description of their religious experience. If they were genuine, wouldn't all people have the same experience?
5   God is totally different from human beings. How, therefore, can there be any communication such as religious experiences?

The argument from miracles

A **miracle** is claimed to be an action of God in the world for the benefit of an individual or group of people.

Many religious people believe that God performs **miracles** or allows some humans to perform them. John 20:30–31 reports:

> Now Jesus did many other signs in the presence of his disciples that are not written in this book. But these are written that you may come to believe that Jesus is the Messiah, the Son of God, and that through this belief you may have life in his name.

Thirty-seven miracles enacted by Jesus are recorded in the Gospels, but only one (the feeding of the 5,000) is included in all four. Jesus is reported as having accomplished healing miracles, miracles over nature, exorcisms and raising of the dead. The Qur'an also mentions miracles performed by Jesus (such as the healing of the blind and lepers) and attributes miraculous events to the Prophet Muhammad, such as the splitting of the moon (54:1–2). The question here is – Do these (and other) miracles prove the existence of God?

A scene from the beatification of Mother Teresa of Calcutta, 2003. Beatification is a stage in the process of being made a saint by the Roman Catholic Church. Mother Teresa is on track to be made a saint because of miracles that have been attributed to her.

Those who say that miracles serve as good evidence that God exists will point to certain factors such as the fact that biblical miracles took place across a wide time span (recorded in at least fifteen books of the Bible) and that at least forty individuals or groups who were not Christian acknowledged that they actually occurred.

In very simple terms, the argument for the existence of God from miracles is as follows:

1   There have been miracles.
2   If there have been miracles, God exists.
3   Therefore God exists.

This is a valid argument, meaning that the premises lead logically to the conclusion. The more important question is whether the premises are true. To take the discussion further, we need to define what a 'miracle' is. Here are three definitions:

> Those things are properly called miracles which are done by divine agency beyond the order commonly observed in nature. (Aquinas)
> A miracle occurs when the world is not left to itself, when something distinct from the natural order as a whole intrudes into it. (J. L. Mackie: *The Miracle of Theism*, 1982)
> . . . an event which is astonishing, unusual, shaking, without contradicting the natural structure of reality . . . an event which points to the mystery of being. (P. Tillich: *Systematic Theology*, 1953)

Task

Look at these definitions of a miracle and note the similarities and the differences. How would you define a miracle? Give reasons for your answer.

Aquinas was convinced that the evidence from miracles proved the existence of God. For him, and for many others, a miracle has to be an act of God and must have a clear purpose and significance. He believed that God intervened in the world when he thought it was necessary for the good of humans. Aquinas identified three types of miracle:

1. where God acts in a way that nature could not. An example given by Aquinas was when God stopped the sun so that the Israelites could win a battle (Joshua 10:13).
2. where God acts in a way that nature could, but that is highly unlikely. An example would be a person recovering from paralysis or a terminal illness. It is possible for these things to happen, but they are very unexpected.
3. where God acts in a way that nature could but without using the principles of nature. For example, someone might recover from having the flu more quickly than expected because they had prayed for God's help.

For Aquinas, then, a miracle is an act of God which is beneficial for the recipient; it may break a natural law, but it does not necessarily have to do so.

Arguments against miracles as proof of God's existence

Many philosophers and others have criticized this type of argument from miracles. The most powerful statement comes from the Scottish philosopher David Hume. He never says that miracles do not happen; instead he bases his criticism on the idea that it would be impossible to prove that they exist.

Hume defines a miracle as 'a transgression of a law of nature brought about by a particular volition of a Deity' and says that nothing that can happen within the laws of nature should be called a miracle. This is what he means by a 'transgression of a law of nature'. He puts forward several arguments against the belief in miracles.

First, he says that miracles are extremely unlikely events. The world works in an orderly and regular way, so that, for instance, night follows day and ill people do not suddenly get better. The vast majority of people do not claim to witness miracles. Hume thought that miracles are so unlikely that it is always more probable that the people who claim to have witnessed them were mistaken than that the miracles had actually occurred. As he says, 'a wise man proportions his belief to the evidence'. As miracles are few and far between, it is difficult to amass enough evidence of them to convince anyone that they are genuine.

Hume's second argument may be thought to be somewhat rude and arrogant: he says that most miracles take place in conditions where they cannot be properly checked and tested. If miracles are going to be accepted, they must be witnessed by credible, well-educated people. However, most of the people who claim to have observed a miracle tend to come from 'ignorant and barbarous' nations! Their evidence cannot be trusted.

Third, Hume says that people naturally tend to exaggerate and love to sensationalize things that have happened. He maintains that this happens with accounts of miracles – things get dramatized and the truth gets lost.

Fourth, Hume argues that every religion has its own miracles and that all are different from one another. This means, for Hume, that it cancels out the truth of any miracles; on the grounds that not all can be true, none of them are. For instance,

Christians believe in the resurrection of Jesus, while Muslims believe in the miracle of the Qur'an being dictated to the Prophet Muhammad. Hume says that both of these cannot be true; if one is true, the other must be false. If Jesus was resurrected, then what the Qur'an says about him must be false, because the Qur'an denies the crucifixion of Jesus. If the Qur'an is true, then Jesus could not have been resurrected. For Hume, each claim cancels out the other, and neither can be true.

> **Task**
>
> What do you think of Hume's criticisms of miracles? Can you think of any arguments against what he says? Give reasons for your answers.

Counter-arguments

Hume's criticisms of miracles have had a very strong influence on many people, both religious and non-religious, and several recent theologians and philosophers have offered suggestions and **counter-arguments**. We will look briefly at one of these.

Counter-argument is a term used when a person argues against someone else's argument.

R. F. Holland (1923–2013) argued that events that do not break the laws of nature may be seen as miraculous. He gives the example of a train speeding round a bend in the track and a young child who becomes stuck on the track in a toy car. The child's mother could not free him from the car, and it looked as if the train would crush him. At that moment, the train driver had a heart attack, took the pressure off the 'dead man's handle' that controlled the speed, and the train stopped just short of the child. Both the driver and the child survived without injury. Holland says that this could be thought of as a miracle, even though no laws of nature were broken.

> **Task**
>
> Explain why this is a counter-argument to Hume's criticisms. Which of Hume's criticisms do you think it applies to?

> **Taking it further**
>
> **Maurice Wiles** (1923–2005), a Christian theologian, argued that miracles were actually damaging to Christian faith. It is contradictory, he says, to believe in an omnibenevolent God who would help only some people in need and do so only some of the time. For instance, why would God allow Jesus to feed 5,000 people but then ignore the starving millions in Africa and other parts of the world? Or why would God save the Israelites by parting the Red Sea and yet ignore the murder of millions in the Holocaust? While Wiles grants that events that break natural laws may be a logically possible idea, he says that God performed only one miracle – that of the creation of the universe. All other accounts of miracles may be explained by other, natural, means. This is particularly so for the miracles recorded in the Bible – Wiles concludes that these stories are theological myths, not originally intended to be taken literally. They come from a culture that valued mythological stories for the way that they explained deep theological truths without attempting to take them as historical accounts.

TICK THE TOPICS

Now you should tick the relevant boxes to check what you have learned in this chapter.

Sections	Topics	Tick
Design argument	Definition	
Christian	Aquinas	
	William Paley	
Islam	Surah 2:164	
	Al-Ghazali	
Criticisms	Criticisms from philosophy (Hume)	
	Criticisms from science (evolution)	
Cosmological argument		
Islam	Kalam	
Christian	Aquinas	
	Leibniz	
Criticisms	Infinite regress	
	Fallacy of composition	
	Like causes resemble like effects	
	Empirical to non-empirical evidence	
Religious experience	Public and private	
	Criticisms	
Miracles	Aquinas	
	Criticisms – Hume	
	Criticisms – Holland	

Sample questions

AQA Religious Studies A (8062)

1 Which of the following best expresses the idea that the divine (God, gods or the ultimate reality) is in the world?
   a) Omnipotent b) Transcendent c) Immanent d) Atheist (1 mark)
2 Give two types of religious experience other than visions. (2 marks)
3 Explain two contrasting beliefs in contemporary British society about miracles. (4 marks)
4 Explain two religious beliefs about visions. (5 marks)
5 'The cosmological argument proves that God exists.'
Evaluate this statement. In your answer, you:
   • should give reasoned arguments in support of this statement
   • should give reasoned arguments to support a different point of view
   • should refer to religious arguments
   • may refer to non-religious arguments
   • should reach a justified conclusion. (12 marks)

Edexcel Religious Studies A (1RA0) and Religious Studies B (1RB0)

a) Give three different types of philosophical argument for God's existence. (3)
b) Outline the philosophical argument from cosmology. (4)
c) Assess whether arguments for God's existence are necessary today. (9)
d) 'God's existence can never be proved.'
Evaluate this statement, considering more than one point of view. (12)

Edexcel International GCSE Religious Studies (4RS0)

a) Define what is meant by 'argument'. (2)
b) Outline how some religious believers attempt to prove God's existence by studying the supposed design of the universe. (5)
c) Explain why some people criticize the argument from design. (8)
d) 'God's existence can never be proved.'
Do you agree? Give reasons for your answer, showing that you have considered another point of view. (5)

OCR Religious Studies Full Course (J625)

a) State three reasons why a religious person might believe in God. (3)
b) Outline the philosophical argument from the First Cause for the existence of God. (6)
c) Explain one argument against the existence of God.
You should refer to sources of wisdom and authority in your answer. (6)
d) 'God is involved with human beings.'
Discuss this statement. In your answer, you should draw on your learning from across your course of study, including reference to beliefs, teachings and practices within your chosen religion. (15)
(SPaG + 3)

The Nature and Characteristics of God

CONTENTS

In this chapter, you will learn about the traditional Christian and Muslim understanding of God. Who or what is God? How can we go about trying to think about what 'He' is like (is it a he?)? How can we describe God? These are questions that Christian and Islamic scholars and believers have explored for centuries. As will be seen, each religion has focused on a range of characteristics of God, and we will look at some of the most important of these.

In Christianity, these are God as Trinity, omniscient, omnipotent, omnibenevolent, omnipresent, eternal and immanent and transcendent.

In Islam, these will be Al-Fatihah, God as creator, Tawhid, Shahadah, Risalah and the ninety-nine names of God.

The Christian understanding of God

In *The Simpsons*, Homer Simpson has several encounters with God. In the episode 'Homer the Heretic', God appears to Homer in a dream, and they have a discussion about how bad the Reverend Lovejoy's sermons are. God does not criticize Homer for missing church, although Marge does.

God is also the only character (other than Jesus) in the animation to have four fingers and a thumb on each hand and ten toes. All other characters have three fingers on each hand and eight toes. The reason for this may be to make God and Jesus different from all 'humans', and it renders them unique, which may be appropriate for divine beings. The God of *The Simpsons* can show anger, as he does in 'Pray Anything', when he sends a flood because the townspeople have broken all Ten Commandments. God is also seen as forgiving, however, when he agrees with Homer (in 'Thank God it's Doomsday') to undo the end of the world by turning back time and restoring Moe's Tavern. God is always portrayed as male.

Task

Make a list of each characteristic of God in *The Simpsons* as described above. Pick one of these that you think is the most important and give reasons for your choice.

In this section, we are going to discuss some of the main characteristics of God in Christianity. Christians use many terms to describe the main characteristics of God, the most important of which are given in table 3.1.

Table 3.1 Characteristics of God in Christianity

The Trinity	God is one, but in three distinct 'Persons': Father, Son and Holy Spirit (sometimes called Holy Ghost)
Omniscient	All knowing
Omnipotent	All powerful
Omnibenevolent	Entirely good
Omnipresent	Present everywhere
Eternal	Without beginning and without end
Immanent and transcendent	God is actively present and involved with our lives (immanent) but also beyond, above and separate from our world (transcendent).

The Trinity

The Trinity is the central belief of nearly all Christians, though it is rejected by some branches, such as the Church of Latter Day Saints (Mormons) and Jehovah's Witnesses. The Trinity is the doctrine that God exists in three separate forms, each form being a distinct person, known as Father, Son and Holy Spirit. Each is different from the others, but they share the same **essence**. Each is fully divine in nature, but they are not identical in their individuality and self-awareness. Each member of the Trinity has a different function in the universe. God the Father is usually seen as the creator, God the Son as the saviour, and God the Holy Spirit as the sustainer of the world.

The **Trinity** describes the Christian belief in one God who exists in three 'persons' – Father, Son and Holy Spirit.

Essence refers to what is essential in a person – what cannot be taken away from someone if they are still to be a 'person'.

An eighteenth-century woodcut showing a representation of the Trinity: God the Father, with triangular halo, holding God the Son (Jesus) on the cross, beneath God the Holy Spirit (the dove).

Although the Trinity consists of three distinct persons, Christians understand it as strictly monotheistic – they believe in only one God. To put this another way:

- God is three persons.
- Each person is divine.
- There is only one God.

While each of the persons in the Trinity is equal to the others in respect of their essence, there is a hierarchy of sorts: God the Father (creator) is not derived from anyone or anything else, but God the Son is 'begotten' from the Father (John 3:16):

'For God so loved the world that he gave his one and only son, that whoever believes in him shall not perish but have eternal life.' According to 1 John 4:10, the Father sent the Son, while the Son and the Father sent the Holy Spirit (John 14:26). The Father creates (Isaiah 44:24), the Son redeems (Galatians 3:13) and the Holy Spirit sanctifies (Romans 15:16).

The word 'trinity' does not appear in the Bible, but Christians point to verses such as Matthew 28:19, 2 Corinthians 13:14, 1 Peter 1:2 and Jude 20–21 as showing the beginnings of the idea of the Trinity.

Omniscience

To be **omniscient** is to be all knowing. God knows everything that can be known, whether it exists now, existed in the past or will exist in the future. Psalm 147:4–5 says: 'God determines the number of the stars and calls them each by name. Great is our Lord and mighty in power; his understanding has no limit.' Isaiah 46:10 says: 'I make known the end from the beginning, from ancient times, what is still to come. I say: My purpose will stand, and I will do all that I please.' Thus God knows every single thing about every single person who has ever lived and who will ever live in the future. God already knows every thought that a person has before that person has it. When someone performs an action, God knows whether that individual's intentions were genuine or not.

Omniscience refers to the idea that God is all knowing.

Omnipotence

To be omnipotent is to be all powerful. Christians believe that God is able to do whatever he wishes to do. There are no limits to his power, except that he cannot do anything that goes against his nature as God. This means that God cannot commit a sin or do anything that is logically contradictory, such as create a stone that he is unable to lift. If God wills that something should happen, he has the power to guarantee that it will happen. When Christians read in the Bible that God promises eternal life to his followers, they believe that this will happen because of God's **omnipotence**. In the story of Job, Job says 'I know that you can do all things, nothing can thwart your purposes', while Revelation 19:6 says: 'Then I heard what sounded like a great multitude, like the roar of rushing waters and like loud peels of thunder, shouting: "Hallelujah! For our God omnipotent reigns."'

Omnipotence refers to the idea that God is all powerful.

Omnibenevolence

God is omnibenevolent – all good or all loving. The Old Testament prophet Hosea taught that God loved his followers as if they were his children, so, when they turned their backs on him, God was upset. Even though the people were continually going against his will, God continued to show his love for them – though, as any parent knows, sometimes that love needs to be 'cruel to be kind', so punishment is a kind of love. Psalm 63 praises God because 'your steadfast love is better than life'. For Christians, God's love is consistent and ever present. They believe that the ultimate expression of God's **omnibenevolence** was in the death and resurrection of Christ, where God sacrificed his only son in order to save humanity from their sins.

Omnibenevolence refers to the idea that God is all loving and good.

Omnipresence

God is **omnipresent** – ubiquitous – in the universe. Christians believe that God fills the universe with his presence: every part of God is present in every part of the universe, and there is nowhere where God is absent. 1 Kings 8:27 says: 'But will God really dwell on earth? The heavens, even the highest heaven, cannot contain you. How much less this temple I have built!' In Matthew 18:20, Jesus declared that 'where two

Omnipresence refers to the idea that God is always present.

or three are gathered together in my name, I am in the midst of them.' For Christians, this is a reassuring idea because, wherever they go and whatever situation they find themselves in, they believe that God will be with them and protecting them.

Eternity

God is said to be eternal because he had no beginning and will have no end. God has always been and will always be in existence. Abraham called God 'the everlasting God' (Genesis 21:33), and Psalm 90:2 says: 'Before the mountains were born, or you had brought forth the whole world, from everlasting to everlasting, you are God.' In the New Testament, the author of 1 Timothy declares: 'Now to the king eternal, immortal, invisible, the only God, be honour and glory for ever and ever, Amen' (1:17). Christians believe that God existed before anything, and this means that God was the cause of everything else, creating the universe and everything in it. God will never cease to exist, so this is a kind of guarantee for Christians that God will look after them and provide them with eternal life after the death of the body.

Immanence and transcendence

Immanence refers to the idea that God is inside the universe and can make relationships with human beings.

These two terms are mirror images of each other. **Immanence** is the idea that God is present in the universe, is involved with the processes of the world and wants to have a special relationship with humans. **Transcendence** is the idea that God is separate

Transcendence refers to the idea that God is outside and remote from the universe and beings in it.

To Christians, God is at the same time both immanent and transcendent. Here, a Christian nun prays to God in the belief that he is close and able to act in her life (he is immanent); yet the setting and act of kneeling show that God is also mighty and to be worshipped (he is transcendent).

and different from the universe, just as a potter is separate and different from the pot that he or she creates. The transcendent God created the universe but is not part of it. In this case, God does not have a close relationship with human beings or guide them in all they do day to day. God is a remote figure who cannot be known in any meaningful way by believers.

For Christians, the belief in both the immanence and the transcendence of God is a difficult concept – that God is both within yet outside the universe, both active yet not active in the world, both in relationship and not in relationship with humans. Christians must balance these two apparently contradictory ideas together.

Tasks

1 Draw a grid with two columns and, on the left-hand side, write the words Trinity, Omniscience, Omnipotence, Omnibenevolence, Omnipresence, Eternity, Immanence, Transcendence. On the right-hand side, write a brief definition of each one with an example of how this might affect a Christian's everyday life or worship.
2 Explain how God can be both transcendent and immanent and why this is important for Christians.
3 Which do you think might be the three most important characteristics of God for Christians? Give reasons for your answer.
4 'The Christian understanding of God is too difficult for anyone to understand fully.' Do you agree with this statement? Give reasons for your answer.
5 'Faith is to believe what you do not see; the reward for faith is to see what you believe' (St Augustine). Do you agree that this is an adequate definition of Christian belief in the nature of God? Give reasons for your answer.

Taking it further

The gender of God

When you talk about God in class or read about God in books, is God usually referred to as 'He'? Do you automatically talk about 'Him' (rather than 'Her')? Is God 'male' or 'female' or something else? Does God have a gender? Christians believe that God has no gender, is neither male nor female. Gender is a biological characteristic and God is not a biological being. According to John's Gospel (4:24), 'God is spirit'. 'Spirit' in this sense does not have corporeal form and has no physical characteristics that can be observed by humans. Every time God is mentioned 'by name' in the Bible, it is always as 'him' or 'he.' One explanation for this is because God is sometimes called 'Father' and Jesus is his 'son'. Also, in the story of Adam and Eve (Genesis 2–3), Adam was created before Eve and was given authority to name the animals. These observations could lead to the conclusion that God must be male.

On the other hand, however, there are sections of the Bible where God is referred to as having female qualities and characteristics. For example, Genesis 1:27 says that humans are created 'in the image of God', and this refers to both male and female: 'And God created man in His own image, in the image of God He created him; male and female He created them.' The Old Testament book of Proverbs talks about God as 'Wisdom' and uses female imagery to describe God:

> Out in the open, Wisdom calls aloud; she raises her voice in the public square; on top of the wall she cries out, at the city gate she makes her speech. (1:20–21)
>
> For wisdom is more precious than rubies, and nothing you desire can compare with her. (8:11)
>
> Wisdom has built her house, she has set up its seven pillars. She has prepared her meat and mixed her wine; she has also set her table. (9:1–2)

Task

Draw a grid like the one below. Find and copy out the references mentioned and show how they may refer to feminine characteristics of God.

Deuteronomy 32:11–12	
Isaiah 66:13	
Hosea 11:3–4	
Psalm 131:2	
Matthew 23:37	

Fundamentalist Christians believe that God wanted humans to understand him as male, and therefore the (divinely inspired) biblical authors used the terms 'him', 'his' and 'he'. More liberal Christians take greater notice of the places where God is given more feminine characteristics and conclude that God has both 'male' and 'female' features and encapsulates both 'maleness' and 'femaleness' in order that all humans can relate to God. As the Catechism of the Catholic Church says: 'God is neither man nor woman: he is God' (Section 239).

Task

Some Christian feminist theologians have attempted to alter some prayers, such as the Lord's Prayer, to avoid the male-centred language used in church services. Do you think the following example is helpful? 'Our nurturing parent who art in heaven, hallowed be thy name.'

The gender of God in Islam

ISLAM

For all Muslims, God is 'one' (Tawhid). In the Qur'an, the terms '*hu*' and '*huwa*' are used to refer to God. These are usually translated as 'him' but may also be rendered as 'it' – i.e., in an impersonal or gender neutral way. The feminine pronoun in Arabic is '*hiya*', but this can also be translated as impersonally as 'it'. Translators have been male and so have always translated each of these terms in the masculine. The fact that God is always referred to as male in the Qur'an, therefore, is because of cultural and historical rather than religious reasons.

The Muslim understanding of God

Muslims believe that God is unique and cannot therefore be described or limited. This is why there are no images or pictures of God in any Muslim home or mosque. Muslims accept that God is beyond human understanding but makes himself known in ways that help humans to apprehend him. One of the ways they do this is by frequently saying **'Allahu Akbar'** – 'God is the greatest' – which reminds them that, although God is completely different from humans, he makes himself known to them in many ways.

Allahu Akbar
is Arabic for 'God is great'.

The core Muslim beliefs about the nature of God are:

- God (Allah) is one God. Muslims are **monotheistic**, believing that Allah is the only God.
- God created everyone and everything that exists or has existed. Humans see God's creative powers every day in the natural world.
- God will judge every person at the time of his or her death. Every action a Muslim does in life is recorded, and if they do more good than bad actions, they will achieve **Paradise**. If not, they will go to hell.
- God is both merciful and compassionate.
- God has given guidance in the Qur'an and through his prophets for how Muslims should behave.

Paradise
is another name for heaven or for a blissful afterlife in God's presence.

One of these ways is seen in the first Surah of the Qur'an, **Al-Fatihah**, and we shall also look at other ways God has made himself known to Muslims, as shown in table 3.2.

Al-Fatihah
is the name given to the first surah in the Qur'an.

Table 3.2   Understanding God in Islam

Al-Fatihah	The first surah of the Qur'an
Tawhid	Surah 112, which the Prophet Muhammad picked out as one of the most important in the Qur'an
Shahadah	Statement of belief, one of the Five Pillars of Islam
Immanence and transcendence	God is actively present and involved with our lives (immanent) but also beyond, above and separate from our world (transcendent)
Risalah	Prophets and angels who act as God's messengers
The ninety-nine names of God	Names of God in the Qur'an and ahadith

Al-Fatihah

Al-Fatihah means 'the opening', and it is a summary of or preface to some of the most important Muslim beliefs about the nature and character of God.

In the name of Allah, the Compassionate, the Merciful
Praise be to Allah, Lord of the Creation,

The Compassionate, the Merciful,
King of Judgement Day!
You alone we worship, and to you alone
We pray for help.
Guide us to the straight path
The path of those whom you have favoured,
Not of those who have incurred your anger
Nor of those who have gone astray.

All Muslims learn this surah by heart and recite it seventeen times per day in their prayers.

The Qur'an states many times that God is the most merciful – every surah except one begins with the phrase 'In the name of Allah, the Compassionate, the Merciful', showing the importance of this idea for Muslims, who understand God's mercy as central to their behaviour in the world. No human is perfect, as only God is perfect, so when a Muslim commits a sin, then asks God for forgiveness, God will show his mercy towards that person. God will change the person's sin into good deeds. God will forgive often because he understands that humans are sinful by nature and are in need of God's mercy and forgiveness.

Surah 6:160 says: 'He that does a good deed shall be repaid tenfold; but he that does evil shall be rewarded with evil.' This means that God is overwhelmingly merciful. Muslims believe that justice and mercy go hand in hand. If a sinful person refuses to repent of his sin, then God will show his justice by punishing that person. The Qur'an states that people who persist in sinning – particularly those who practise oppression and who rebel against God's laws of justice – will be punished. Muslims understand punishment as being 'earned' by the sinners themselves, and the Qur'an refers to such people as 'those who oppress their own souls'. God does not exact his punishment until the sinner has had a chance to repent and return to God.

God's mercy extends beyond Muslims to members of other religions or of none. If a non-Muslim decides to convert to Islam, God will forgive all his previous sins.

Tawhid

Tawhid
is the Muslim belief
in the oneness of
God.

Tawhid is a key **doctrine** in Islam that teaches the unity and oneness of God. The Prophet Muhammad described Surah 112 as one-third of the whole Qur'an, even though it is only four verses long, because it contains such an important meaning about the nature of God:

Say: He is one God, the Unique,
the Uncaused Cause of all being.
He does not give birth, and nor was he born;
and there is nothing that is equal to him.

One of the key elements of God which this surah stresses is God as Creator. Muslims believe that God is the creator of the entire universe and is in control over everything in it. Surah 7:54, 57–8 says:

Surely, your Lord is Allah. Who created the heavens and the earth in six periods; then He settled Himself on the Throne. He makes the night cover the day, pursuing it swiftly. He

has created the sun and the moon and the stars, all made subservient by His command . . .
He it is who sends the winds . . .
Good land brings forth vegetation plentifully by the command of the Lord.

In this account, there is no indication of how long the 'periods' of time lasted. It is clear, however, that the creation was deliberate and that God created the universe according to a particular order.

More information about the Islamic creation account may be found on pp. 113–17.

Shahadah

The **Shahadah** is a statement of belief. It is the first of the **Five Pillars** of faith in Islam. The Five Pillars are the five most important duties for Muslims and a lifelong commitment. The Shahadah declares that 'There is no God but Allah and Muhammad is his prophet.' Muslims believe that having faith in God will help them to live their lives in a way that is consistent with God's will. This in turn will make Islam a stronger religion. The Shahadah therefore reminds Muslims that it is God who is in control of the universe and has created everything and that Muhammad is the prophet chosen by God to reveal his truth to humans.

Immanence and transcendence

Muslims believe that God is both **transcendent** and **immanent**. Transcendence is the idea that God is outside the universe and cannot be known because he is totally different from humans. Humans can have no understanding of God because their minds cannot cope with the enormity of his nature. God is also immanent – the idea that he is present within the universe and wishes to have a relationship with humans. This is how Muslims can know about the nature of God, because he has revealed himself to the Prophet Muhammad (as the Shahadah makes clear), to whom he gave the Qur'an. For Muslims (as for Christians), God is both transcendent and immanent. This is very difficult to understand but is the means by which God allows himself to be known.

Risalah

Risalah is the channel by which a transcendent God communicates with humans. God's message and commands come in two ways – through the prophets and through the **angels**. According to Muslim tradition, there were 124,000 prophets, twenty-five of whom are mentioned in the Qur'an:

Adam	Moses	David	Elisha	Ishmael	Jacob	John	Job	Noah	Ezekiel	Abraham	Elijah	Lot	Zachari'ah
Enoch	Aaron	Solomon	Isaac	Jonah	Joseph	Jesus	Hud	Shuaib	Salib	Muhammad			

Apart from the final four names on this list, these prophets also appear in the Christian Bible. The most important are called 'messengers', so that Moses was the

Shahadah
is one of the Five Pillars in Islam, the declaration of faith that there is only one God and Muhammad is his messenger.

The **Five Pillars**
are the guiding principles of Islam: belief in one God, prayer, giving money to the poor, fasting during Ramadan and pilgrimage to Mecca.

Risalah
refers to prophecy in Islam.

Angels
are heavenly, semi-divine beings who are seen, in both Islam and Christianity, as messengers of God.

prophet of the Jews, Jesus was the prophet of the Christians, and Muhammad was the prophet of Islam. Each of these was given a book by God – the Torah, the Gospel and the Qur'an. Muslims must treat all of these with respect and follow the example of the prophets who were given them:

> We believe in Allah, and the revelation given to us, and to Abraham, Ismael, Isaac, Jacob and the Tribes, and that given to Moses and Jesus, and that given to all prophets from their Lord. We make no difference between one and another of them. (Qur'an 2:136)

However, only the Qur'an is the absolutely correct message given by God, as the Torah and Gospels were not recorded correctly and have changed over time.

An Islamic image of an angel, from a Persian manuscript dated 1555.

The second channel by which God communicates is the angels. Angels are supernatural beings who were created by God out of pure light. All angels worship God and never tire of doing so. Some have appeared to humans – for example, Abraham and Maryam (Mary) – in human form, others have taken other forms. Some angels record everything that humans think and do and report these to God. The most important angel is Jibril (Gabriel), who delivered God's message to the prophets, particularly the Qur'an to Muhammad.

The ninety-nine names of God

According to Muslim tradition, God has ninety-nine Glorious names which he has revealed in the Qur'an and ahadith. These names are an important way of knowing about God's nature – for example:

- the Most Holy
- the Ever Forgiving
- the All Hearing
- the All Seeing
- the Magnificent
- the Infinite
- the Preserver
- the Giver of Life
- the Strong
- the Most Kind and Righteous
- the Bringer of Death, the Destroyer.

All ninety-nine names appear in the Qur'an. Although some lists have slightly different names, all show the various characteristics of God and help Muslims to have a greater understanding of God.

The ninety-nine names of God are very important for Muslims. Some understand that reciting the names will help their hopes of entering Paradise, while others believe that knowledge of God's names is the basis of all other knowledge. The respected

The ninety-nine Names by which God is known in Islam, found in the mihrab of the Jamia Masjid mosque in Nowhatta, India.

fourteenth-century scholar of the Qur'an Ibn Qayyim al-Jawziyya said: 'The key to the call of the Messengers, the essence of their message, is knowing God through his Names, his attributes and his actions, because this is the foundation on which the rest of the message, from beginning to end, is built' (*Sawa'iq al Mursalah*, 1/150–51). For Ibn Qayyim, therefore, knowing God's names is the essential basis of understanding everything else about God and Islam.

Tasks

6 Draw a grid with two columns and, on the left-hand side, write Al-Fatihah, God as creator, Shahadah, Tawhid, Transcendence, Immanence, Risalah. On the right-hand side, write the meaning of each one.

7 Explain how God can be both transcendent and immanent and why this is important for Muslims.

8 In a search engine, look up all ninety-nine names of God. Which do you think are the most important for understanding how Muslims think of God? Give reasons for your answer.

9 'The Muslim understanding of God is too difficult for anyone to understand fully.' Do you agree with this statement? Give reasons for your answer.

Tick the topics

Now you should tick all the relevant boxes to check what you have learned in this chapter.

Sections	Topic	Tick
Christianity	The Trinity	
	Omniscience	
	Omnipotence	
	Omnibenevolence	
	Omnipresence	
	Eternity	
	Immanence	
	Transcendence	
Islam	Core characteristics of God	
	Al-Fatihah	
	Tawhid	
	Shahadah	
	Risalah	
	The ninety-nine names of God	

Sample questions

AQA Religious Studies A (8062)

1 Which of the following best describes the idea that the divine (God, gods or the ultimate reality) is all-knowing?
   a) Omnipotent b) Transcendent c) Immanent d) Omniscient   (1 mark)
2 Give two ideas about the divine (God, gods or the ultimate reality) that religious believers would see as necessary.   (2 marks)
3 Explain two contrasting beliefs in contemporary British society about omniscience.   (4 marks)
4 Explain two religious ideas about nature.   (5 marks)
5 'God cannot be known by humans.'
Evaluate this statement. In your answer, you:
   - should give reasoned arguments in support of this statement
   - should give reasoned arguments to support a different point of view
   - should refer to religious arguments
   - may refer to non-religious arguments
   - should reach a justified conclusion.   (12 marks)

Edexcel Religious Studies A (1RA0) and Religious Studies B (1RB0)

a) Give three characteristics of God.   (3)
b) Outline the evidence for God being creator.   (4)
c) Assess whether God's character is consistently shown in religious holy books.   (9)
d) 'Humans can never know God.'
Evaluate this statement, considering more than one point of view.   (12)

Edexcel International GCSE Religious Studies (4RS0)

a) Define what 'transcendence' means.   (2)
b) Describe three characteristics of God in Christianity (other than God as Trinity).   (5)
c) Explain why Christians understand God as Trinity.   (8)
d) 'God cannot be known.'
Do you agree? Give reasons for your answer, showing that you have considered another point of view.   (5)

OCR Religious Studies Full Course (J625) and Short Course (J125)

a) Name the three persons of the Trinity.   (3)
b) Outline the meaning of the term 'omnipotent' as applied to God.   (6)
c) Explain why some religious believers do not like the idea of God as eternal.
You should refer to sources of wisdom and authority in your answer.   (6)
d) 'The most important characteristic of God is his immanence.'
Discuss this statement. In your answer, you should draw on your learning from across your course of study, including reference to beliefs, teachings and practices within your chosen religion.   (15)
          (SPaG + 3)

Revelation and Religious Experience

In this chapter, you will learn about an important concept in religious belief from both Christian and Muslim viewpoints. Revelation, or how God allows humans to know about the divine nature, happens in two ways. General revelation is when humans can understand God through the way in which the world works. In Islam, this is called Fitrah. 'Special' revelation is where individual believers undergo conversion, visions or mystical experiences.

You will also learn about the major problems with religious experience.

Revelation

> **Revelation**
> is the making known
> of something that
> was previously
> hidden.

The word '**revelation**' means to 'show' something that previously could not be seen or was hidden from view. It is used particularly in discussions about God. Some people believe that God is beyond human knowledge and cannot be known. Many philosophers argue that humans cannot know God because there is such a wide disparity between God and humans, not just in space but in terms of knowledge and understanding. Others believe that God can be known because God has 'revealed' himself to humans in various ways. Both Christians and Muslims believe that God created humans to be in a relationship with him, and so it is logical that humans can know him. Humans have a natural desire to know God, so it would be odd or cruel if God did not provide the means to fulfil this desire.

There seem to be two options for how religious believers may know God. The first is by using our brains and our powers of reason. Philosophers have attempted to do

Table 4.1   Types of revelation

General revelation	This is where God makes himself known to humans through establishing general truths, such as the laws of nature. Humans can see these natural laws and work out that they could not have come about randomly but must have been put in place by some greater being. The design argument for the existence of God is an important example of general revelation (see pp. 28–34).
Special revelation	This is the direct communication of God with humans and refers to the specific ways in which God has chosen to reveal himself to particular individuals or to humanity as a whole.

this for many centuries, but they often disagree with one another about whether it is possible to know God or whether people can be sure if he even exists. The closest these philosophers can get by using their reason is only a probability of the existence of a supreme being or force – see, for instance, chapter 2 on the existence of God. They look at the complexity of the universe, both at the microscopic and the macro level and conclude that something must have brought it into being. This is quite distant from the Christian and Muslim belief in a God we can know personally.

The second way of knowing God is by revelation. Believers say that we can know God only if he shows himself to us. Again, it seems likely he would do this if he exists and, given the disparity between God and his creation, it would seem necessary for him to do this.

Christians and Muslims suggest that God reveals himself in two distinct ways, known as 'general' and 'special' revelation (see table 4.1). We will look at these in turn for each religion.

General revelation in Christianity

The idea of general revelation is seen in the Bible. Psalm 19:1–4, for example, states:

> The heavens are telling the glory of God;
> And the firmament proclaims his handiwork.
> Day to day pours forth speech,
> And night to night declares knowledge.
> There is no speech, nor are there words;
> Their voice is not heard;
> Yet their voice goes out through all the earth,
> And their words to the ends of the earth.

CHRISTIANITY
ROMAN
CATHOLICISM

The Psalmist is saying here that the wonder, power and glory of God is seen everywhere in the universe for those who look. However, he sets up an apparent contradiction between 'day to day pours forth speech' and 'there is no speech'. This means that the order and complexity of the world can be understood just by looking at nature. Nature, in all its beauty, glory and power points to the existence of God.

The same idea is seen in the New Testament, in Romans 1:20: 'Ever since the creation of the world his eternal power and divine nature, invisible though they are, have been understood and seen through the things he has made. So they are without

Many passages in the Bible, particularly in the Psalms, describe how God can be experienced and seen in his works, such as the awe-inspiring beauty of the natural world.

excuse.' Here, St Paul says that God's creative power may be clearly seen and understood just by looking at the world around us. There is no excuse for not accepting that God has made everything in the universe.

General revelation, therefore, is about looking at the world and understanding it as being made and controlled by God. No other explanation can be given for the way the world is. Everything seems to be interconnected – for instance, honey is produced by bees, which collect pollen from a range of plants that need to grow in certain conditions – conditions that are dependent upon the correct amount of sun and rainfall. This level of interconnectedness and complexity must mean that any such God has to be supremely powerful, supremely intelligent and supremely good.

Of course, in order for humans to see properly and understand the power and majesty of God in nature, God must have created humans in such a way that they were able to do this. Part of human nature is the ability to reason, to look at specific things in the world and then to work out more general principles or truths from them. For example, humans are able to look at how crops grow and observe that they need a certain amount of sunlight, rain and type of soil to flourish. Not all crops will flourish under the same conditions. Humans can therefore work out the general principles for growing crops so that farmers can obtain the best harvests possible.

Fitrah is the natural tendency for humans to believe in and worship God.

ISLAM

General revelation in Islam

Fitrah is the name for general revelation in Islam. It is the idea that, when a child is born, it has an inbuilt and natural sense of and belief in God. Even if the child did not have any parents or a religious upbringing, it would still naturally believe in God. The Prophet Muhammad said: 'Each child is born in a state of "Fitrah", but his parents make him a Jew or a Christian. It is like the way an animal gives birth to a normal offspring.' Each child will be affected by many influences – the people he meets, the physical environment and the circumstances in which he finds himself as he grows up, and so on. All these influences will shape his beliefs and have an effect on how he understands the world.

For instance, if twin boys are separated at birth and one is placed with a Christian family while the other is placed with a non-religious family, the one who grows up in the Christian family will be taught Christian ideas of God, while the one brought up in a non-religious family will be taught different beliefs and ideas. Muslims say that neither child is strong enough at this early stage of his life to judge whether what he is taught is true. Only later in life will he be able to analyse and evaluate what he has been taught. The person's Fitrah will become active at this point, using both his conscience and his ability to reason to find the correct path through life to come to believe in God. Muslims believe that God will help people to overcome any negative influences so that they will turn to God.

Fitrah in Islam is the idea that every human has, inbuilt from birth, a natural sense of and belief in God.

Using their reason means that a person can study nature to work out that God has created and designed the universe and everything in it, and that he continues to look after it. People can see evidence of this in the everyday working of a human body and also in investigating the furthest reaches of the cosmos. Studying these things can help a person to discover belief in God.

Muslims believe that, while it can help people to come to an understanding and acceptance of the existence of God, Fitrah by itself is not sufficient. This why special revelations, given through the prophets and especially in the revelation of the Qur'an, are necessary in order to provide a full understanding of God's holy nature (see below, pp. 77–9).

Special revelation in Christianity

**CHRISTIANITY
ROMAN
CATHOLICISM**

Christians believe that the Bible is of primary importance as a record of God's revelation to humans. God spoke directly to some humans, such as Abraham (Genesis 17), and through dreams and visions to others, such as Joseph (Genesis 37:5–11; and chapters 40 and 41) and Daniel (Daniel chapters 2, 7, 8, 9, and 10–12). For fundamentalist Christians, the Bible contains the actual words of God and is 'living and active' (Hebrews 4:12). The Bible is 'inspired by God, useful for teaching, for reproof, for correction and for training in righteousness, so that everyone who belongs to God may be proficient, equipped for every good work' (2 Timothy 3:16–17).

The supreme example of God's special revelation was in the person of Jesus, when God revealed his own person rather than just a message. In John's Gospel (14:9), Jesus says: 'He who has seen me has seen the Father [God].' Many Christians believe that Jesus was the fullest and final revelation from God because he was God in human form. As it says in Hebrews 1:1–3, 'Long ago, God spoke to our ancestors in many and various ways by the prophets, but in these last days he has spoken to us by a Son . . . he is the reflection of God's glory and the exact imprint of God's very being.' This belief is called the **Incarnation**.

Incarnation is the Christian belief that God came down to earth in the form of a human being and lived a fully human life.

Many Christians believe that God did not reveal himself only in the Bible but continues to give special revelations today. This happens in two ways. The first is through the Bible, where the Holy Spirit opens human hearts to know God through the truths contained therein. Because Christians believe that God inspires the words of the Bible, it means that believers may know God personally by studying the Bible regularly.

The second way is through direct special revelations to individual believers and (sometimes) non-believers. Some people claim that they have had a revelation from God that has a dramatic effect on their life. Such religious experiences are obviously very subjective, as they are encountered only by the individual, not anyone else. Occasionally, however, a group of people can have a special revelation together.

Direct special revelations have been experienced by many thousands of people across countries, centuries and denominations. They are of several different types, summarized in table 4.2.

Table 4.2 Types of religious experience

Conversion experience	Conversion is when an individual makes a radical change in his or her life. This change has a long-lasting and permanent effect.
Visionary experience	This is a religious experience that someone 'sees', either physically through their eyes or in their mind. Visionaries can hear words being spoken.
Mystical experience	This can be a sense of the presence of God rather than a physical experience. Mystics sometimes receive a message from God.

Conversion experiences

The best-known conversion experience is that of Saul of Tarsus, who experienced the risen Jesus while on a journey from Jerusalem to Damascus. St Paul (he adopted the Roman form of his name) wrote many of the books (mostly letters) that are included in the New Testament and is a key figure in early Christianity. The story of his genuine and long-lasting conversion is told three times in the New Testament (Acts chapters 9, 22 and 26). There are slight differences in the details of each, but all tell of how a man who had previously persecuted Christians became a Christian himself.

Blasphemy
is when someone uses God's name in an inappropriate way – e.g., to swear using God's name – to show lack of respect.

Saul was a militant Pharisaic Jew from Tarsus, born at about the same time as Jesus. He believed in strict observance of the commands of the Torah and thought that, if Israel would be faithful to the Torah, then God would rule the earth, evil would be defeated, and the Jews would be vindicated as the people of the one true God. But God would direct his anger against Israel if it did not fully keep his commandments. Saul was committed to promoting zeal for observance, Torah and God.

Saul is introduced to readers of the New Testament in Acts chapter 7. This passage describes the death of the first Christian martyr, Stephen, who, after preaching the message of salvation through Christ, was stoned to death by the crowd and his clothes lay at the feet of Saul. We can presume that Saul had some kind of direct influence on this killing, as he is described as 'giving his approval to his death' (Acts 8:1). Immediately after Stephen's death Saul initiates a great persecution against the Christian Church, and believers scatter far and wide to escape his anger. He begins to round up any Christians and throw them in prison and is described as 'breathing out murderous threats against the Lord's disciples' (Acts 9:1). Immediately before his conversion, Saul sets out on the road to Damascus with the intention of rounding up any professing Christians there and imprisoning them in Jerusalem.

Saul probably persecuted the Christians because he believed that honouring God and the Torah necessitated stamping out any form of disloyalty or **blasphemy** among the Jews. To him, the Christians were heretical, blasphemous Jews who were attempting to lead Israel astray from worship of the one true God. While on his way to Damascus, at the height of his persecution of the Christians, Saul had a dramatic experience that resulted in his conversion to Christianity, symbolized by his adoption of the new name Paul. According to the first nine verses of Acts 9:

Meanwhile, Saul was still breathing out murderous threats against the Lord's disciples. He went to the high priest **2** and asked him for letters to the synagogues in Damascus, so that if he found any there who belonged to the Way, whether men or women, he might take them as prisoners to Jerusalem.

3 As he neared Damascus on his journey, suddenly a light from heaven flashed around him. **4** He fell to the ground and heard a voice say to him, 'Saul, Saul, why do you persecute me?'

5 'Who are you, Lord?' Saul asked.

The Conversion of St Paul on the Road to Damascus, an eighteenth-century French painting.

'I am Jesus, whom you are persecuting,' he replied. **6** 'Now get up and go into the city, and you will be told what you must do.'

7 The men travelling with Saul stood there speechless; they heard the sound but did not see anyone. **8** Saul got up from the ground, but when he opened his eyes he could see nothing. So they led him by the hand into Damascus. **9** For three days he was blind, and did not eat or drink anything.

There are several key features in a conversion experience, all of which are seen in Paul's story.

- It has an immediate effect (though this is not universal for all conversions; some involve a gradual realization).
- The effect must be long-lasting.
- It is not sought out by the person involved.
- It has a transforming aspect, and the individual becomes noticeably different – a new person.

First, Paul's experience had a huge and lasting effect on him. He immediately ceased his persecution of the Christians and began to preach the Christian message of salvation through Christ. Naturally he renounced his life as a **Pharisee**. His new faith was

A **Pharisee** was a memebr of a Jewish religious sect who opposed Jesus' attempts to reform Judaism. St Paul was trained as a Pharisee.

in the risen Christ, and his new religious practice was that of a Christian. He believed that he had been particularly called by God to spread the message of the living Christ to the non-Jewish world, and for the next thirty years he was dedicated to the conversion of the gentiles. A huge proportion of the New Testament comprises Paul's teachings to the gentile churches.

As a direct result of Paul's conversion, the Christian Church was saved from the onslaught of persecution in which he had been involved. In the medium term, he was involved (directly and indirectly) in the conversion of thousands of people (particularly gentiles) and devoted his life to teaching and supporting new churches as far away as Greece and Italy. The letters he sent to them directly affected their religious practice. In the long term, Christian theology is largely based upon Paul's teachings.

Tasks

1 Describe the conversion of Saul of Tarsus. What are the key features of his conversion experience?
2 What effect did the conversion experience have on Saul's life?
3 In what ways did Paul's conversion experience provide a source of faith and influence the religious practice of others?

Another famous example of a conversion experience in Christianity comes from the experience of **John Wesley** (1703–1791), the founder of Methodism, who described a turning point in his life in his journal:

> In the evening, I went very unwillingly to a meeting in Aldersgate Street, where one was reading Luther's preface to the epistle to the Romans. About a quarter to nine, while he was describing the change which God works in the heart through faith in Christ, I felt my heart strangely warmed. I felt I did trust in Christ, Christ alone for salvation; and an assurance was given me that he had taken away my sins, even mine, and saved me from the law of sin and death. (*Journal of John Wesley*, entry for Thursday 24 May 1738).

Wesley's conversion had been preceded by days of 'continual sorrow and heaviness in my heart', so his experience on the Thursday came as a complete shock to him and he had to take some time to come to terms with the truth that it was a genuine transformation. After he had done so, he spent the rest of his life preaching the truth of Christ's life, death and resurrection and the salvation that Christ offered to all people.

Task

Research another conversion experience – for instance, that of the former gang member Nicky Cruz, the hip-hop rapper Jin Au-Yeung (MC Jin) or Dave Mustaine, lead guitarist of Megadeth, and compare them with that of Paul. How many of the key features can you see in these accounts?

Visionary experiences

A visionary experience, as the name suggests, is something that a person 'sees' and that has to do with God. Sometimes people will 'see' a vision physically through their eyes, while others will see it in a dream.

An example of a vision is that of the French peasant girl **Bernadette Soubirous** (1844–1879), who, aged just fourteen, claimed to have experienced many visions of the Virgin Mary and that the Virgin had told her of the healing power of the water in a spring near a grotto in Lourdes. Bernadette saw the Virgin with her eyes and heard the words she told her. She remembered many details of what the Virgin looked like and the clothes she wore and recorded the words that were spoken to her. Her visions were investigated thoroughly by the Roman Catholic Church and declared to be authentic. The grotto at Lourdes is now one of the most visited Christian sites in the world. Bernadette joined the Sisters of Charity in 1866 and dedicated her life to religious and charitable work. She was **canonized** (made a saint) in 1933.

Canonization is the process of making someone a saint. Recent examples include Mother Teresa of Calcutta and Padre Pio of Pietrelcina.

Another example of a visionary experience was that of St Teresa of Ávila (1515–1582), who had 'inner visions' of Christ – that is, she saw Christ in her mind rather than with her eyes. She told people afterwards that she could not see his physical form, but she just knew that he was there. St Teresa offered two tests to prove whether such experiences were genuine:

- does it fit in with Christian teachings?
- does it leave the individual feeling at peace?

If the experience did not have these effects, then it means that the vision came from the Devil, not from God.

Perhaps the most interesting and important example of visionary experience has been at the Roman Catholic pilgrimage site of Medjugorje, near Mostar in Bosnia-Herzegovina. In 1981, six children started having visions of the Virgin Mary.

Statue at Apparition Hill in Medjugorje, where the Virgin Mary is said to have appeared. It is now an important site of pilgrimage for many Roman Catholics, with over 1 million visitors a year.

These visions, which the children experienced together, continued for several years. While four of the children have now ceased to have the visions, the other two claim to experience them regularly. Marija Lunetti (Pavlović) receives messages on the 25th of each month and Mirjana Soldo (Dragičević) has them on the 2nd of each month. Medjugorje is in a war-torn area and has experienced many battles and political upsets over the years. The visions started to occur while the village was still under the communist government in the former Yugoslavia, when the children, their families and the village were all subject to various restrictions. The government initially tried to stop pilgrims visiting the village but eventually gave up because there were so many of them. It is estimated that over 30 million people have visited Medjugorje. The Vatican has not confirmed that it is an official pilgrimage site but is still conducting an investigation into whether the apparitions were genuine. Medjugorje constitutes an important example both because it involved six young people who experienced the same visions of the Virgin Mary and because the visions continued for such a long time.

Task

Look up the Medjugorje website (www.medjugorje.org) and find out more about the stories of the children and the messages they claim to have received. Do you think the children's stories are genuine? Are the messages important for all Christians? Do you think the children were happy to have visions every day? How would you feel if it happened to you?

Mystical experiences

A person who has a mystical experience feels a sense of being overwhelmingly aware of the presence of God. They have feelings of being totally swept up by God's power and holiness. Many people have claimed to have a mystical experience, and these can be quite wide-ranging. There are, however, some characteristics that are common:

- a profound sense of union with God
- a loss of the sense of time (the experience may last only a few seconds but seems much longer)
- something is revealed, usually a message of some kind
- a strong sense of joy and well-being.

There are many examples of mystical experiences in the Bible, such as that of the prophet Isaiah, recorded in Isaiah 6:1–8. Isaiah saw God in all his glory and observed the worship given to him by the angels. It was totally different from any worship he had experienced previously:

> In the year that King Uzziah died, I saw the Lord sitting on a throne, high and lofty; and the hem of his robe filled the temple. Seraphs were in attendance above him; each had six wings: with two they covered their faces, and with two they covered their feet, and with two they flew. And one called to another and said: 'Holy, holy, holy is the LORD Almighty; the whole earth is full of his glory.' At the sound of their voices the doorposts and thresholds shook and the temple was filled with smoke. 'Woe to me!' I cried. 'I am ruined! For I am a man of unclean lips, and I live among a people of unclean lips, and my eyes have seen the King, the LORD Almighty.' (Isaiah 6:1–5)

Isaiah felt overwhelmed because he suddenly understood the majesty of God and became aware of his own insignificance, and he confessed his sinfulness and unworthiness in God's presence. God forgave him through the actions of the Seraphim (six-winged angels who existed in God's presence). Isaiah felt that his sins had been taken away immediately and stood before God cleansed and forgiven. Then he heard God's voice asking the question: 'Who shall I send? And who will go for us?' Isaiah's immediate answer was 'Here am I, send me.' Isaiah was to become the prophet of God, the messenger who would speak God's message to the sinful people of Israel.

Taking it further

The French philosopher Blaise Pascal had a religious experience in 1664. As he describes it: 'From about half past ten in the evening until half past midnight, Fire! . . . The God of Abraham . . .. Certainty, certainty, heartfelt, joy, peace. . . . Joy, joy, joy, tears of joy. . . . Let me never be cut off from him!' What kind of religious experience do you think this was? Give reasons for your answer.

Special revelation in Islam

Visionary experiences

A visionary experience, as the name suggests, is something that a person 'sees' and that has to do with God. Sometimes people will 'see' a vision physically through their eyes, while others will see it in a dream.

In Islam, the best example of a vision is when the Prophet Muhammad received the Qur'an from the angel Jibril. Muhammad had become weary of the society he lived in, with its social unrest, its injustice and the immorality of the people. He used to get away from them to meditate and pray in a cave on Mount Hira, just north of Mecca, where he used to have dreams filled with spiritual significance. These led to his first special revelation, which was in the form of a vision.

This story is recorded in the Qur'an (Surah 96:1–5):

Read! In the name of thy Lord and Cherisher, Who created –
Created man, out of a (mere) clot of congealed blood:
Proclaim! And thy Lord is Most Bountiful, –
Who taught (the use of) the pen, –
Taught man that which he knew not.

Muhammad saw the angel, who squeezed him almost to the point of suffocation three times when Muhammad told him that he could not write. After this, Muhammad found that he could recite the beautiful poetry of the Qur'an as if it were 'inscribed on his heart'. For Muhammad, this was an actual event where Jibril was actually present with him. His experience was puzzling for Muhammad, but his wife, Khadija, believed and supported him and took him to her cousin Waraqa ibn Nawfal. Waraqa was a holy man and immediately declared that Muhammad was a prophet and that the vision was truly from God. This was the first vision that Muhammad received during a period

The Dome of the Rock in Jerusalem covers the Foundation Stone, or Sakhrah, from which, according to a hadith, the Prophet Muhammad ascended to heaven on the Night Journey in a vision.

of about twenty-three years when the entire Qur'an was given to him. One distinctive aspect of his vision is the receiving of texts rather than simply oral messages. These messages that make up the Qur'an are believed by Muslims to be the recording of the actual words of God. The experience for Muhammad himself was personally profound and is thought by Muslims to be the final, complete and universal revelation from God. Muhammad's vision, therefore, is central to the existence of Islam and is fundamental to the development of Muslim belief and practice.

Mystical experiences

A person who has a mystical experience feels a sense of being overwhelmingly aware of the presence of God – of being totally swept up by God's power and holiness. Many people have claimed to have a mystical experience, and these can be quite wide-ranging. There are, however, some common characteristics:

- a profound sense of union with God
- a loss of the sense of time (the experience may last only a few seconds but seems much longer)
- something is revealed, usually a message of some kind
- a strong sense of joy and well-being.

In Islam, **Sufism** teaches and practises **mysticism**. Sufis work to be constantly aware of God's presence, emphasizing spiritual development over obedience to laws,

Mysticism
is a form of religious experience where a person has a feeling of union with God.

contemplation over action in the world, and the cultivation of the soul over interaction with other people. Sufis see the religious experience of the Prophet Muhammad as centrally important to how they understand humans and their relationship with God.

Sufism grew out of a reaction to the increased **secularism** in Islam, and Sufis make much of the simplicity and prayer that had characterized the Prophet Muhammad's life. They practise meditation, ritual and a simple lifestyle to become as close to God as they can, using music, rhythmic movements and chanting to put them in a trance-like state. Their aim is to achieve a higher level of awareness of God and to purify their souls. The movement has also produced a large body of writings that include teaching and poetry. One famous Sufi was the mystic and philosopher **Al-Ghazali**.

> **Secularism**
> is the principle that there should be a complete separation of the state from religious institutions.

Problems with religious experiences

There are many difficulties with the idea that religious experiences are real. Some of these are listed and briefly discussed below.

- Why do people have visions that fit only within their own tradition? Christians are highly unlikely to report having had a vision of the Buddha, and Buddhists are just as unlikely to have had a mystical experience of Hinduism. This might suggest that their experiences are culturally based and not actually from God.
- Why do so few people have religious experiences? Surely, if God wished to impart important messages, he would do so to more people in a way that they would be more likely to accept. It seems very strange that God would send messages to humans via a medium that is doubted by the majority.
- Might there be physical or psychological reasons for religious experiences? Some individuals who claim to have had religious experiences are known to suffer from mental illness or psychological problems, such as split personality. A schizophrenic might hear voices in his head that he genuinely believes to come from God. Why should people who claim to have had a religious experience be believed when there are alternative explanations for what they have encountered? What is the difference between a real religious experience and a hallucination or the result of having eaten something that disagrees with you?
- There is scientific evidence that mystical states and visionary states can be induced by certain chemicals or by electrical stimulation of the brain. **Michael A. Persinger** (b. 1945) designed a 'God helmet' to stimulate people's temporal lobes in order to induce a religious state. Many of his subjects reported a sensation of 'an ethereal presence' in the room, very similar to a religious experience. Some of the volunteers were religious while others were not. Not all volunteers experienced this feeling.
- Religious experiences are purely subjective – a single individual has an experience that he or she thinks is an experience of God. But no one else has that same experience. So how can anyone else confirm that the person has seen God?

- Many people who claim to have had a mystical experience cannot explain what it was like. They have real difficulty trying to give a rational account that would make sense of it and can only express what they have undergone in vague terms, such as 'feeling at one with God' or having a sense of 'awe and wonder'. St Teresa of Ávila described her visions as like being in a dark room and sensing that there is someone there with you, although you cannot see them. This kind of description does not help sceptics to understand what has happened to the person or to believe that the experience has a divine origin.

The points above all pose problems about accepting that religious experiences are valid and genuine. But revelations (whether they come from God or not) can be very dangerous if someone believes they have been given by God. There are instances of people who claim that they have been told by God to commit murder, or a suicide bombing, or some other 'atrocity'. Examples include the Ku Klux Klan (KKK), founded in the nineteenth century to 're-establish Protestant Christian values in America by any means possible', who murdered, lynched, raped or tarred and feathered many Jews, Roman Catholics and others. Another example is the **genocide** of Roman Catholics in East Timor by the Fretelin government of Indonesia between 1975 and 1999. About one in every three Catholics in the country was killed. Clearly, these examples raise a huge problem of how believers can justify the validity of religious experiences. If they are genuinely from God, and if God is 'good', all religious experiences must necessarily have a 'good' outcome that is positive and helpful. It would seem to be impossible for any genuine religious experience to have negative effects, such as the death of many innocent people.

> **Genocide**
> is the deliberate killing of a whole race of people, especially of a religious, cultural or ethnic group.

The real problem is how to interpret a religious experience. Different denominations in both Christianity and Islam will interpret not only their religious texts differently (see pp. 7–9; 18–20 on the different ways of interpreting scripture) but also the other ways by which God is claimed to speak, particularly through religious experiences.

In Christianity, for example, those who take the biblical documents literally might try to justify genocide by appealing to the story of the capture of Jericho (Joshua 6), where God commanded the Israelites to kill all the inhabitants of the city without exception. Those who interpret this story differently will argue against it as a justification for mass murder, saying that it is an idealized account showing the power of God in bringing a fulfilment to his promise of providing a land for them to live in. Muslims throughout the world are also at pains in recent times to counter extreme interpretations of the Qur'an used by Islamist terror groups, such as the attacks in Paris in November 2015.

How to interpret religious experiences is extremely difficult because they are almost always personal and individual and therefore not accessible to others. If only one person has a religious experience, no one else will see or hear it, so it is impossible for them to say whether it is genuine or not. It all comes down to how the individual explains their experience and whether or not they can persuade others to believe it.

Tasks

1 Describe the main characteristics of the three main types of religious experiences – conversions, visions, mystical experiences.
2 What if your friend claimed that your RS teacher is really an alien, badly disguised as a human? Would you believe her? If you would, what reasons or evidence could you give to support her conclusion? Explain how this relates to a problem with religious experience.
3 If several people have the same religious experience together, does this make it more likely to be true? Does it depend on the number of people who experience it? What else might it depend on to make it 'real'?

TICK THE TOPICS

Now you should tick all the relevant boxes for what you have learned in this chapter:

Sections	Topics	Tick
General revelation	Christianity	
	Islam (Fitrah)	
Religious experience/special revelation	Conversions	
	Visions	
	Mystical experiences	
	Problems with religious experiences	

Sample questions

AQA Religious Studies A (8062)

1   Which of the following best expresses the idea that the divine (God, gods or the ultimate reality) is all-powerful?
     a) Omniscient b) Omnipotent c) Omnibenevolent d) Omnipresent   (1 mark)
2   Give two types of special revelation.   (2 marks)
3   Explain two contrasting beliefs in contemporary British society about enlightenment.   (4 marks)
4   Explain two religious beliefs about visions.   (5 marks)
5   'Religious experience is of no value to anyone.'
     Evaluate this statement. In your answer, you:
     ● should give reasoned arguments in support of this statement
     ● should give reasoned arguments to support a different point of view
     ● should refer to religious arguments
     ● may refer to non-religious arguments
     ● should reach a justified conclusion.   (12 marks)

Edexcel Religious Studies A (1RA0) and Religious Studies B (1RB0)

a)   Give three types of religious experience.   (3)
b)   Outline one type of revelation.   (4)
c)   Assess whether religious experiences can be shown to be real.   (9)
d)   'God has not revealed himself adequately.'
      Evaluate this statement, considering more than one point of view.   (12)

Edexcel International GCSE Religious Studies (4RS0)

a)   What is meant by 'general revelation'?   (2)
b)   Outline the characteristics of a visionary experience in Islam.   (5)
c)   Explain how Muslims understand the concept of Fitrah.   (8)
d)   'Conversions are more important than visions.'
      Do you agree? Give reasons for your answer, showing that you have considered another point of view.   (5)

OCR Religious Studies Full Course (J625)

a)   Give three types of religious experience.   (3)
b)   Outline the main characteristics of one type of religious experience.   (6)
c)   Explain why religious experiences are not important to some religious believers.
      You should refer to sources of wisdom and authority in your answer.   (6)
d)   'The only true believers are those who have had a religious experience.'
      Discuss this statement. In your answer, you should draw on your learning from across your course of study, including reference to beliefs, teachings and practices within your chosen religion.   (15)
                                                                                       (SPaG + 3)

5 The Problem of Evil

In this chapter you will see both why the existence of suffering and evil in the world is a philosophical problem when thinking about the existence of God and how Christians and Muslims understand evil. We will look at Christian arguments from Irenaeus and Augustine which ask whether evil is God's fault and what purpose it might serve. In Islam we will look at various attitudes to evil, including evil as a test of faith, and Fitrah, or humans' ability to choose good over evil.

Suffering and evil

The 'problem' of the apparent existence of 'evil' and 'suffering' in the world is probably the strongest argument against the existence of God.

The word 'evil' comes from the Old English word 'yfel' and had the meaning of something or someone who was 'bad', 'terrible', 'disgusting' or 'shameful'. Evil is a very strong word that goes beyond simply describing something as 'bad', or even 'very, very, very bad', which is not strong enough to express the depth and extent of the wrongness, harmfulness and disgust caused by a particular action or event. Such events as the Holocaust, the attack on the World Trade Center on 11 September 2001, or the devastating earthquake in Nepal in April 2015, which killed more than 9,000 people and injured another 23,000, would merit the term 'evil', as they go beyond our normal understanding of what human beings are like and of how nature can change from being supportive to being a very destructive force that kills and destroys.

Earthquakes – such as the one in Nepal in 2015 – and other natural disasters which destroy human lives and livelihoods can cause problems for those who seek to believe in a loving, all-powerful God.

Many people cannot understand why, if God is good, he would allow so many humans and animals to suffer a great deal of pain, torment and death throughout history. There are countless examples of suffering and evil:

- Genocide – not only the Jewish Holocaust, but more recent 'ethnic cleansings', e.g., in Bosnia
- Pol Pot's Year Zero in Cambodia
- Stalin's pogroms in Russia
- famine in Ethiopia and other parts of Africa
- earthquakes that kill thousands of people and destroy houses and crops
- tsunamis such as the one in the Indian Ocean on 26 December 2004, which killed 230,000 people in fourteen countries
- burglary with violence against pensioners
- life-shortening diseases where the person suffers great pain
- dementia-related illnesses
- rape, murder, torture, child abduction
- stillborn babies
- genetic illnesses
- teenage pregnancy
- acts of terrorism, such as that on the World Trade Center on 11 September 2001, which killed over 3,000 people.

> **Task**
>
> Read the following statement and write down your response.
>
> In sober truth, nearly all the things which men are hanged or imprisoned for doing to one another are nature's everyday performances. Killing, the most criminal act recognized by human laws, nature does once to every being that lives and in a large proportion of cases after protracted tortures. (J. S. Mill: 'Nature', 1874)

Moral and natural evil

Philosophers often distinguish between what they call 'moral' and 'natural' evil. Moral evils, on the one hand, are those things that people do to each other by a deliberate act of will. Murder would be an example of this. Natural evils, however, are those sufferings inflicted on people by nature over which we have no conscious control. Earthquakes, famines and epidemics of disease would count as examples.

The philosophers who make this distinction between moral and natural evil use the term 'evil' only in order to classify and categorize the kinds of thing that do harm to humans, not to describe some malignant superhuman power.

> **Tasks**
>
> Write down four examples of moral evil and four of natural evil and explain how and why they are evil. You should use the list above as a starting point, but try to think of your own examples too.
>
> Read the following statement by C. S. Lewis and summarize what he thinks about the origins of evil.
>
> God created things which had free will. That means creatures which can go wrong or right. Some people think they can imagine a creature which was free but had no possibility of going wrong, but I can't. If a thing is free to be good it's also free to be bad. And free will is what has made evil possible. Why, then, did God give them free will? Because free will, though it makes evil possible, is also the only thing that makes possible any love or goodness or joy worth having. A world of automata – of creatures that worked like machines – would hardly be worth creating. The happiness which God designs for His higher creatures is the happiness of being freely, voluntarily united to Him and to each other in an ecstasy of love and delight compared with which the most rapturous love between a man and a woman on this earth is mere milk and water. And for that they've got to be free.
>
> Of course God knew what would happen if they used their freedom the wrong way: apparently, He thought it worth the risk.
>
> (*The Case for Christianity*, radio talk, 1942, published in book form 1956)

Evil and the characteristics of God

The real problem with the existence of evil in the world has been clarified by many philosophers and theologians and set out logically. It is generally accepted that God (at least the God of the monotheistic religions of Christianity, Islam and Judaism) has three main characteristics:

- omnipotence (God has all the power that it is possible to have)
- omniscience (God has all the knowledge that it is possible to have)
- omnibenevolence (God has all the goodness that it is possible to have).

The problem arises with the acknowledgement that evil and suffering exist in the world, which challenges these characteristics of God.

Several philosophers have stated this problem very concisely. The twentieth-century atheist philosopher **John L. Mackie** (1917–1981), in a famous essay entitled 'Evil and Omnipotence', saw the problem of evil as a piece of mistaken thinking. According to Mackie, the following three claims are logically inconsistent:

- God is omnipotent.
- God is omnibenevolent.
- Evil exists.

Mackie commented that, if God is omnipotent, he is aware that evil and suffering exist and has the power to stop it. If God is omnibenevolent, he will want to stop it. And yet it is abundantly clear that evil and suffering exist. According to Mackie, if you believe that omnibenevolence and omnipotence are essential characteristics of God (i.e., God *must be* both omnipotent and omnibenevolent), then the existence of evil in the world actually *disproves* the existence of God.

Mackie agrees with the eighteenth-century Scottish philosopher David Hume that at least one of the following claims must be true:

- God is not omnipotent.
- God is not omnibenevolent.
- Evil does not exist.

In Mackie's view, agreeing with any one of these statements will do away with the problem of evil but will have very serious implications for claims about God's existence. Monotheist believers will not accept either of the first two claims, because they conflict with Christian, Muslim and Jewish doctrines about God's nature. We have lots of evidence, however, that evil exists in the world, so (for Mackie) it must follow logically that, if God exists, he is either not omnipotent or not omnibenevolent. If God exists in this scheme, he is clearly not the God of classical theism. Mackie says that it is still possible that God exists, but he would be a God who has limited powers or limited goodness. No monotheist would wish to accept this claim, because it contradicts every doctrine that has been formulated about the nature of God. According to Mackie (and Hume), the evidence for evil in the world is so overwhelming that he concludes that the God of classical theism does not exist.

Taking it further

One of the earliest philosophers to discuss this so-called inconsistent triad was the Greek Epicurus (341 BCE–270 BCE). A triad is a set or group of three things – in this instance, the three statements 'God is omnipotent', 'God is omnibenevolent', 'Evil exists'. If all three of the statements cannot logically be true, it is called an inconsistent triad. Epicurus said: 'If the gods have the will to remove evil and cannot, then they are not all powerful. If they are neither able nor willing, they are neither all powerful nor benevolent. If they are both able and willing to annihilate evil, why does it exist?' Another was the fifth-century African Christian philosopher St Augustine, bishop of Hippo: 'Either God is not able to abolish evil, or not willing; if he is not able then he is not all powerful; if he is not willing then he is not all good.'

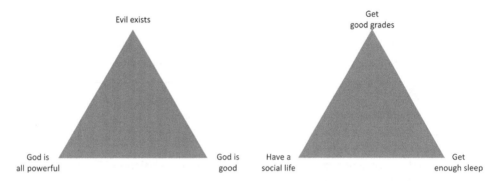

Two examples of what is called an 'inconsistent triad' – a set of three statements which can't all be true. If two of them are true, then the third must be false.

Non-religious responses to evil

Non-religious people acknowledge that the existence of evil is a particularly difficult problem for theists and understand the consequences for them if its existence cannot be explained. Non-religious people can also understand that personal experience of suffering or evil can cause believers to question or even reject their belief in an omnipotent and omnibenevolent God.

Groups such as humanists do not believe that suffering is some kind of punishment or a test for religious believers. This is obviously because humanists believe neither in God nor in an afterlife where punishment or reward will be handed out. Instead, they think that human beings have the ability to make free choices and take control over their lives. This means that they must take some personal responsibility for the way in which their life develops. Some evils and much suffering, such as wars, famine and poverty, are brought about or made worse because of human greed. Others, such as illness, floods and earthquakes, have natural causes that come about just because that is the way the world is. Sometimes these may be made worse because of human action or inaction. For example, the failure to send aid during an epidemic of disease will make things worse for those suffering and increase the death toll.

If there really was a God, humanists say, then why did he not make the world so that natural disasters do not happen, where viruses and cancers do not exist, and where tsunamis do not kill thousands of people?

Humanists believe that it is up to human beings to fight evil and suffering and solve the world's problems as far as possible. They are generally optimistic about human nature, saying that, although a lot of bad things happen to ordinary people, the majority show care and respect for others and for nature. The atheist philosopher **A. J. Ayer** (1910–1989) wrote, in *The Humanist Outlook* (1968): 'If the capacity for evil is part of human nature, so is the capacity for good.'

Humanists and other non-religious people do not wish to see the continuance of suffering and evil in the world. Further, they do not want the desire for punishment or revenge to dominate the minds of those who have suffered or been victims, because that would cloud their view of human nature and could make them ill and permanently unhappy. Humanists say that people must realize that evil is always going to be present in society because humans are not perfect creatures. What they can do, though, is try to help those who suffer, perhaps by offering personal or financial assistance, thus attempting to bring happiness to themselves and others.

Tasks

1 List three points made by humanists about their response to evil.
2 Explain what A. J. Ayer meant when he said 'If the capacity for evil is part of human nature, so is the capacity for good.'
3 'Humanist and other non-religious responses to evil are not satisfactory.' Do you agree? Give reasons for your answer.

Christian responses to evil

CHRISTIANITY
ROMAN
CATHOLICISM

Several Christian theologians have attempted to explain the problem of evil, taking into account the difficulties posed by the fact that evil exists despite God being loving and all powerful (the inconsistent triad). These responses are known as 'theodicies'.

The word **theodicy** comes from two Greek words, *theos* meaning 'God' and *diké*, meaning 'justice', so a theodicy attempts to show how God has good or just reasons for allowing evil to continue to exist in the world. Evil does not therefore contradict God's characteristics of omnipotence, omniscience or omnibenevolence. The term theodicy was first used by the German philosopher Gottfried Leibniz in his book *Theodicy*, published in 1710, though various responses to the problem of evil had been put forward long before then.

There have been two major theodicies in the Christian tradition: one by St Augustine and the other by St Irenaeus. Both are important, as each focuses on a different aspect of the problem.

The Irenaean theodicy

Theodicy
means an attempt to justify God's goodness despite the existence of evil in the world.

St Irenaeus (c.130–202 CE) was the second bishop of Lyons in France during the second half of the second century. He was one of the first Christian theologians and attempted to defend Christian ideas against a number of groups who claimed to be Christian but who did not believe the most important doctrines.

Irenaeus begins his theodicy by going back to the book of Genesis, especially the section where the creation of humans is discussed (1:26). He wondered why the author wrote that, when God created humans, he says 'Let us make humankind in our image, in our likeness.' Because Irenaeus considered the Bible to be the word of God, he thought that there was an important point being made here. He concluded that all humans were made in the 'image' of God but are not yet in God's 'likeness'. All humans are made in God's image, both holy and morally good people and unholy and morally bad people, such as Pontius Pilate (who sentenced Jesus to death) and Judas Iscariot (who betrayed Jesus to the authorities). For Irenaeus, being made in God's image has to do with being a rational creature, having the ability to make choices, and showing compassion and love towards others. But, sometimes, people fail to do good things and do very bad things. Being made in the 'image' of God does not guarantee moral perfection. To become in God's 'likeness' is a much longer journey for humans; it is a privilege and not automatic. If a positive free choice for God is made, then Christians, by doing good actions such as showing love and compassion for others, may eventually become in God's 'likeness' and achieve moral perfection. They will then become spiritual beings with God in heaven.

The Irenaean theodicy suggests that a Christian's life is a process of suffering, struggle and self-improvement to become more like God – much like a long and difficult trek or climb to a mountain peak.

As we will see shortly, Irenaeus' view concentrates on the creation of humans by God, not on their fall from grace, which is the focus of Augustine's theodicy.

Irenaeus goes on to show that evil is the result of **free will**. This means that, for Irenaeus, God is partly responsible for the existence of evil. God created humans imperfect – in his own 'image' but not in his 'likeness'. God did this deliberately because he wanted humans to grow and develop in order to reach moral and spiritual perfection. God had to make humans with free will so that they could freely decide to

Free will
is the idea that human beings are able to make their own decisions about what they do without being limited by outside factors.

do this. Giving humans freedom of choice, however, meant that God had to accept that they would sometimes make wrong choices and go against his intentions and will. God had to permit evil and suffering to take place. As Irenaeus said: 'How, if we had no knowledge of the contrary, could we have instruction in that which is good?' (*Against Heresies*, 4, xxxix, 1).

In other words, God had to allow the existence of evil so that humans would understand what good was. If God had intervened, humans would have lost their freedom and therefore their distinguishing characteristic. In Irenaeus' view, God created the world with the possibility of good as well as suffering and evil. Evil is necessary so that humans can exercise their free will and, in doing so, show their capacity for care, compassion and love for their fellow human beings and for the rest of the created world. For Irenaeus, suffering is cathartic – that is, it enables good to come into the world, as people who see suffering try to help by giving their time and using their skills to turn suffering into a positive and good outcome.

Irenaeus may have got this idea from some passages in the Bible. St Paul said: 'Not only so, but we also glory in our sufferings, because we know that suffering produces perseverance, character; and character, hope' (Romans 5:3). Irenaeus would also have known the book of Revelation (21:4): 'God will wipe every tear from their eyes. Death will be no more; mourning and crying and pain will be no more, for the first things have passed away.' This seems to suggest that, until God comes at the end of time to bring His Kingdom, suffering is a normal and expected part of life on earth.

Taking it further

The English philosopher Richard Swinburne follows up on this idea of the positive value of suffering:

> My suffering provides me with the opportunity to show courage and patience. It provides you with the opportunity to show sympathy and to help alleviate my suffering. And it provides society with the opportunity to choose whether or not to invest a lot of money in trying to find a cure for this or that particular kind of suffering. . . . Although a good God regrets our suffering, his greatest concern is surely that each of us shall show patience, sympathy and generosity and, thereby, form a holy character. ('Christianity Predicts a Negative Result', 2006)

Many philosophers and religious believers have found Swinburne's words here quite upsetting, if not insensitive. They ask why a good God would have to allow such horrific suffering for so many people in order for them to find a 'holy character'. The atheist biologist Richard Dawkins is very indignant on this point in his widely read book *The God Delusion* (2006), where he describes a TV debate between Swinburne and the Oxford professor of chemistry Peter Atkins: 'Swinburne at one point attempted to justify the Holocaust on the grounds that it gave the Jews a wonderful opportunity to be courageous and noble. Peter Atkins splendidly growled, "May you rot in hell".' Supporters of Swinburne might reply that there have been some significant outcomes from the Holocaust, such as Holocaust Memorial Day, the Yad Vashem Holocaust History Museum in Jerusalem, many books on the subject, inclusion in many history specifications in schools, and a much greater recognition throughout the world of the evils and dangers of anti-Semitism.

> **Task**
>
> Read the following statement and discuss whether you think it is a successful criticism of Irenaeus' theodicy.
>
> 'A God who deliberately plans suffering into the fabric of nature is not a being worthy of worship but rather a divine monster, randomly and horribly cruel, worthy only of fear and contempt. If, on the other hand, God is being totally indifferent to the fate of the human race, then he cannot be the sort of being with whom we can have any sort of relationship at all.'

Strengths of the Irenaean theodicy

Irenaeus provides important insights into human personality and moral development.

- He has a positive view of human beings, because they have the capacity to do good deeds and improve themselves morally and spiritually.
- He believes that things are worth more if one has to work hard and struggle for them than if they come naturally.

When Irenaeus discusses the phrase in Genesis 1:26 about how humans are made 'in the image and likeness of God', he uses the two-stage process of moral development to show that humans must make an effort to become like God.

- Being created in God's image, humans can make real moral decisions for themselves, but they are not yet *like* God – that is, they do not have his moral perfection. As they are made in God's image, however, they have the potential to attain it. In order to do this, they must endure evil and suffering.
- Irenaeus' theodicy can be understood in the light of modern evolutionary theory, which supports the idea of humans being made for growth and development towards morality and spiritual awareness.

Irenaeus makes no attempt to deny either the real existence of evil in the world or that God can use evil as a tool to help humans to develop towards godliness. The Irenaean approach takes a positive approach to evil. It looks to the future for the purpose that evil serves and the good that can come from it. Evil is the means to a greater end. Irenaeus has a forward-looking solution to the problem, where humans can rise towards God.

The Fall is the name given by Christians to explain the idea that humans were originally created perfect but then 'fell' from this state and became imperfect by going against God's will. Genesis chapters 2 and 3 tell the story of how Adam and Eve disobeyed God and their punishment for doing so.

> **Tasks**
>
> 1 Define the term 'theodicy'.
> 2 Explain, in your own words, three important strengths of Irenaeus' theodicy.
> 3 Do you agree that having to work hard to achieve something (such as good grades at GCSE) is worth more than not having to work hard because you have a natural talent for the same thing? Give reasons for your answer.

Weaknesses of the Irenaean theodicy

Irenaeus' arguments have not been very well received by many Christians because his 'positive' view of evil downplays the importance of **the Fall** as the point at which evil and suffering entered the world.

- He seems to ignore the idea expressed in Genesis 3 that sin (and therefore suffering and evil) came about as a result of Adam and Eve's choice to disobey God's command.
- As a result, he makes Jesus into little else than a great moral role model. This seems to go against mainstream Christian teaching that Jesus was the saviour of the world who brought forgiveness and reconciliation with God through his crucifixion and resurrection.

Irenaeus believed that *all* humans would eventually reach moral perfection – even such evil people as Hitler or Saddam Hussein would eventually become perfect. For many people who have lived good moral lives, this seems like an unfair suggestion. Irenaeus' theodicy does not really solve the problem of why many 'innocent' individuals suffer terribly through their lives.

Taking it further

For Irenaeus' theodicy to be successful, he has to have a theoretical idea that a state of moral perfection actually exists. He says that it is possible for all humans to reach the 'likeness' of God, but not all will achieve this state during their physical life. There must, therefore, be some form of life after bodily death so that all humans can reach moral perfection. Irenaeus does not give any evidence for this idea, so this is a serious weakness.

Tasks

1 Explain, in your own words, the main criticisms of Irenaeus' theodicy.
2 Do you think that Irenaeus' idea that everyone will eventually achieve moral perfection is a good one? Give reasons for your answer.
3 'Irenaeus' theodicy does not explain the problem of evil satisfactorily.' Do you agree? Give reasons for your answer, showing that you have thought about another point of view.

The Augustinian theodicy

St Augustine (354–430 CE) developed four themes in his discussion of the problem of evil, as shown in table 5.1.

1 *The privation of good* Augustine argued, from studying the Bible, that God was totally good. In Genesis 1, God is described as having created a world that was perfect in every respect; it was therefore free from any defective things, such as suffering and evil: 'God saw all that he had made and it was very good' (1:31). Importantly for Augustine, 'evil' is not a substance or a thing, so God did not create it; evil occurs when something goes wrong with something good. An example he uses is of blindness. Blindness happens when the eye stops working correctly, where there is an absence of sight. Augustine used the term '**privation**'

Privation
is Augustine's idea that what might be called 'evil' is only a 'lack' of goodness.

Table 5.1   St Augustine on the problem of evil

Theme	Brief explanation
The privation of good	Augustine says that something called 'evil' does not exist. What people call evil is actually only a lack of goodness.
The free will defence	Humans are responsible for evil actions because they use their free will wrongly. Evil is not God's fault.
The principle of plenitude	God created a world that contained every variety of creature so that it showed the 'fullness' of his creation. This means that some imperfections will exist.
The aesthetic theme	The universe is totally good when seen from God's point of view. Humans have only a partial view, so see such things as earthquakes as evil, while they may have some positive function for God.

to describe this state (a privation of something is an absence or lack of that thing). For example, 'evil' is an absence of 'good', so the blind eye is lacking its proper function of seeing. Blindness is not an evil in itself; it is simply the loss of function of the eye. Darkness is not a real thing in itself; it is simply the absence of light. Augustine says, in the *Enchiridion*:

> What, after all, is what we call evil except the privation of good? In animal bodies, for instance, sickness and wounds are nothing but the privation of health. When a cure is effected, the evils that were present (i.e. the sickness and the wounds) do not retreat and go elsewhere. Rather they simply do not exist any more.

As God made only things that exist, and because 'evil' is not an existing thing, so God cannot be responsible for any evil or suffering in the world.

2 *The free will defence* Augustine says that evil came not from God but from entities that have free will. God created all humans with free will. The story of 'the Fall' of Adam and Eve in Genesis 3 is key to understanding what Augustine means about free will. In his book *The City of God*, he discusses this story at length. Adam and Eve (who represent all humans) are tempted by the serpent (not an evil character) to eat the fruit of the tree of knowledge of good and evil (which Adam and Eve want). They choose to ignore what God has said about this fruit and freely decide to eat it. The result is their shame and corruption and, through them, of all human beings.

   Augustine says that God foresaw that this misuse of free will would happen, because God is omniscient and planned to redeem humans by sending Christ, who would die and rise again for their sakes. He argued that some people will still go to hell, but this will be because of their abuse of their free will. Others will repent by using their free will, will turn to Christ and so will be saved.

3 *The principle of plenitude* The term '**plenitude**' means 'fullness', 'abundance' or 'completeness'. The term is not Augustine's but was coined by the American philosopher and historian of ideas Arthur Lovejoy, in his book *The Great Chain of Being* (1936). The principle is traced back to Plato in the *Timaeus*.

Plenitude
is Augustine's idea the the world is 'full' of all varieties of experience, events and objects and that there is more goodness than evil.

A seventeenth-century Italian painting of the Fall: according to the Book of Genesis, Adam and Eve disobeyed God and were cast out of the Garden of Eden. For many Christian theologians, this explains the origins of evil and suffering in the world.

Augustine argued that the best type of world is one that contains every possible variety of creature and not one that consists only of the highest kind of being. It is a universe where all possibilities of existence are realized. Some creatures are, therefore, imperfect. This results in a principle of variety, so that some creatures are stronger, some are more beautiful, some are more intelligent than others. Variety therefore entails inequality and, it could be argued, injustice.

So, if we ask: 'Why don't butterflies live as long as elephants?' or 'Why aren't elephants as beautiful as butterflies?', the answer is simple: if they were, they would not be butterflies and elephants. Why did God create such an imperfect creature as humans and not just angelic beings? The answer is that, if he had, it would not be a world but, rather, the highest heaven. For Augustine, this principle of plenitude explains the problem of why God would have created such seemingly horrible, useless and destructive creatures as slugs or such natural events as earthquakes or tsunamis.

4   *The aesthetic theme* When the British philosopher of religion **John Hick** (1922–2012) refers to Augustine's '**aesthetic** theme', he has in mind the latter's belief that the universe is entirely good when seen in its totality, from God's

Aesthetics is the name given to the study of 'beauty'.

perspective. He argues that humans see only part of the picture. Only God sees the total view. In one of his works, Augustine points out that such 'evils' as a substance which poisons, the fire which burns, and the water which drowns are evil only in a relative sense. So, for instance, if a famous art gallery burns down, it may be seen as a great tragedy by art lovers but not by many other people who do not like or appreciate art. Poisons are not 'evil' in themselves but are harmful only when brought into conjunction with other substances with which they react. A tidal wave is not 'evil' in itself but is 'evil' only when it damages buildings or kills humans. Augustine acknowledged that good things can come from evil actions. For instance, although a powerful cyclone may destroy a city, the city will be rebuilt with stronger houses that do not collapse in the future, meaning that the people who live in them will be safer.

Taking it further

The aesthetic theme is also an idea influenced by neo-Platonism, particularly in the works of Plotinus, who writes: 'We are like people ignorant of painting who complain that the colours are not beautiful everywhere in the picture: but the Artist has laid on the appropriate tint to every spot.' Augustine himself writes:

> All have their offices and limits laid down so as to ensure the beauty of the universe. That which we abhor in any part of it gives us the greatest pleasure when we consider the universe as a whole. . . .The very reason why some things are inferior is that though the parts may be imperfect the whole is perfect . . . the black colour in a picture may very well be beautiful if you take the picture as a whole.

Strengths of the Augustinian theodicy

An important strength of Augustine's theodicy is that it takes the responsibility for evil away from God and lays it at the feet of humans.

- The fact that humans have free will means that God is not responsible for evil. This is especially relevant for moral evil.
- For Augustine, free will explains the existence of natural evil. Angels have free will as well as humans, and some angels decided to go against God's will. This resulted in such things as earthquakes, tornadoes and disease that bring death and suffering to humans. God is not responsible for natural evil.
- Although God created everything, Augustine says that evil is not a substance, therefore God did not create it. So God is not responsible for evil in the world.
- The aesthetic theme and the principle of plenitude show that human sin is a by-product of God's creation. Humans use it to do evil, but God reworks it for good, like an artist who uses shadows to illuminate the beauty and colour in their work.

Augustine uses the existence of evil to emphasize his views about salvation. Human evil meant that God had to send Jesus to absorb the sins of the world on the cross so that humans could be brought back to God. This creates a greater world.

For Augustine, complete happiness is not the point of this lifetime. Life is really a test for souls where their destiny in the next life will be decided. The existence and hope for life after death is crucial for Augustine.

Weaknesses of the Augustinian theodicy

Many people do not accept that Augustine's argument takes the responsibility for evil away from God, because it seems that God created the possible conditions in which evil could thrive.

- Augustine says that God created a world that was perfect, but the existence of evil shows that the world is not perfect. This is a contradiction in his argument. Evil cannot have created itself from a perfect world, so God must have created it. If this is true, either God must be not perfect or he intentionally created evil. This would mean that God was not omnibenevolent.
- The scientific theory of evolution shows that the world was not created perfect. Instead, it has been evolving and changing for many millions of years. Evolutionary theory shows that every living thing has a selfish desire for survival, and this does not fit with the biblical account of the Fall in Genesis chapters 2 and 3. Also, the idea that all humans inherit 'original sin' from Adam that predisposes them to do evil doesn't fit with modern scientific ideas about inheritance or the psychology of human behaviour.

For Augustine, the afterlife would be a place of eternal punishment for those who had committed sin and evil. This raises a serious problem for believing that God is omnibenevolent. It seems to make a mockery of God sending Jesus to die on behalf of humans to take away their sins and bring them back to God. Augustine believed that hell was a necessary part of God's creation, but why would God do this if his creation was perfect? If God is omniscient, why would he create a world that was imperfect?

Task

Read the following short extract below from Elie Wiesel's book *The Gates of the Forest*. Wiesel survived the horrors of Auschwitz and Buchenwald concentration camps during the Second World War. In this novel he writes about an argument between a rabbi and Gregor, whose faith in God has been destroyed by experiencing the Holocaust.

> Gregor was angry.
> 'After what has happened to us, how can you believe in God?'
> With an understanding smile on his lips, the Rebbe answered, 'How can you not believe in God after what has just happened?'

Discuss your response to the rabbi's question. Is it still possible to believe in an all-powerful, all-loving God after the Holocaust?

Muslim views on suffering and evil

Muslim views on evil and suffering in the world begin with the concept of God. The Qur'an mentions God (Allah) 2,692 times and asserts frequently that there is no God but Allah. For example, Surah 1 says:

ISLAM

In the name of Allah, the Compassionate, the Merciful
Praise be to Allah, Lord of the Creation,
The Compassionate, the Merciful,
King of Judgement Day!
You alone we worship, and to you alone
We pray for help.
Guide us to the straight path
The path of those whom you have favoured,
Not of those who have incurred your anger
Nor of those who have gone astray.

There are ninety-nine names for God which express various characteristics of the divine. All of these names are based on the idea that God is One and is ultimately unknowable. This is a strict and uncompromising monotheism and teaches Muslims that 'oneness' is central to the idea of God. This is the idea of '**Tawhid**'. God has given life to humans and will cause them to die and then raise them up again. Nothing is impossible for God because he gives everything its order and place in the universe. In return for his blessings, God requires only that believers acknowledge that there is no God but him. The belief in Tawhid is seen in the first and most important of the Five Pillars of Islam, the duties expected of all Muslims: 'I bear witness that there is no god but God and that Muhammad is the Messenger of God.'

One of the ninety-nine names for God is 'omnipotent', all powerful. God is also 'omnibenevolent', all good. Muslims believe that God is omnipotent and all good, but they believe that God is much more than this. Among the other names of God are 'the Just', 'the Severe in Punishment', 'the Wise', 'the Avenger' and 'the Compassionate'. Because they believe in Tawhid, Muslims do not separate the names and attributes of God from one another but understand them all together. If God were only 'the Compassionate' and 'the Merciful', there would be a significant difficulty in reconciling the problem of suffering and evil in the world with the existence of God. This would be because it implies that God was not in complete control of the universe and perhaps did not create it. Evil could have come into the world because God was not omniscient (all knowing) or omnipotent (all powerful). God would not then be able to do anything to alleviate the suffering of believers or to get rid of the evil in the world. Muslims believe, however, that God is all knowing and all powerful, so there must be reasons why he allows evil to exist.

Islam provides several reasons why God allows evil to exist in the world.

God has a purpose for suffering

Suffering and evil can test the belief of anyone, and God allows this to happen because suffering shows the inner self to God. Through the experience of human suffering, God can see who is truly righteous. In other words, God has a positive reason for allowing suffering and evil. God uses suffering to look deep with the human soul to test and correct those who fail to live up to his commands and laws.

Suffering is the result of sin

In Islam, sin is directly linked with lack of belief in God. The term 'Islam' means 'surrender', and this is what observant Muslims do throughout their lives – they surrender their own wishes and desires to God's will. Sometimes, Muslims forget to do this and so fail to serve God. This is called '**Kufr**', the state of unbelief. There are three main meanings of Kufr in Islam.

Kufr
is the Islamic term for disbelief in God.

- It can mean denying or rejecting what one knows to be the truth – pretending that everything is fine, but knowing that this is not really the case.
- It can mean permitting what is forbidden or turning away in arrogance. This is what **Iblis** (Satan) did when he turned away from God.
- It can mean **hypocrisy** – going through the actions of being a Muslim but not inwardly believing in God.

Iblis
is the Muslim name for the Devil.

To be in a state of Kufr means to become self-centred rather than God-centred. People become so preoccupied with their own desires and needs that they 'forget' God and fail to obey God's commands. They begin to misuse the gifts they have been given by God and so do evil things such as crave money or pleasure. This kind of behaviour can become destructive, and people grow further apart from God. When they finally realize what they have done, they suffer because they feel guilty and at a distance from God. This kind of rejection of God can happen to anyone and, when they realize their mistake, their suffering may be painful, but they will see it as a lesson to serve God in the future, not themselves.

Hypocrisy
means saying one thing but doing the opposite.

Evil is not permanent

Muslims believe that evil is a temporary condition. God did not make the world a permanent world. It is temporary and everything in it has a limited existence. Everything in the world lives for a time and then comes to an end. This applies to both good things and bad things. Humans are in the world for a relatively short time and then die. During a person's life, God will test them. Those who 'pass' the test will be taken to an eternal world that is perfect and permanent. Those who 'fail' the test will see the evil consequences of their sin and will suffer punishment.

Evil is a test

Following from the previous point, several passages in the Qur'an teach that God sends the existence of evil in the world as a test for believers.

> Do you think that you will enter paradise without any trials while you have known the examples of those who passed away before you? They were afflicted with suffering and adversity and were so violently shaken up that even the Prophet and the believers with him cried out: 'When will God's help come?' Be aware, God's help is close. (Surah 2:214)

> Surely with every difficulty there is relief. (Surah 94:5)

A nineteenth-century Russian painting of Job, known in the Islamic tradition as the prophet Ayyub. The Qur'an tells how he suffered many trials and setbacks but kept his faith in God and was rewarded for his patient acceptance of his lot.

Suffering can be a real test of endurance. Muslims believe that God allows some people to suffer in order to test their patience and steadfastness. Even God's prophets and messengers were affected in this way. For example, Ayyub is mentioned in the Qur'an as a prophet who was very patient. Good people sometimes suffer, but their ordeals have a benefit for those who see how the sufferer puts up with their pain or illness. The people who observe this feel humbled, and it may make them more unassuming and believe in God even more strongly than before. Such witnesses may learn lessons from the good example of the person who suffers.

In a slightly different way, God may sometimes allow some people to suffer in order to test others. When a Muslim sees someone else suffering, it is seen as a trial from God, because it may test his or her charity or his or her faith.

The role of Iblis

Shaytan is the Muslim name for Satan.

A **djinni** is an invisible spirit in Islam which can affect humans.

The role of Iblis – the name of the Devil – in Islam is to tempt humans to go against the will of God and commit sins. Iblis is referred to in the Qur'an eleven times in eleven verses. Another name for Iblis is **Shaytan**, who is mentioned in the Qur'an eighty-seven times. Iblis was a **djinni**, an invisible creature made from smokeless fire, unlike humans, whom God made from clay. Djinn (plural of djinni) were made by God and had free will. Iblis used his free will to disobey and was forced to leave

Paradise and was thereafter called Shaytan. On earth, he tricked Adam and his wife (she is not given a name in the Qur'an) into eating the fruit from the forbidden tree. After this, he was condemned by God to **Jahannam** (hell) but was allowed to roam the earth tempting humans to defect from God. Surah 7:22 says:

> Then he caused them to fall by deceit; so when they tasted of the tree, their evil inclinations became manifest to them, and they both began to cover themselves with the leaves of the garden; and their Lord called out to them: 'Did I not forbid you both from that tree and say to you that the Shaytan is your open enemy?'

The role of Iblis is to seduce humans by whispering sinful ideas in their ears. Muslims understand Iblis in different ways: he is an evil being who exists independently, or he is the personification of evil in human terms. His goal in life is to make humans loyal to him and lead them away from the worship of the one true God. Many Muslims now will say a special prayer before reading the Qur'an or participating in other activities: 'I seek refuge with Allah from the cursed Shaytan.' They believe that those who are seduced by Iblis and perform evil actions or have evil thoughts will join him in Jahannam. It is also believed that Iblis is in some ways still within God's control. This is because God is the sovereign lord of all creatures, which would include even Iblis. Justice will eventually be done to Iblis, and he will be condemned for ever to Jahannam, as will those humans who have been under his power.

Jahannam
is the Muslim name for Hell.

There are a number of duas or prayers in Islam to invoke protection against djinn and Iblis.

Taking it further

There is a different tradition concerning Iblis in the Sufi tradition of Islam. Sufis believe that Iblis had a great deal of love for God but did not want to take second place to Adam. God instructed all the angels and Iblis to bow down before Adam, but Iblis refused. When God asked Iblis why this was, he said: 'I am better than Adam: you have created me from fire, while him you created from clay' (Surah 7:12).

Sufis ask why God would want the angels (and Iblis) to bow down to anything other than God himself, particularly something younger and inferior to them. Sufi scholars and mystics were confused by this and could not find a satisfactory answer. They came to the conclusion that God could not really have wanted Iblis to bow down to Adam and argued instead that God was testing not Iblis's obedience, but his love. They see Iblis as being predestined to go against God's will, playing the role of a tragic and jealous lover of God who was compelled to disobey God's command to bow down to Adam because he could not see God's image in Adam. Sufis think that, rather than being criticized, Iblis should be praised for this disobedience. They praise him for his dedication to what he sees as a just cause, even in the face of difficulties and suffering.

Fitrah as applied to suffering and evil

God created humans with free will, giving them the ability to choose whether to do right or wrong, good or evil actions. This depends on the idea of **fitrah**, an innate moral sense of right and wrong. Islam is '*din al-fitrah*', meaning that human beings are naturally inclined to do good rather than evil. Their inner nature is to submit to the will of God (as shown in the meaning of 'Islam' – submission). Fitrah makes an unbreakable bond between God and humans, a harmony between creator and created. It is in tune with the nature of creation and the role of humans in that creation. This is shown in the Qur'an:

> Therefore, stand firm in your devotion to the upright faith – the natural disposition [fitrah] made by Allah, the one on which mankind is created – and the laws of Nature ordained by Allah cannot be changed. That is the standard of true faith, but most among mankind do not know. (Surah 30:30)

Humans have an instinct that leads them to intuit the difference between right and wrong. They can acknowledge the truth of God's existence, a truth that is inscribed on their soul. Even those who reject God's guidance have this instinct. For some Muslims, however, fitrah is not a strong instinct because its influence can quickly be lost by all a person's other instincts, as well as any other influences. In other words, humans can use fitrah for good or for evil. Those who use it for good will endeavour to live according to the laws of Islam; those who ignore fitrah will turn against God's laws and commit sin and do evil acts.

Tasks

1   A person using their innate instinct to know what God's commands are is in obedience to the **Five Pillars**. Find out what these are and show how they link to the idea of fitrah.
2   Do you think Muslims see themselves as being essentially sinful? Give reasons for your answer.
3   In what ways is 'sin' different from 'evil'? How is this important to the way Muslims act in the world?
4   Read the following passage from the Qur'an and, in your own words, explain why Muslims think that God allows evil and suffering in the world.

   Surely I will test you with something of fear and of hunger, and of loss of wealth, and lives, and produce: Yet give good tidings to the patient who, when calamity afflicts them, say 'We belong to God, and to Him we are returning'.
   (Surah 2:155–6)

Now think about this passage critically. Given what you know about the nature of God, is there anything inconsistent or wrong with this kind of answer?

TICK THE TOPICS

Now you should tick the relevant boxes to check what you have learned in this chapter.

Sections	Topics	Tick
Terms	Moral and natural evil	
Characteristics of God	Omnipotence	
	Omniscience	
	Omnibenevolence	
Non-religious responses to evil	Humanists	
Christian responses to evil	Irenaean theodicy	
	– strengths	
	– weaknesses	
	Augustinian theodicy	
	– strengths	
	– weaknesses	
Muslim responses to evil	Tawhid	
	Purpose of suffering	
	Suffering as a result of sin	
	Evil is not permanent	
	Evil is a test	
	The role of Iblis	
	Fitrah applied to suffering and evil	

Additional tasks on the problem of evil

1 In your own words, explain the distinction that philosophers make between moral and natural evil.
2 Explain the term 'theodicy'.
3 Read the following statements and put a tick next to the ones that seem to be in line with what an atheist might say.
   a) God allows evil because he is indifferent to human suffering.
   b) God uses evil to punish people for their sins.
   c) God allows evil to exist so that people can make genuine moral choices.
   d) God cannot control all the evil in the universe.
   e) Human beings need evil to stimulate them to grow into mature spiritual beings.
   f) In a world without suffering, nothing would ever matter.
   g) Good and evil are opposing concepts that need each other to exist. Nothing is good unless you have evil to compare it with.
4 If God is omnipotent, why can he not:
   • create beings that are already morally and spiritually perfect
   • create beings who are free but will only ever choose to do good.
5 Imagine that you are a minister writing a letter of sympathy to parents who have lost their child in a tragic accident. In the letter you must try to explain to the parents why God allows such things to happen.

Sample questions

AQA Religious Studies A (8062)

1 Which of the following is a religious theory about the problem of evil?
   a) Theology b) Theodicy c) Theogony d) Theophany (1 mark)
2 Give two examples of evil.   (2 marks)
3 Explain two contrasting beliefs in contemporary British society about suffering.   (4 marks)
4 Explain two religious beliefs about natural evil.   (5 marks)
5 'Evil is God's fault.'
Evaluate this statement. In your answer, you:
   • should give reasoned arguments in support of this statement
   • should give reasoned arguments to support a different point of view
   • should refer to religious arguments
   • may refer to non-religious arguments
   • should reach a justified conclusion.   (12 marks)

Edexcel Religious Studies A (1RA0) and Religious Studies B (1RB0)

a) Outline the inconsistent triad.   (3)
b) Explain two reasons why evil is a problem for religious believers.   (4)
c) Assess the success of Augustine's theodicy.   (9)
d) 'The problem of evil cannot be solved.'
Evaluate this statement, considering more than one point of view.   (12)

Edexcel International GCSE Religious Studies (4RS0)

a) Define 'natural evil'. (2)
b) Outline what is meant by the 'inconsistent triad'. (5)
c) Explain how some Christians attempt to solve the problem of moral evil. (8)
d) 'The problem of evil shows that God is either evil or incompetent.'
Do you agree? Give reasons for your answer, showing that you have considered another
point of view. (5)

OCR Religious Studies Short Course (J125)

a) Give three examples of natural evil. (3)
b) Outline the problem of evil. (6)
c) Explain how religious believers try to solve the problem of evil.
You should refer to sources of wisdom and authority in your answer. (6)
d) 'The existence of evil means that God does not exist.'
Discuss this statement. In your answer, you should draw on your learning from across
your course of study, including reference to beliefs, teachings and practices within your
chosen religion. (15)
(SPaG + 3)

WJEC Eduqas Religious Studies

a) Giving one example, state what is meant by moral evil. (2)
b) With reference to one religion you have studied, explain views about original sin. (5)
c) From two different religions or two religious traditions, explain views about
forgiveness. (8)
d) 'If God is just, he will punish evil people.'
Discuss this statement, showing that you have considered more than one point of view.
(You must refer to religion and belief in your answer.) (15)
(SPaG + 6)

6 Religion and Science

In this chapter, you will be studying the interaction between religion and science on the topics of the origins of the universe and the theory of evolution. From the scientific side, you will look at the main theory for the origins of the universe and reactions to this from both Christian and Muslim points of view. You will give special attention to Genesis chapters 1 and 2, the Jewish/Christian creation account, and the relevant surahs in the Qur'an on creation in Islam.

   You will then go on to look at another aspect of the interaction between religion and science – the debate about evolution and the origins of life. Richard Dawkins's more radical views will be discussed as a forceful statement of the atheist evolutionary position, and Christian and Muslim responses to these will be examined.

In the first part of this chapter, we will be looking at the relationship between religion and science in relation to the origins of the universe. There are several ways of looking at the interaction between religion and science. Some people see them as polar opposites, where they have nothing in common and they disagree with each other entirely – there is no common ground. Others see religion and science as being more compatible: both are looking for meaning in the universe but use different methods to search for it, so that they are like railway lines that run parallel to each other but never touch. We will be exploring the relationship between science and religion by focusing on two of the most important aspects of their interaction – the origins of the universe and the origins of life – which we will use to draw out some of the core features relevant to religion and science more broadly.

The origin of the universe

The Big Bang theory

The **Big Bang theory** is the most widely accepted scientific account of the origin of the universe. It suggests that the universe came about as the result of something like a large explosion that created space and time itself and caused matter to be projected in all directions. As this matter began to slow down, the stars, galaxies and planets began to form. Eventually, the conditions were suitable for life to begin to evolve.

> The **Big Bang theory** is the scientific theory that the universe began with a huge explosion which expanded over billions of years to create galaxies, solar systems and planets.

The Big Bang theory is a scientific explanation for the creation of the universe.

At the 1924 meeting of the American Astronomical Society in Washington, the astronomer **Edwin Hubble** (1889–1953) read a paper that showed that stars existed beyond the Milky Way. This does not seem very astonishing to us now, but at the time it changed the way that scientists saw the universe, as then most astronomers believed that it consisted entirely of the Milky Way. Beyond this, nothing existed. Hubble had identified a Cepheid variable star – the one kind of star that could provide a means of determining the distance to the galaxy. Over the next several months Hubble determined that the star was 7,000 times brighter than the sun and that it was 900,000 light years away. Given that almost all astronomers thought that the universe (the Milky Way) was only 100,000 light years across, this was an extraordinary discovery. In 1929, Hubble published a paper that was to prove that the universe was expanding from a single point from which everything in the universe had all started, at the moment of a 'Big Bang'. Fairly soon, it became obvious that, by measuring how fast the universe was expanding, it was possible to date the origin of the universe.

Hubble's ground-breaking work changed the understanding of the place of humans in the universe and had huge implications for religion, as we shall see later.

Taking it further

The Big Bang theory claims that the entire universe began to condense out of the initial explosion about 15 billion years ago and is still expanding.

- After about 300,000 years, as the intense heat from the explosion started to cool, the uniform space in which matter and energy existed started to divide and differences in temperature and density appeared.
- Around the same time, the four fundamental forces used by physics to relate everything that exists – gravity, electro-magnetism and the strong and weak nuclear forces – began to emerge as recognizable entities governing the behaviour of the cosmic material created by the Big Bang.
- After approximately 400,000 years, atoms of hydrogen and helium started to form out of sub-atomic particles created earlier.
- About 1 billion years after the Big Bang, galaxies and stars formed out of the cooling cosmic material produced by the explosion.
- At 10 billion years, planets started to form. After another 2 billion years, the earliest life forms developed, as did the start of evolutionary biology.

Task

Draw a timeline or other diagram to provide an outline of how the universe began and developed according to the Big Bang theory.

There are three important strands of evidence that cosmologists use in favour of the Big Bang being the correct explanation for the beginning of the universe.

1 It is a fact that the universe appears to be expanding at a rapid rate as if in the aftermath of a large explosion. Very distant galaxies seem to be moving apart from each other, and those furthest away are moving faster than those nearest to us. From this evidence it can be inferred that, at one time, they were closer together and are now moving further and further apart. It is possible to calculate how far away a galaxy is by measuring how fast it is moving. Because we can measure how far away the stars are, how fast they are moving and how old they are, we can also calculate the age of the universe.

2 The theory states that the conditions at the beginning of time must have been very hot indeed. In effect, the Big Bang was a huge fireball. Scientists believe that they have detected the remnants of this fireball in the background microwave radiation in the universe. Andrew McKellar (1910–1960) made an accidental discovery in 1941 that was observed again in 1964 by Arno Penzias (b. 1933) and Robert Wilson (b. 1936) and finally confirmed by satellite observations in the 1990s. This radiation seems to be coming from all points of space at the same time. This observation is consistent with the Big Bang theory because all parts of the universe came about equally from the same initial explosion.

3 It takes time for the light from distant galaxies to reach earth. This means that

observing objects through a telescope is like looking back in time. We are now seeing the distant parts of the universe as they were a long time ago. Observations show that it looked different then from how it does now. This is exactly what we would expect from the Big Bang.

> **Tasks**
>
> 1 What do scientists mean by the 'Big Bang'?
> 2 Find out what cosmologists mean by a 'singularity' when they talk about the beginning of the universe. How does this relate to the Big Bang?

We will look at Christian and Muslim responses to the Big Bang theory when examining their creation accounts in the sections which follow.

Genesis creation accounts in Christianity

Some Christians believe that the account of creation in Genesis is literally true, but many do not. Among this latter group, it is widely accepted that Genesis has combined two different origin stories, one in chapters 1:1–2:4a and the second from chapters 2:4b–3:24.

- The first account emphasizes the order and regularity by which God created the universe. Everything that exists came into being as a direct result of the words and acts of God.
- The second account reverses the order of creation, with man appearing first, then plants and animals, and woman appearing later. Man and woman are servants of God, whereas in the first story they are created together and raised to the dignity of God's agents in creation.

There are some points of connection between the two stories.

- In both, wholeness is a key aspect: in the first, God rests when creation is complete; in the second, the creation of woman brings completion to God's work. It is particularly significant that humans are created 'in the image' of God, which gives human beings immense value and dignity.
- Both stories reflect a monotheistic theology: one shows God's **transcendence**, the other his **immanence**. For more information on these characteristics of God, see pp. 57–8.

The theologian **Keith Ward** (b. 1938) thinks that the two creation accounts come from different tribal origin stories that have been placed side by side by the editor of Genesis. They express different and important spiritual truths. Ward believes that the editor was not worried by the fact that, taken literally, they are incompatible. This is not a problem because different stories can depict different spiritual truths. Like metaphors, they cannot contradict each other – only literal accounts can be contradictory – but they can complement each other. The two Genesis origin stories offer important complementary truths, and the editor did not want to lose any of these truths, so included them both.

CHRISTIANITY
ROMAN
CATHOLICISM

Genesis 1

The structure or literary framework of Genesis 1 is interesting, and many scholars and others have suggested differing ways in which the chapter may be better understood. One such scheme is the 'shape and fill' structure to explain the six days of creation, as shown in table 6.1.

Table 6.1 The 'shape and fill' structure of Genesis 1

Prologue: The earth was formless and void (empty)	
SHAPE (by separation)	**FILL (each form)**
Day 1: Separating day and night	Day 4: Sun and moon for day and night
Day 2: Separating 'waters' into sky and sea	Day 5: Birds and fish created for sky and sea
Day 3: Separating land and sea; land plants are created	Day 6: Animals and humans fill the lands and eat the plants
Day 7: The heavens and earth are finished; God rested	

In what we are calling the 'prologue', the phrase 'formless and void' in Hebrew is a rhyming phrase – *tohu wa-bohu.* This sets the scene for the format of the chapter,

The Book of Genesis in the Bible recounts how God created the earth and all living things, as shown in this woodcut from Martin Luther's Bible of 1545.

where in the first three days the 'shape' of the universe is created and in the next three days things and creatures are created to 'fill' the void. The two trios of days follow a logical structure and show that God's creative work is both *complete* (as it covers everything that exists) and *ordered* (as it follows a logical structure). The prologue and day 7 frame the six productive days of creation and show the beginning and end of God's creative work.

One other point about the structure of Genesis 1 suggests that it was intended to be spoken or proclaimed orally rather than to be read silently. We have to remember that most people could not read or write, so they would have had the story told to them. To help with this, the editor of Genesis 1 deliberately wrote in a particular way, using the same pattern for each day's creative activity, so that the person who recited or proclaimed the story found it easier to understand and learn it. It has been suggested that the creation story was proclaimed at the Jewish New Year festival every year to thank God for creating the universe. The repeated structure also gives the reader/hearer some specific theological ideas about the nature of God. It presents God's power, freedom and unchallenged control over the world he created.

> **Task**
>
> Read Genesis 1 and see if you can spot the particular structure the editor uses that would help people to remember the story. Hint: you should look for repeated phrases.

There are several other theological themes in the first creation story.

- God created a perfect world which has order and purpose, showing his omniscience (knowing all things).
- God created the world from nothing (***ex nihilo***), showing his power and creativity.
- Humans are given the highest place in God's creation, as they are the final part of the creative process. This shows that God wishes to have a special relationship with humans.
- Genesis 1 mentions that God rested on the seventh day. Christians have taken this to mean that the **Sabbath**, God's holy day, is grounded in the act of creation.

Genesis 2

This account of the origin of the universe is quite different from the first one. Where Genesis 1 builds up to the creation of human beings, Genesis 2 starts with their creation, then describes a world that God gives them to live in. Genesis 1 is highly structured, whereas Genesis 2 is really a story in two halves: one half is about one human being, who is in need of a companion, and God provides first a garden, then animals, then a woman to create a human community. The other half shows how God gave the humans responsibility over the garden and made everything perfect for them.

Keith Ward sees four important spiritual truths in the second creation story.

- Humans are formed 'from the dust of the ground', enlivened with the 'breath of life'. They are not immortal souls that have fallen into the material world but creatures made of matter. Their life depends entirely on God, who gives it and takes it away.

Ex nihilo
is the Latin phrase for 'out of nothing' and refers to the idea that God created the universe from nothing.

The Sabbath
is now a rather old-fashioned way of referring to Sunday (or, in some Christian traditions, Saturday, which is the Jewish Sabbath day), the special day of rest that used to be observed by Christians (some still hold to the tradition). It meant that Christians should not do any work on that day, so that they could concentrate on worshipping God, reading the Bible and spending time with their family.

- The proper home of humans is a garden, a place of life and joy (Eden), in which all creatures can flourish in total dependence on God. At its centre is the tree of eternal life.
- Humans have to look after the garden. They are given this responsibility by God. In the garden there is also the 'tree of the knowledge of good and evil', which symbolizes wisdom. God forbids Adam to eat the fruit of this tree. When the serpent (which is not the same as the Devil or Satan and is not intrinsically evil) tempts Adam and Eve to eat this fruit because it will give them autonomy, knowledge and power, the humans brought destruction upon themselves. This saw the beginning of sin (which is going against the will of God) and its consequent punishments: having to leave the garden, the loss of the sense of the presence of God, and a slow but inevitable spiritual death.
- God made Adam a 'helper and a partner'. To be human is to be in relationship to other people. True personhood can be found only in community. Adam gave names to all the animals, but a full moral and responsible relationship can exist only between humans. With the creation of Eve, a special relationship is established between men and women so that they can live together in the deepest form of union.

In conclusion, then, the two biblical creation stories can be understood as having different functions.

- The first story focuses on the ordering of the elements of the universe, with humans emerging as the pinnacle of the creative process.
- The second story focuses more specifically on human nature, which is understood as being material and relational, finding its fulfilment in total dependence on God.

Christian responses to the Big Bang

Some Christians view the Big Bang theory with scorn, as it is unbiblical. There are problems with the dating of the universe to 15 billion years ago. **Archbishop James Ussher** (1581–1656) used the dates given in the Bible to calculate the age of the universe from its creation by God. In his book *The Annals of the World*, published after his death (1658), he worked out that the earth was created on 22 October 4004 BCE. Interestingly, this date was also calculated by **Dr John Lightfoot** (1602–1675) years earlier, in 1644. Lightfoot added that creation occurred at 9.00 a.m.

There are many Christians who maintain that the universe came into existence between 6,000 and 10,000 years ago. These are the **Young Earth Creationists**. They believe that the 'apparent' age of the universe (evidence of fossils, etc.) was added by God deliberately. It is not clear to many people why God would wish to do this – unless it was to be a 'test of faith' for believers.

Many believers think that 'Big Bang' scientists seek to overthrow the biblical understanding of the origin of the universe found in Genesis 1. There are a number of scientists who support the Big Bang theory, however, who are also committed Christians, such as **John Polkinghorne**. There are also non-Christian scientists who believe that, although the Big Bang theory can answer many questions concerning the origins of the universe, there is a need for God to be acknowledged as a possible 'author' of the Big Bang. The English physicist **Paul Davies** (b. 1946) is one such person. Even the world-famous cosmologist **Stephen Hawking** (b. 1942) concluded his *A Brief History of Time* with the statement 'I thought I had left the question of a supreme being completely open . . .. It would be perfectly consistent with all we know to say that there was a being responsible for the laws of physics.'

The essential problem with the difference between these Christians and scientific views of the origin of the universe lies in the interpretation of the biblical account of the creation of the 'heavens and the earth' in Genesis 1. Those who understand it as literally true, as a 'historical' account of *how* God created the universe, will never accept the Big Bang or any other scientific theory that conflicts with the biblical account. Others, who interpret the Genesis account differently, are more open to believing that both science and religion are searching for ways to describe and understand the universe.

Some theologians point to several similarities between the biblical and scientific accounts. The universe is not infinitely old – it had a beginning. Just as Genesis 1 explains that the universe came into existence suddenly out of nothing, so does the Big Bang theory. The agnostic physicist **Robert Jastrow** (1925–2008), in an interview in the journal *Christianity Today* (6 August 1982), said:

> Astronomers now find they have painted themselves into a corner because they have proven, by their own methods, that the world began abruptly in an act of creation to which you can trace the seeds of every star, every planet, every living thing in this cosmos and on the earth. And they have found that all this happened as a product of forces they cannot hope to discover. That there are what I or anyone would call supernatural forces at work is now, I think, a scientifically proven fact.

Jastrow argued that the scientific and biblical accounts are complementary. Both could be 'true', although they may appear to be superficially different. They represent different approaches to describing aspects of the same reality.

God of the Gaps is a theory arguing that science provides almost all the answers to the origins of the universe, and that God is needed only to fill in the gaps that science cannot (yet) answer.

Taking it further

If the universe came into existence from nothing, it raises the question of what caused the Big Bang. Atheist cosmologists answer this by saying that, before time and space existed, it does not make sense to talk about a 'cause' because the rules of physics (including the laws of cause and effect) did not exist at that moment of creation (causes can be understood only *within* space and time). This idea, however, can itself be used to argue for the role of a divine creator. For some thinkers, the moment of creation represents the point at which physics must stop. It is impossible to go any further back. Physicists acknowledge that there is something real beyond this but that it is not accessible to physics. For some theologians, this scientifically inaccessible point is where God is. This view is criticized, however, as using God to 'fill in the gaps in scientific knowledge' – it is known as the '**God of the Gaps**' theory, coined by **Charles A. Coulson** in *Science and Christian Belief* (1954). The phrase is used to describe attempts to fill the gaps in scientific knowledge, indicating the limits of human knowledge. This recognition in turn points to the necessity for and existence of God.

Tasks

1 Outline two ways in which the Big Bang theory and Genesis 1 and 2 can be seen as complementary.
2 Explain what Charles Coulson meant by 'God of the Gaps'.

ISLAM

Muslim creation accounts

References to creation are spread across several surahs in the Qur'an, and the Qur'anic understanding of creation is not recounted in one continuous story. The ahadith also have references to creation. In the eighth century, the various references to creation were drawn together by Muslim scholars and a more continuous narrative began to be assembled. Because the Muslim creation accounts are not easily found in one place, this narrative has been summarized here.

The universe was a formless indivisible unit until God's act of creation split it into two parts, heaven and earth. According to the Qur'an, creation took six long 'days' or eras of time. During these eras, God made everything in the heavens and the earth, from angels and animals to all the vegetation, including the grape, the olive and the palm tree. He created everything for the sake of humans. They are his 'guardians' on earth, and God created everything for their physical and spiritual good.

Taking it further

There has been some confusion over the years about the use of the word 'days' in connection with the creation of the world. The Arabic word used for 'days' is '*youm*', which appears several other times in the Qur'an, at each instance denoting a different measurement of time. In Surah 70:4, it means 50,000 years; in Surah 22:47, it means 1,000 years. So, the word '*youm*' essentially always means a long period of time, such as an 'aeon' or an 'era'. Hence, most Muslims think of each 'day' of creation to mean an era, the exact length of time of which is not precisely defined.

Surah 32:7 states that God created humans out of clay. He moulded Adam from clay, then breathed life and power into him (15:29). When God took Adam to Paradise, he made a wife for him from his side. She is not given a name in the Qur'an but is called 'Hawa' in some later commentaries. Hawa is the Arabic form of Eve. God taught Adam the names of everything in the universe and instructed the angels to bow down to Adam. One of the angels, Iblis (a name for Satan in the Qur'an), refused to do so.

> We made a covenant with Adam, but he forgot and showed himself lacking in steadfastness. And when we said to the angels: 'prostrate yourselves before Adam', they all prostrated themselves, except Satan, who refused. (Surah 20:115–16)

In Islamic tradition, this is the first refusal to obey any of God's commands. While this was going on in Paradise, Adam and his wife were allowed to eat anything except the fruit from the forbidden tree.

Surah 20:120–21 tells the story of Adam's temptation by Satan to eat the fruit of the forbidden tree:

> Satan whispered to him [Adam], saying: 'Shall I show you the Tree of Immortality and an everlasting kingdom?' They both ate of its fruit, so that they beheld their nakedness and began to cover themselves with leaves. Thus Adam disobeyed his Lord and went astray.

Adam and his wife are equally guilty in eating the forbidden fruit, and their punishment is to be ejected from Paradise and condemned to live on earth. They both ask God for his forgiveness and admit that 'we have sinned against our own souls' (Surah 7:23).

Tasks

1 Summarize Muslim teaching about the creation of the universe.
2 Why do you think God made humans out of clay?

The Qur'an is first and foremost a spiritual book, intended to engage readers to contemplate what God has done and continues to do for them. It should not be a surprise, then, that comments in the Qur'an about the creation should not be understood as history. References to the creation of the world are intended to prompt the reader to ask what they can learn from them and to remind them about God, who is all knowing, all powerful and the source of the created world. Surah 45:3–5 says:

> Surely in the heavens and the earth there are signs for the faithful; in your own creation, and in the beasts that are scattered far and near, signs for true believers; in the alternation of

According to Islam, God's work of creation continues with the birth of each new creature and the appearance of new species – for instance, this hybrid of a donkey and a zebra.

night and day, in the sustenance Allah sends down from heaven with which he revives the earth after its death, and in the marshaling of the winds, signs for men of understanding.

The Qur'an makes some other important points about God in his work of creation.

- After completing the creation, God 'settled himself on the throne to oversee his work' (Surah 57: 4).
- God was not weary after creating the universe, and his work is ongoing because every new-born child and every new species of plant is an example of an act of creation brought about by God (Surah 50:38).

Muslim responses to the Big Bang theory

Many Muslims believe that the Qur'anic account of creation is consistent with the modern scientific understanding of the origin of the universe. While acknowledging that the universe took a very long time to develop as it is today, Muslims understand the phrase 'the heavens and the earth were joined together as one unit, before we clove them asunder' (Surah 21:30) as suggestive of a huge explosion such as the Big Bang. Following this, God 'turned to the sky and it had been like smoke. He said to it and to the sky: "Come together, willingly or unwillingly." They said: "We come together in willing obedience"' (Surah 41:11). In this way, all the elements that were to become the stars and planets began to cool and form in accordance with the laws of nature that God had laid down. Surah 21:33 further states that God created the sun, moon and planets and gave them their own orbits: 'It is he who created the night and the day, the sun and moon; all [the heavenly bodies] swim along, each in its rounded course.'

Muslims also see the confirmation of the expansion of the universe, in the form of the Big Bang explosion, in the Qur'an. Surah 51:47 says: 'the heavens, we have built them with power. And truly, we are expanding it.' There has been some scholarly discussion about what this verse means, because the expansion of the universe was discovered only recently. For people in the early days of Islam, the word 'heavens' referred to what was above the sky. In the verse just quoted, 'heavens' is understood to relate to space and the universe. If this understanding of the word is taken, the verse seems to confirm the modern scientific view that the universe is expanding. Given that the early Muslims did not have telescopes to see what Hubble observed, this is a remarkable conclusion.

> **Task**
>
> Explain how many Muslims believe that the Islamic account of creation is compatible with the Big Bang theory.

Evolution and the origins of life

Apart from debates concerning the origins of the universe, a major interface between science and religion is in the area of religious belief and evolutionary theory as explaining the origins of life – and human life in particular.

The theory of evolution argues that all life on earth developed via the process of

natural selection, where small differences and genetic mutations within the same species can make one individual stronger or better suited to its environment so that it survives for longer. These traits are inherited by its offspring. Over millions of years, these small differences are enhanced and developed many times, sometimes leading to whole new species. Species which do not adapt will die out. This idea is called 'the survival of the fittest'. In this whole process of evolution, there is no suggestion of design; change and mutations happen randomly. This point is the main challenge to religious believers, who insist that everything in the universe was purposefully and intentionally designed by a divine being.

Charles Darwin and natural selection

Charles Darwin (1809–1882) was born and brought up in the small town of Shrewsbury. He did not excel at school but managed to gain a place at Edinburgh University to study medicine. However, he found that he did not like the sight of blood or suffering, and his father advised him that he should study to be a priest in the Church of England. Darwin then went to Cambridge University, thinking that the fairly easy life of a country vicar would fit in well with his growing interest in natural history (the study of animals and plants, which is now called biology). He became an avid collector of beetles and made friends with the professor of botany **John Stevens Henslow** (1796–1861). It was Henslow who gave Darwin the opportunity to take part in the five-year journey around the world on HMS *Beagle*. Darwin's position on the ship was as the 'scientific person' or naturalist, and it was on this journey that he collected most of the evidence that formed the basis of his ideas on natural selection and evolution.

During the *Beagle*'s voyage, Darwin studied the geology and zoology of all the countries he visited. He witnessed evidence of erosion, earthquakes, volcanoes and other natural phenomena, collected organisms of all sorts, and found many fossilized creatures. This made him wonder why some fossils were very similar to ones already known and others were very different. He began to think that species were created to adapt to their particular environments. But, if this were true, why were jungle species different in Asia, Africa and South America when the climate was very similar?

Darwin was not able to answer this question until some years after his return. He learned that some of his collected plants and animals, particularly from the Galapagos Islands, were unique while others were already known, leading him to think that plants and animals evolve. In coming to this conclusion, he took advice from farmers, animal breeders and pigeon-fanciers, among others, in order to understand how distinct breeds of plants and animals were made. He determined that natural selection worked to preserve advantageous genetic changes. For instance, if an animal was born with very powerful legs so it could jump high in the air to catch its prey, this would be passed on to its young and they, in turn, would pass it on to theirs. Those members of the species that did not inherit this advantageous mutation would die out, leaving only the 'superior' members of the species. Darwin discovered that natural selection is the process that helps a species have a better chance of survival in its environment. He also realized why animals have many offspring: this was to maximize the possibility that at least some would survive to produce the continuance of the species.

Darwin later summarized this idea in *On the Origin of Species* (1859):

> As many more individuals of each species are born than can possibly survive; and as, consequently, there is a frequently recurring struggle for existence, it follows that any being, if it vary however slightly in any manner profitable to itself, under the complex and sometimes varying conditions of life, will have a better chance of surviving, and thus be naturally selected. From the strong principle of inheritance, any selected variety will tend to propagate its new and modified form.

According to modern Darwinists, life on earth is concerned primarily with the passing on of genetic information. When any species of animal reproduces, it passes on the DNA contained in its genes to the next generation. Quite frequently, however, there are small variations in this genetic message so that the offspring differ slightly from their parents. This is why we don't exactly resemble our parents. For the most part these variations are irrelevant or a disadvantage for an animal, but occasionally they will give an animal a small advantage in a certain environment. For example, in an environment where the main source of food consists of leaves high up on trees, an animal born with a longer neck than other members of its species will have access to food the others cannot reach. It will therefore have a clear advantage in the struggle to survive.

Another example would be an insect that, because of a small genetic change, looks a little more like a twig than the others of its kind. This insect will be a little less likely to be eaten by a predator and therefore have a greater chance of reproducing and passing on this advantageous gene to its offspring. This twig-like characteristic may become more and more pronounced in successive generations – an actual example being the stick insect.

According to Darwin, evolution by natural selection is like a race where only the

According to the Darwinian theory of evolution, the stick insect (left – can you see it?) has evolved to mimic the plants on which it lives in order to hide from predators, while curlews (right) have evolved long, thin bills which enable them to dig into the sand for food.

winner is visible. Over millions of years species either produce genetic traits that are advantageous in their environment or die out. These survival characteristics, such as long necks in giraffes or sonar-like hearing in bats, reach such a refined point of adaptation that they appear to us as if they have been designed by some intelligent mind to fit perfectly into their environment.

Darwin's theory of evolution caused a storm of controversy when it was published in 1859. Darwin was writing in a Christian society, and the traditional Christian view was that God had created a perfect world and therefore there was no need for change in nature. The essence of his researches showed that this was not the case; life forms had to adapt to their situations if they were to survive, and this process was the action of natural selection. If they did not adapt, life forms would not survive. Darwin's theory ran counter to the Bible.

Taking it further

Was Darwin religious?

Some people assume that, because of his work on the theory of evolution, Darwin must have been an atheist. This is not the case, however. When he was aboard the *Beagle* on his voyage to the Galapagos Islands, he used to quote verses from the Bible to the sailors, but by the time he returned to England in 1836 he no longer thought the Bible was literally true and believed that many of the events in it were allegorical. When he studied at Cambridge University, he was convinced by the design argument for God's existence put forward by William Paley (see chapter 2, pp. 31–2), but by the time he wrote *On the Origin of Species* he realized that this argument failed:

> The old argument of design in nature, as given by Paley, which formerly seemed to me as conclusive, fails, now that the law of natural selection has been discovered. We can no longer argue that, for instance, the beautiful hinge of a bivalve shell must have been made by an intelligent being, like the hinge of a door by man. There seems to be no more design in the variability of organic beings and in the action of natural selection, than in the course which the wind blows. Everything in nature is the result of fixed laws.

Because his theory of evolution was in conflict with Genesis, this had a significant effect on his religious beliefs.

Darwin was never an atheist. In his *Autobiography*, he says that he was a theist when he wrote *On the Origin of Species* and that he believed in an intelligent First Cause. It was his belief, though, that humans could not understand the nature of this First Cause. The death of his daughter Annie in 1851 was a crushing blow to his religious beliefs, and he stopped attending church services after that. He eventually became an agnostic. Darwin never thought in terms of a conflict between religion and science; religion was a personal matter and science was something completely different, as it was objective and could be shown to be true by using reason and experiment.

Task

Do you think that Darwin was religious? Give reasons for your answer.

Even some eminent scientists believed Darwin to be wrong. **Philip Gosse** (1810–1888), a naturalist and the inventor of the aquarium, thought that Darwin was wrong because God had placed fossils in the ground in order to test people's belief. Gosse was a member of the **Plymouth Brethren**, a theologically conservative Christian denomination. Other scientists also rejected the theory, among them **Adam Sedgwick** (1785–1873), one of the founders of modern geology, who had taught Darwin. He wrote to Darwin saying that parts of it were admirable, some parts made him laugh and some filled him with sorrow. In a letter to another correspondent, Sedgwick was even harsher on Darwin's book, calling it 'utterly false', and wrote that 'It repudiates all reasoning from final causes; and seems to shut the door on any view (however feeble) of the God of Nature as manifested in His works. From first to last it is a dish of rank materialism cleverly cooked and served up.'

The astronomer **Sir John Herschel** (1792–1871) also rejected Darwin's theory, saying that it was 'the law of higgledy-piggledy'. Darwin was deeply saddened by his friend's reaction, saying 'what this means I do not know, but evidently it is very contemptuous. If true this is a great blow and discouragement.'

Task

Summarize Darwin's theory of natural selection.

Christian reactions to evolution

There are two different kinds of reaction to Darwin's theory of evolution from Christians, one saying that Christianity and evolution can coexist, the other saying that they cannot.

Christianity and evolution together

Some Christians see no difficulty in accepting Darwin's theory of evolution. This is because they can understand the evidence for the theory and how Darwin's conclusions seem to fit this. They do not see a split between religion and science on this issue, nor do they see a contradiction in believing both in evolution and in God. They do not take the Bible literally, so they appreciate that Genesis 1, the creation story of the beginning of the universe, needs to be understood in its literary and theological context. That context is (as we have seen on pp. 110–11) as a mythical story that was intended to be taken figuratively. It was an explanation for *why* there is a world rather than for *how* the world came into existence. The Bible was never intended as a science textbook but, rather, as the thoughts of an ancient people over 3,000 years ago.

Such Christians might point out that Darwin was a religious person yet he studied for many years to understand the evidence before finally concluding that evolution was the correct way of understanding how life developed on earth. They see the theory of evolution and the biblical creation story as running in parallel: science gives one explanation while religion gives another. God could have created a process by which the whole universe could develop into ever more complex states; life could emerge on earth, and eventually this life could become conscious in human beings with free will. There is nothing illogical in this suggestion. Evolution is an essential part of this process and has a purpose in God's plan. Far from undermining the argument, evolution actually demonstrates that there is a designing mind of immense wisdom that has created a system shaping life on earth to produce intelligent creatures who can appreciate beauty, understand moral values and eventually come to recognize their creator.

Christianity and evolution separate

Conservative evangelicals and fundamentalist Christians will not agree with the theory of evolution. This is because they read the Bible literally as the actual words of God. The creation story in Genesis 1 states that God created the entire universe in six days. He created a perfect world, which means that there was no need for anything to evolve. Evolution theory is therefore wrong.

Some fundamentalists will point out that Jesus apparently dismissed evolution when he answered the Pharisees about divorce. He quoted Genesis 5:2: 'He created them male and female and blessed them. And when they were created, he called them man.' Here, it is clear that Jesus believed in creation – and therefore not evolution. Jesus refers to the first male and female being created – and fundamentalists take this to mean that they were created as humans immediately and did not evolve from primates into humans over a period of many thousands of years. God's creation happened without any delay.

The Gospel of John begins:

> In the beginning was the Word, and the Word was with God, and the Word was God. He was in the beginning with God. All things were made through Him, and without Him nothing was made that was made.

The key point for fundamentalists is the phrase 'without Him nothing was made that was made': the word 'made' in the Greek means 'created', so this obviously refers to a creation. They believe that the Bible plainly says that God created everything that has ever existed (John 1:3).

Fundamentalists might also argue that the theory of evolution is just that – a 'theory'. As such, it has not, unlike Newton's three laws of motion, been proven after more than 150 years. By definition, a theory is hypothetical and subject to proof. As such, the theory of evolution cannot be believed to be true, so it is subjective. 'Science' is defined as quantifiable (you can show your findings in numerical form), measurable (you can set out to gather hard evidence) and repeatable (you will get the same results time and time again), but, because it is subjective, evolution is not on the same level as science. It is just as likely that the Bible is correct and that the theory of evolution is wrong.

It is impossible to repeat the origins of life in a laboratory, say fundamentalists. This means that the theory of evolution, which has to assume the origins of life, cannot give an explanation for the origin of the universe. In this case, the biblical account is just as good as any other theory, if not more satisfactory. In fact, evolution required matter and the existence of life for evolution to begin. Evolutionists do not explain where life came from.

The idea that life might have evolved was first mentioned by St Augustine in the early fifth century, when he said that God probably created very simple life forms and that these developed over time.

Creationism and intelligent design

Creationism
is the idea in fundamentalist Christianity that God created the earth between six thousand and ten thousand years ago.

Creationism is the belief that all species of living creatures, rather than evolving, were created separate and distinct from one another from the beginning. There are two varieties of creationists: **Young Earth Creationists** and **Old Earth Creationists**.

Young Earth Creationists believe that the Bible must be taken as literally true as it was dictated by God. God created the earth between 6,000 and 10,000 years ago, a figure arrived at via a system rather like that used by Archbishop Ussher when he decided on the date of 4004 BCE (see p. 111). Young Earth Creationists believe that all life was created in six days of 24 hours each and that death came about because of the sin of Adam and Eve. However, they do accept that the earth moves around the sun.

A potential problem for Young Earth Creationists is how to explain the existence of fossils that show the earth to be much older than they believe it is. They say that scientists who study fossils use faulty dating methods, that God created the earth in six days as a perfect and complete entity, and that this would have made it look old. Noah's flood (which they believe was a worldwide event) would have deposited the remains of dead creatures around the globe and covered them in layers of rock, making them look much older than they really were.

Young Earth Creationists reject the Big Bang and evolutionary theory because:

- there are gaps in the fossil record, meaning that there is no direct evidence that evolution took place
- natural selection cannot make an organism into a higher life form
- no evidence has been found for the link between apes and humans.

Old Earth Creationists agree with scientists about the ancient age of the universe and understand the six days in the Genesis 1 creation story as six long periods of time. This solves the problem of having to explain fossils. If there is conflict between science and biblical teaching, they will always accept the Bible's literal truth. Progressive Old Earth Creationists argue that God allows certain natural processes such as gene mutation and natural selection to occur and affect how life on earth develops. However, they say that God sometimes intervenes directly to create new species in ways that science cannot explain. They reject the evolutionary view that new species can evolve.

Some creationists contest the fossil evidence that shows that the earth is much older than calculations based on the Bible.

> **Tasks**
>
> 1 List the main beliefs of Young Earth Creationists.
> 2 Explain two differences between Young Earth and Old Earth Creationists.
> 3 'Creationism is an acceptable theory to explain how the universe began.' Do you agree? Give reasons for your answer.

> **Taking it further**
>
> ## The Scopes trial
>
> John Scopes, a 24-year-old Tennessee schoolteacher, was put on trial in 1925 for teaching evolution to American schoolchildren. The trial – nicknamed 'the monkey trial' because of the (mistaken) idea that evolution implies human beings are descended from monkeys – attracted huge publicity. The legendary defence lawyer Clarence Darrow, who was an agnostic in religious matters, defended Scopes. A one-time presidential candidate and a devout Christian (he believed that the Bible should be interpreted literally), William Jennings Bryan led the case for the prosecution. He believed that teaching evolution led to dangerous social movements.
>
> As the trial developed, the main issue became the authority of the Bible versus the soundness of Darwin's theory. 'Millions of guesses strung together', is how Bryan characterized evolutionary theory, adding that it made man 'indistinguishable among the mammals'. Darrow, in his attacks, tried to make holes in the Genesis story according to modern thinking, calling them 'fool ideas that no intelligent Christian on earth believes'.

The jury found Scopes guilty of violating the law and fined him $100. Bryan and the anti-evolutionists claimed victory, and the Tennessee law did not change for another forty-two years. But Clarence Darrow had succeeded in publicizing scientific evidence for evolution, and the press reported that, although Bryan had won the case, he had lost the argument. The verdict had a chilling effect on the teaching of evolution in the classroom, however, and it was not until the 1960s that it appeared in school science textbooks.

Today, there is still controversy about teaching evolution in some places. In the United Kingdom, for example, the teaching of evolution is compulsory, and it is a requirement of the National Curriculum at Key Stage 4 for fourteen- to sixteen-year-olds to be taught that the fossil record is evidence for evolution and how variation and selection may lead to evolution or extinction. Teaching evolution is unlawful in a few parts of the USA and in several fundamentalist Islamic countries.

Task

Find out more about the Scopes trial and summarize the arguments used on both sides. You may find it helpful to watch the 1960 film *Inherit the Wind*, which portrays the characters in the trial remarkably well.

Task

Using the information above about Darwin's theory of evolution, create a grid that shows the points of similarity and difference between Darwin and Christianity.

Muslim reactions to evolution

ISLAM

Most Muslims believe that they are descendants of Adam and Eve. Surah 49:13 says:

> O mankind! We have created you from a male and a female, and made you into nations and tribes, that you may know one another. Truly, the most honorable of you with God is the one who is the most God-fearing.

Surah 4:1 also states clearly that Adam and Eve were the parents of all human beings who have ever lived:

> O mankind! Be careful of your duty to your Lord Who created you from a single soul and from it created its mate and from these two has spread abroad a multitude of men and women.

Many Muslims believe that this is a direct revelation from God.

Muslims say that, as it was a unique event, the creation of Adam cannot be confirmed (or denied) by science. They believe it is true because it is in the Qur'an, which is a special revelation from God. Neither the Qur'an nor the Sunnah mentions anything about the creation of plants or animals, but Surah 21:30 says that 'God made from water all living things'. God created all creatures according to his own will. The Qur'an neither affirms nor denies the theory of evolution or the process of natural selection. The question remains purely a matter of scientific enquiry and separated from religious belief. Evolution must stand or fall on its own scientific merits – and that depends upon whether the physical evidence confirms or conflicts with the theory.

For Muslims, the role of science is to observe and describe the patterns that God places in his creation. If scientific observation shows a pattern in the evolution of species over time that can be described as natural selection, this is not in itself unbelief. It is only unbelief to think that this evolution took place on its own, and not as a creation of God. A Muslim who accepts evolution or natural selection as a valid scientific theory needs to be aware that the theory is merely an explanation of one of the many observed patterns in God's creation. As for the fossil remains of bipedal apes and the tools and artefacts associated with those remains, their existence poses no problem for Islamic teachings. There is nothing in the Qur'an or the Sunnah that either affirms or denies that upright, intelligent, tool-using apes ever existed or evolved from other ape-like ancestors. Such animals may very well have existed before Adam's arrival on earth. The only conclusion that Muslims can draw from the Qur'an and the Sunnah is that, even if those animals once existed, they were not the forefathers of Adam.

Some Muslims believe that the theory of evolution is compatible with the Qur'an. One such is **Usama Hasan**, an imam, academic and fellow of the Royal Astronomical Society. He caused controversy in the Islamic community when he described the story of Adam and Eve in the Qur'an as showing a 'children's madrasa-level understanding' of human origins, and he argues that versions of evolutionary theory were already present in such medieval Muslim philosophers as Ibn Miskawayh (932–1030)

Ibn Khaldun (1332–1406) was a Tunisian historian who is recognized as one of the greatest philosophers of the Middle Ages.

and **Ibn Khaldun** (1332–1406). For instance, Ibn Khaldun, in his work *Muqaddimah* ('Introduction to History'), talks about the origin of plant, animal and human life as developing gradually in an ascending order through various stages, until 'the higher stage of man is reached from the world of the monkeys, in which both sagacity and perception are found, but which has not reached the stage of actual reflection and thinking. At this stage we come to the first stage of man.'

> **Task**
> Summarize how Muslims can see evolution and Islamic accounts of creation as compatible.

Non-religious reactions to evolution

Critics of a religious understanding of evolution could ask why a benevolent and loving God would create such a seemingly random and brutal process. Natural selection is blind and utterly indifferent to suffering. Approximately 98 per cent of all animal species that have ever existed on this planet have become extinct. This seems to be too incredibly wasteful for it to be the product of a loving creator.

It also seems to critics that the means by which some animals adapt to survive are very cruel. One example that horrified Darwin and troubled his faith concerns a species of wasp that will paralyse its victim and then lay its eggs in its living flesh. After a short time the eggs will hatch and the wasp larvae will begin to eat the still living host. This may well be a useful evolutionary adaptation, as the wasp larvae will get an advantageous start to their lives. It is difficult, however, to understand why an all-loving God would create a process which actually contained so much suffering.

Richard Dawkins

Richard Dawkins is a former professor for the public understanding of science at Oxford University and a very well-known lecturer and writer on the interface between science and religion. He believes strongly in the truth of Darwinian evolution and argues against Christian teaching on both the creation of the universe and the arguments for God's existence. On religion, for example, he says:

> Much of what people do is done in the name of God. Irishmen blow each other up in his name. Arabs blow themselves up in his name. Imams and ayatollahs oppress women in his name. Celibate popes and priests mess up people's sex lives in his name. Jewish shohets cut live animals' throats in his name. The achievements of religion in past history – bloody crusades, torturing inquisitions, mass-murdering conquistadors, culture-destroying missionaries, legally enforced resistance to each new piece of scientific truth until the last possible moment – are even more impressive. And what has it all been in aid of? I believe it is becoming increasingly clear that the answer is absolutely nothing at all. There is no reason for believing that any sort of gods exist and quite good reason for believing that they do not exist and never have. It has all been a gigantic waste of time and a waste of life. It would be a joke of cosmic proportions if it weren't so tragic. (Excerpt from an article in *Free Inquiry Magazine*, Vol. 18, no. 3; also at www.richarddawkins.net).

Dawkins thinks that evolution, as discovered and developed by Darwin, is a fact that cannot reasonably be denied. He says: 'One thing all real scientists agree upon is the fact of evolution itself. It is a fact that we are cousins of gorillas, kangaroos, starfish, and bacteria. Evolution is as much a fact as the heat of the sun.' Failure to accept this, as some fundamentalist Christians do, is to fail to look at the overwhelming evidence in favour of evolution. Dawkins points to such things as fossil evidence. Millions of fossils have been found exactly where they would be expected if evolution were true, and at just the depth in the earth that would be expected. No fossils have been found in places where evolutionary biologists would not expect them to be. For example, a fossilized mammal has never been found in rocks so old that fish have not yet arrived. If even a single one did, it would disprove the theory of evolution.

Dawkins makes many other forceful points about the evidence in favour of evolution. For instance:

- The way that plants and animals are distributed around the world is exactly what should be expected if evolution is correct.
- The pattern of resemblance among animals and plants is exactly what should be expected.
- The fact that the genetic code is the same in all living creatures shows overwhelmingly that all beings are descended from one single ancestor that lived over 3,000 million years ago.

Task

Summarize Dawkins's views in favour of evolution

TICK THE TOPICS

You should now tick the relevant boxes to check what you have learned in this chapter.

Sections	Topics	Tick
Origins of the universe	Big Bang theory	
	Genesis creation accounts	
	Christian responses to the Big Bang	
	Muslim creation accounts	
	Muslim responses to the Big Bang	
Evolution	Charles Darwin and natural selection	
	Christian responses to evolution	
	Muslim responses to evolution	
	Non-religious responses to evolution	

Sample questions

AQA Religious Studies A (8062)

1   Which of the following is a non-religious theory about how the universe began?
    a) Creation b) Little Bang c) Big Bang d) Big Fizz   (1 mark)
2   Give two examples of what religious believers might do to stop abuse of the
    environment.   (2 marks)
3   Explain two contrasting beliefs in contemporary British society about
    evolution.   (4 marks)
4   Explain two religious beliefs about responsibility for the earth.   (5 marks)
5   'Religious views on the origin of the universe make no sense.'
Evaluate this statement. In your answer, you:
   - should give reasoned arguments in support of this statement
   - should give reasoned arguments to support a different point of view
   - should refer to religious arguments
   - may refer to non-religious arguments
   - should reach a justified conclusion.   (12 marks)

Edexcel Religious Studies B (1RB0)

a)   Outline the Big Bang theory of the origins of the universe.   (3)
b)   Explain two responses to the Big Bang theory.   (4)
c)   Assess whether religious belief is weakened by sin.   (9)
d)   'Religious accounts of the origin of the universe cannot be taken seriously.'
Evaluate this statement, considering more than one point of view.   (12)

Edexcel International GCSE Religious Studies (4RS0)

a)   What is meant by 'creation'?   (2)
b)   Outline one religious account of the origins of the universe.   (5)
c)   Explain how some Christians believe that religion is compatible with scientific
     theories of the origins of the universe.   (8)
d)   'Religion has myths, science has facts, about how the universe began.'
Do you agree? Give reasons for your answer, showing that you have considered
another point of view.   (5)

WJEC Eduqas Religious Studies (Full Course and Short Course)

a)   Describe what is meant by 'creation'.   (2)
b)   With reference to one religion you have studied, explain views about the origin of the
     universe.   (5)
c)   From two different religions, or two religious traditions, explain views about
     stewardship.   (8)
d)   'Religious and scientific views of the origin of the universe are compatible.'
Discuss this statement, showing that you have considered more than one point of view.
(You must refer to religion and belief in your answer.)   (15)
                                                                                     (SPaG + 6)

7 Death and Life after Death

Death is the one thing that happens to every living creature in the world. It is a certainty that everyone will die at some point. No one can avoid it. This is probably why people are often afraid of death. Very few individuals actually wish to die or actively look forward to dying, unless they are in great pain that cannot be relieved by drugs. People are afraid of death because they do not know what, if anything, it will be like. We have experience of being alive but not of being dead. What is being dead like? It does not matter whether we are religious or non-religious for this question to be an unknown quantity. No one who has died has come back to report what it is like – or have they? This is the big question in the discussion about death and life after death that we will be exploring in this chapter.

What is death?

We will begin our discussion with some medical definitions of death. The definition has actually changed over time, as scientists and medical practitioners have discovered more about the human body and the processes involved in death. In the UK, two medical doctors must agree that a person has died before a death certificate can be issued. In almost every case, this is just a formality because it is very clear that the person is dead. The legal requirement is in place so that no errors are made. Before the 1960s, death was generally understood in terms of the failure of the two vital organs – the heart and the lungs. When these stopped working, the person was declared dead. This was obviously because the heart and lungs work together to provide oxygenated blood for all the other organs. The rest of the body could not survive without the heart and lungs. So, if the person had stopped breathing and if no pulse could be felt, he or she was declared dead.

Brain death, when there is no brain activity, is the modern definition of when a person is dead.

Developments in medical technology forced a change in the definition of death. The year 1967 saw the first successful human heart transplant. If the heart could be replaced, then it meant that it was not the essence of a human being. In fact, every organ except one – the brain – could be replaced successfully. The legal definition of death – '**brain death**' – then changed to when brain activity stopped. In 1979, the Royal College of Physicians published a definition of death: 'brain death represents the stage at which a patient becomes truly dead.' During the 1980s and 1990s, more research and evidence was amassed by medical professionals and, in order to make it more precise, they adapted their previous definition to become 'brainstem death'. 'Death', then, is when no activity can be detected in a person's brainstem. It is not possible for anyone to come back to life if their brainstem has died.

PVS is an abbreviation of permanent vegetative state, a condition in which a person lacks brain function and has to be kept alive by machines.

Taking it further

The change from 'brain death' to 'brainstem death' was important because, previously, patients who were in a permanent vegetative state (**PVS**) could have been defined as dead. It has been found, however, that, although these patients cannot communicate, their brainstem is still alive. *The Telegraph* newspaper reported on 2 February 2010 that one in five of PVS patients could respond meaningfully to stimuli and that about 1,000 PVS patients in British hospitals were being kept alive in the hope that they might recover. One patient, Rob Houben, a Belgian man who had been injured in a car crash, 'woke up' from a PVS after twenty-three years and was able to tell doctors that he had been conscious throughout his time in hospital.

A famous case in Britain was Tony Bland, a victim of the Hillsborough disaster in 1989, who suffered severe brain damage after being crushed when a barrier gave way at a football match. He was kept in a PVS until 1993, when his parents won the legal right to withdraw life-prolonging treatment, including food and water. His was the first case in English legal history that allowed a person to die. It is highly unlikely that he would have benefited from the change in death definition as he was in an extreme form of PVS.

Personal identity

In the 2003 film *Freaky Friday*, an overworked mother (Jamie Lee Curtis) and her daughter (Lindsay Lohan) switch bodies and have real difficulty in understanding how the switch happened and knowing whether they were young or old. The mother had to adjust to being treated as a teenager, while the daughter had to cope with being in her mother's shoes. This story is a twist on a tale told by the English philosopher **John Locke** (1632–1704) about a prince and a cobbler (shoemaker) who wake up one morning to find themselves in each other's body. Locke told the story to highlight some of the problems concerning the argument for a continued 'personal' existence after death.

> ### Task
>
> Find and read Locke's story of the Prince and the Cobbler. Try to work out what it says about what makes a person. Do you think 'memory' or 'appearance' is more important? Discuss the issues with your classmates.

The discussion of what constitutes a person is central to the debate about whether life after death is possible and, if so, what form it might take.

Dualism is the philosophical idea that the body and the mind/soul are separate but interact. The soul is a 'spiritual substance' that can live on its own without the body. On this view, the real 'me' is not my body (for this changes over time) but my soul (which does not change). It is the soul that survives death and which, according to Plato, also existed before birth.

The French philosopher **René Descartes** (1596–1650) gave the classic argument in support of the dualist position:

> My essence consists solely in the fact that I am a thinking thing. It is true that I may have (or, to anticipate, that I certainly have) a body that is very closely joined to me. But nevertheless, on the one hand I have a clear and distinct idea of myself, in so far as I am simply a non-extended thinking thing, and on the other hand I have a distinct idea of body, in so far as this is simply an extended non-thinking thing. And accordingly, it is certain that I am really distinct from my body and can exist without it. (*Meditation* 6, 54)

Descartes argues that, if he considers himself to be a 'thinking thing', then that is what he must actually be. He can think of himself as not having a body but cannot think of himself as not having a soul. Therefore, it follows that the body and soul cannot be one and the same thing. Descartes wrestled with the problem of how the body and soul are connected to each other. He used the current knowledge of anatomy and wrongly decided that the point of connection between body and soul was in a part of the brain called the pineal gland. This sits near the centre of the brain, between the two hemispheres, and is now known to influence sleep rhythms. One difficulty with the dualist argument is that, for example, just because I can think of myself as being sober does not actually mean that I am sober. Similarly, just because I can think of myself as intelligent and handsome does not necessarily mean that I have either of those qualities. The dualist view would understand life after death as being a non-physical existence, without a body. This would go against the traditional Christian and Islamic view of a resurrected body after death.

Dualism
is a philosophical position that says that humans are made up of two elements: body and soul.

What makes us the same person that we were in the past? The cells of our bodies are replaced over time and so are not the same as they were when we were younger. Our memories? What about those who lose their memory? Or do we have a soul?

Monism is a philosophical view that there is only one substance (e.g., matter) and that all mental states can be explained as a product of physical brain states. The key issue in discussions about life after death is 'identity' – how do we know that Mr X in the afterlife is the same Mr X who lived on earth? Various ideas have been put forward.

- Some philosophers have suggested that we should look at 'memory' as the most important criterion. If I remember certain incidents in the afterlife, I can be sure that I was the same person who had those experiences before I died. An obvious objection to this criterion is that many people suffer memory loss from amnesia or dementia. Such people will have no memories that they can take into the after-life, so identifying them would be impossible.
- What if two people claimed that they were the same person? Both cannot be correct. How, then, would we decide which is the 'real' or 'genuine' person in the afterlife?
- What about continuity in time and space? The thing that connects a person from being a baby, a teenager, a mature adult and a senile old person is not memory but living in time and space. The problem with this view, however, is that, while it would work in this life, the act of dying and the destruction of the body would break this continuum.

Thinkers such as the Oxford philosopher **A. J. Ayer** argued that the language of life after death has to do with matters that are beyond the scope of empirical science.

The notion of life after death cannot be tested in any way, so it is unverifiable and unfalsifiable – i.e., it cannot be proven to be either true or false. Religious believers will typically continue to believe in life after death as a necessary part of their faith, so will not accept any counter-arguments. An atheist will just be able to criticize this view as being the same as saying that unicorns exist or that 'black' is 'white'.

By contrast, the philosopher **John Hick** argued for the idea of '**eschatological verification**'. It was clear to Hick that any proof of life after death is impossible while we are still alive, so this must be a simple matter of faith for religious believers. It cannot be a matter of reason or empirical evidence.

Hick tells that parable of the Celestial City. Two people are travelling along a road. One is a theist and believes that it leads to the Celestial City; the other is an atheist and does not. The believer is convinced that the road she is travelling along is headed towards the Celestial City and greets hardships and suffering along the way as encouragements and trials of faith. The other does not believe that the road heads towards the Celestial City but enjoys the journey nevertheless. The only way that both travellers will know if they are correct or not is when they turn the final corner on the road. Hick constructs this story to explain how the different belief systems of the theist and the atheist affect their understanding of the evidence they come across on their journey through life. If the theist is correct, this will be proven when they arrive, after death, in the afterlife. On the other hand, if the atheist is correct, they will just be dead, so nothing can be verified. Hick, then, concludes that humans will be able to verify that a belief in life after death is true only after death.

The **eschatological verification** is John Hick's idea that Christians will only know after death if God exists.

Logical behaviourism is a philosophical view claiming that mental concepts can be explained in terms of behaviour.

A **category mistake** is a logical term where a person confuses the properties of the whole with the properties of a part.

Taking it further

Logical behaviourism is another philosophical view which argues that things can be called meaningful only if they can be verified – that is, if some kind of test can be performed to check whether a statement is true or false and therefore whether that statement has any meaning. If a statement cannot be shown to be either true or false, it has no meaning – it is literally 'nonsense'. Behaviourists such as **Gilbert Ryle** (1900–1976) take the view that any discussion of the mind/soul as separate from the body is a '**category mistake**', a mistaken use of language. In his famous book *The Concept of Mind* (1949), he argues that our actions are simply physical events; there is no mental activity involved. The idea that there is such a thing as the 'mind' – the 'doctrine of the ghost in the machine' – is based on a confusion of concepts. Ryle uses the example of the phrase 'team spirit' to show that it would be quite wrong to interpret it as something to do with ghosts – this would be to make a category mistake about the meaning of the term 'spirit'. When we talk about mental events, we use abstract language to refer to a person's behaviour, not to actual physical events. Ryle uses the phrase 'Jim desires a drink' to mean that Jim is displaying a disposition to behave in a 'having-a-drink' way. There is no mind where desires and beliefs exist. So, in terms of believing in life after death, Ryle would claim that this belief is simply a disposition to believe that, when we die, there is some different form of life from the one we know now. It does not actually exist.

Immortality or resurrection?

There is a long-standing debate among philosophers and theologians as to the form that life after death might take. The two main candidates are '**immortality of the soul**' and '**resurrection of the body**'.

Immortality of the soul

The immortality of the soul is an idea that stems from the dualist view that humans have a body and a soul. At death, the body dies, as it is temporary and changing, but the soul lives on, because it is immortal and unchanging. In *Phaedo*, **Plato** (427–347 BCE) argues that the body belongs to the physical world and will decay and turn to dust. The soul, however, belongs to the eternal world, where infinite ideas such as justice, truth, beauty and goodness exist. He calls these the 'Forms', which he sees as the archetypes or perfect versions of important ideas. On earth, we have only copies or imperfect versions of true justice, truth, beauty and goodness. Plato says that human souls are immortal and are part of the realm of the Forms. A soul enters a human body, and its aim is to break away from the body in which it is trapped and return to the eternal world of the Forms. Here, it will be able to spend eternity contemplating what is perpetually true, beautiful and just.

Immanuel Kant believed that the purpose of human life was to achieve the *summum bonum* or 'highest good'. No matter how hard they try, however, no human beings can achieve this highest good in only one lifetime. This meant, for Kant, that there must logically be a moral obligation on God to provide a way for humans to reach the *summum bonum*, and this requires eternal life. If this does not exist, there would be no point in people acting morally. People do act morally, however, so there must be eternal life. As Kant said: 'the summum bonum is only possible on the presupposition of the immortality of the soul' (*The Critique of Practical Reason*, Book 2, chapter 4, section 4). John Hick echoed this thought when he said: 'If the human potential is to be fulfilled in the lives of individuals, these lives must be prolonged far beyond the limits of our present bodily existence' (*Death and Eternal Life*, 1985, p. 156).

Problems with immortality

There are many problems associated with the dualist view of the afterlife, among which are the following.

- How do the body and soul interact with each other? Descartes thought that they were linked by the pineal gland in the brain. This has been disproved by medical science, however, so the problem remains.
- **H. H. Price** (1899–1984) tried to answer this criticism by arguing that the soul will find itself in a dream world of mental images and memories from its physical life. It may be able to create new mental images, and the dream world will not be limited by the laws of physics, just as ordinary dreams are not. Not many people have been convinced by Price's argument.
- How could disembodied souls recognize each other and how could they communicate with each other?

Immortality
refers to the belief in an everlasting existence after the death of the body.

Resurrection
is the bodily form of the afterlife in both Christianity and Islam.

Summum bonum
is Kant's term for the 'highest good' of which humans are capable.

Resurrection of the body

The resurrection of the body is the mainstream view in both Christianity and Islam.

The resurrection of the body is a central belief of Christian theology, coming from the view that it is an act of God's love for humans. God loved humans so much that he 'gave his only begotten son' (John 3:16) to die on their behalf, to save them from sin so that they could live forever with God. In Christian thought, resurrection is not about resuscitating a dead body – bodies disintegrate and turn to dust. It is about re-creating humans as spiritual individuals. The Gospels attempt to explain what this means in the case of Jesus, who appeared to his disciples in bodily form but was somehow different. He is physical: 'Look at my hands and feet . . . touch me and see; a ghost does not have flesh and bones as you see that I do' (Luke 24:39). However, the resurrected Jesus is different: he disappears after seeing the two disciples on the road to Emmaus: 'Then their eyes were opened and they recognized him, and he disappeared from their sight' (Luke 24:31). The same distinction between the physical and different aspects of the resurrected Jesus is seen in John's Gospel too, when Jesus somehow comes through a locked door to appear in the upper room where the disciples are: 'On the evening of that first day of the week, when the disciples were

The Bible tells how Jesus appeared after rising from the dead. Examples include on the road to Emmaus and the apparition to St Thomas and the Apostles (shown in this fifteenth-century altarpiece), where Jesus explicitly pointed out the wounds he suffered during the Crucifixion.

together, with the doors locked for fear of the Jewish leaders, Jesus came and stood among them and said, "Peace be with you!" After he said this, he showed them his hands and side' (John 20:19–20).

St Paul also struggles to explain the phenomenon of the nature of the resurrected Jesus when he describes Jesus as having a 'spiritual body' (*sarx pneumatikon* in Greek). This expresses, as best he can, the idea that, after his resurrection, Jesus was still in a physical form but was not just physical – he also had a spiritual (i.e., non-physical) aspect that was different from his physical body. He states that all Christians will experience this dual nature: 'For the trumpet shall sound, the dead will be raised imperishable, and we shall be changed. For the perishable must be clothed with the imperishable, and the mortal with immortality' (1 Corinthians 15:52).

The Qur'an discusses the resurrection of the body in Surah 56:62, which says that the first thing God created was the universe, and in Surah 53:47, which says that the second thing to be created was the raising of the dead. Surah 21:104 uses the analogy of a scroll to describe the beginning and end of the universe. The creation of the universe is like the unrolling of a scroll, which reveals God's absolute power, and the rolling up again of the scroll is when God's power will be seen again in creating a new universe, when the dead will be brought back to life. Surah 46:33 makes this clear: 'Do they not see that Allah, Who created the heavens and the earth and was not wearied by their creation, has the power to raise the dead to life? Why not! Surely He has the power over everything.'

The Qur'an uses another analogy to explain that the dead will be resurrected in bodily form. Just as plants die in the winter and then come back to life in springtime, so God will give new life to the dead:

The Qur'an uses the analogy of new life sprouting in springtime after winter as a sign of the resurrection of the dead.

And among His other signs is the earth that you see barren; but when We send down rain upon it, it stirs to life and its yield increases. Surely He Who gives it life, will raise the dead to life. Surely He has power over all things. (Surah 41:39)

Task

Look up the following references in the Qur'an and summarize what they say about the resurrection of the dead: surahs 22:5–6; 30:50; 36:51; 71:17–18; 75:36–40.

Problems with resurrection

There are problems with the idea of the resurrection of the body, just as there are with the idea of the immortality of the soul.

- If death is really the end of the human body, a resurrected body must be a *replica*, not the original body of the person who has died. So, is the replica really the same?
- Will the resurrected body look the same as it did at the point of death? What if a person died as a young child? Or if the person died in a fire, or was disabled in some way, or had been dead for hundreds of years? Would their resurrected bodies reflect the ways in which they had died or when they had died? If so, this seems cruel of God. If not, are they the same persons?
- Following on from the previous point, if the resurrected body is different from the dead body, how will the person be recognized by his or her loved ones?

Replica theory is Hick's theoretical idea showing that it is logically possible for someone to disappear from one location and simultaneously reappear in another.

Taking it further

John Hick attempted to address some of these problems by developing a '**replica theory**'. He puts this forward only as a logical possibility and is at pains to say that he does not believe that it is physically possible. His idea is that, when a person dies, God creates a replica of that person in heaven, an exact copy of the person who has died. This replica lives forever with God. Hick sets out three hypothetical examples to show the logical possibility of the theory.

1 'John Smith' is at a conference in London, and in the blinking of an eye he finds himself transported to a conference in New York. He has continuity of body (including stomach contents), memory and personality (so, he is the same person). Friends of his from London travel to New York to see him and verify that it is the same person.

2 Hick then takes the example a stage further. The man at the conference in London dies and an exact 'replica' of him appears alive in New York. There is continuity of memory, body (including stomach contents) and personality. A 'replica' of a dead man lives in another country.

3 A person dies and is 'replicated' in another world that is populated with other dead persons who have been 'replicated'. God enables this resurrection/'replication', so there is life after death.

Hick therefore argues that it is logically possible for human 'replicas' to exist in a different world populated by resurrected people who are brought back to life by God. He thinks that the person in the resurrected world is quite different from the one being transported from one city to another.

Obviously this idea is dependent on a belief in an omnipotent God. Hick's example is also based on a physical resurrection, not a disembodied soul. However, would this 'replica' really be the same person, even if the 'replica' thought of himself as the same person?

Task

Summarize the ideas covered so far on a) the immortality of the soul, b) the resurrection on the body, c) Hick's replica theory.

Evidence for life after death

On 7 October 2014, *The Independent* newspaper reported that there was scientific evidence that life can continue after death. A UK-based team of researchers spent four years interviewing survivors of cardiac arrests (heart attacks) to analyse their experiences and found that nearly 40 per cent of them described having some form of 'awareness' after they had been declared clinically dead. The brain usually shuts down 20 to 30 seconds after the heart stops beating, and it is not normally possible to be aware of anything at all after that happens. The researchers heard that patients had experienced real events up to 3 minutes after this had happened and could recall them accurately after they had been resuscitated. One man gave a 'very credible' account of what was going on while the doctors and nurses tried to bring him back to life: he said that he felt as if he was looking at his own resuscitation from the corner of the room. The study involved 2,060 patients from hospitals in the UK, the USA and Austria. Of those who survived, 46 per cent experienced a broad range of mental experiences, 9 per cent had experiences similar to traditional definitions of near death experiences (NDE) and 2 per cent showed full awareness with explicit recall of 'seeing' and 'hearing' events – or out-of-body experiences. The researchers believed that what happens at death merits further investigation.

There are accounts of many other different types of 'evidence' suggesting that the death of the body is not necessarily the end of a person's existence – that there may be life after death.

Reincarnation is a dualist idea that, when someone dies, their soul moves into a different body, often carrying memories with it.

Memories of past lives

Dr Ian Stevenson (1918–2007) was a psychiatrist at the University of Virginia Medical School who was internationally recognized for his research into **reincarnation**. He discovered evidence which suggested that memories of physical injuries may be transferred from one lifetime to another and travelled around the world investigating

3,000 cases of children who recounted having lived before. His research presented evidence that such children had unusual abilities, illnesses and fears that could not be explained by their environment or heredity.

Stevenson's first case was a boy in Sri Lanka who reported remembering a past life. He questioned the child and the child's parents thoroughly, including the people whom the child recalled were his parents from his past life. This led to Dr Stevenson's conviction that reincarnation was a reality. In the following years, he wrote many books and articles based on his case studies. He found it significant that these children frequently showed lasting birthmarks which supposedly related to the murder or death they suffered in a previous life. Stevenson's research into birthmarks and congenital defects has particular importance, since it furnishes objective and graphic proof of reincarnation, superior to the often fragmentary memories and reports of the children and adults questioned, which, even if verified afterwards, cannot be assigned the same value in scientific terms.

In many cases presented by Stevenson, further proof is also available from medical documents, which have usually been compiled after the death of the person. Stevenson adds that, in the cases he researched and 'solved' where birthmarks and deformities were present, he believed that reincarnation was the only possible explanation. Between 30 and 60 per cent of these deformities can be put down to birth defects related to genetic factors, virus infections or chemical causes. Apart from these demonstrable causes, the medical profession has no other explanation for the other 40 to 70 per cent of cases other than mere chance. Stevenson concluded that the only rational explanation is reincarnation (excerpted from www.near-death.com/experiences/reincarnation01.html).

Task

'Reincarnation is not possible.' Try to find reasons to agree with this statement and therefore show that Stevenson's research is incorrect.

Spiritualism

Spiritualism is the belief that the spirits of people who have died are able and willing to communicate with the living. The afterlife – the 'spirit world' – is understood to be evolving and changing, just like the physical world. Communication between the two worlds may be enabled by 'mediums'. The spiritualist movement began in 1848 in Hydesville, New York, when the Fox sisters claimed to receive messages from the spirit world. In the nineteenth and early twentieth century, people who wanted to contact dead relatives or friends would gather at a séance, but they now meet either in a public demonstration of mediumship at a spiritualist church service or at a private sitting with a medium. Any communication received is either verbal (the medium speaking the words of the spirit) or through tapping noises. Spiritualism is classed as a new religious movement rather than a traditional religion. It has rituals and a belief system as well as an experiential aspect. The Spiritualists National Union in the UK adheres to Seven Principles, which all full members must accept:

Spiritualism is the belief that the spirits of dead people have the abilty to communicate with the living.

- the Fatherhood of God (by which is meant the non-personal creative force in the universe)
- the Brotherhood of Man
- the Communion of Spirits and the Ministry of Angels
- the continuous existence of the human soul
- personal responsibility
- compensation and retribution hereafter for all the good and evil deeds done on earth
- eternal progress open to every human soul.

One famous spiritualist was Sir Arthur Conan Doyle, the author of the Sherlock Holmes novels. Conan Doyle also wrote many books about spiritualism and spoke to many audiences around the world on the subject. Once, however, he had a clash with the famous illusionist Harry Houdini, who argued that any competent magician could replicate all the tricks of spiritualists.

> ### Task
>
> Undertake some research on what 'mediums' do and their claims that they can communicate with the dead. Do you think these claims are justified? What other reasons might you give for the messages mediums claim to bring from the dead? You might want to start with the musical medium Rosemary Brown (1916–2001), who claimed to receive new musical compositions from famous classical composers such as Beethoven, Chopin and Liszt.

Apocalyptic is a type of literature in the Bible that talks about the end of the world.

CHRISTIANITY ROMAN CATHOLICISM

Christian views on death and life after death

Apocalypse and eschatology

There are two important traditions in the Bible, '**apocalyptic**' and '**eschatological**'. Apocalyptic literally means 'the revealing of secret or hidden things' and refers to writing about things that will happen at the end of the world. It typically contrasts the present age, which is temporary and imperfect, with a new age that will be permanent and perfect. This kind of writing is seen particularly in the book of Daniel in the Old Testament and in the book of Revelation in the New Testament. Apocalyptic literature has many distinctive characteristics, such as detailing dreams and their interpretation, visions, strange and shocking imagery, an emphasis on secrets, and the imminent expectation of an end to the present age and the beginning of a better new age.

Eschatology (pronounced 'es-ka-to-lo-jee'), which means 'doctrines about the last things', concerns the teachings that arise from apocalyptic writings. Eschatology, therefore, is *teaching* about the end of the world. Its emphasis is on the future rather than the past. In Christian eschatology, the present is often an unstable, dangerous and destructive time that is seen as preparing the way for a better future, when God will appear in the world and save the righteous believers. God will bring about the end of the world, judge every human, and usher in a new age of happiness and the end of

Eschatology is doctrine and teaching about the end of the world.

any kind of suffering. Revelation 21:1–4, for instance, talks about a 'new Jerusalem' that will be brought about by God:

> Then I saw a new heaven and a new earth, for the first heaven and the first earth had passed away, and there was no longer any sea. I saw the Holy City, the new Jerusalem, coming down out of heaven from God, prepared as a bride beautifully dressed for her husband. And I heard a loud voice from the throne saying, 'Look! God's dwelling place is now among the people, and he will dwell with them. They will be his people, and God himself will be with them and be their God. He will wipe every tear from their eyes. There will be no more death or mourning or crying or pain, for the old order of things has passed away.'

The theologian **Oscar Cullmann** (1902–1999) described eschatology as being like the time during the Second World War between D-Day in 1944, when the decisive allied landings in France occurred, and VE Day in 1945, when Germany surrendered and the war ended. To live in the present day is still to see casualties, still to know defeats along the way, but the eventual hope of victory is secure. Amid the presence of injustice, suffering and death, Christian faith must take the form of hope for the future, until the end of time comes and God intervenes triumphantly.

For many Christians, the apocalypse and eschatology are important in thinking about the way the world is now and the way it will be after God brings about the end of the present world and the beginning of a new era – in other words, the end of this life and the beginning of life after death.

Tasks

1 Try to summarize Christian beliefs about the apocalypse and eschatology. Can you think of a more recent example that expresses the tension that Cullmann talks about? What kind of images might you use to explain the idea?

2 Look at the following passages from the Bible and explain how they are eschatological:

- Isaiah 2:2–4: 'In the last days . . . they will beat their swords into ploughshares.'
- Isaiah 11:6: 'The wolf shall dwell with the lamb, and the leopard shall lie down with the kid, and the calf and the lion . . . together; and a little child shall lead them.'
- Isaiah 65:17: 'For behold I create new heavens and a new earth . . .'
- Revelation 7:14–16: 'These are they who have come out of the great tribulation . . .. Never again will they hunger, never again will they thirst . . .. God will wipe away every tear from their eyes.'

For Christians, there is a more general tension between the importance of living a holy life now, in this life, and the promise of the life to come, in heaven with God. This idea is seen in the Bible. The prophet Isaiah, for instance, says: 'All men are like grass, and all their glory is like the flowers of the field. The grass withers and the flowers fall, because the breath of the Lord blows on them' (Isaiah 40:6–7). This passage is saying that God is in control of all the processes of the universe and implies that God creates human beings with a specific purpose or 'telos' in mind. For Christians, human life is temporary and transitory; people live out their lives in the world, but they believe that death is not the end of life. The classic statement of this belief is made by St Paul:

But if it is preached that Christ has been raised from the dead, how can some of you say that there is no resurrection of the dead? If there is no resurrection of the dead, then not even Christ has been raised. And if Christ has not been raised, our preaching is useless and so is your faith. . . . you are still in your sins. Then those also who have fallen asleep in Christ are lost. If only for this life we have hope in Christ, we are to be pitied more than men. But Christ has indeed been raised from the dead, the first fruits of those who have fallen asleep. (1 Corinthians 15:12–20)

Christians believe that the present life is important: Jesus taught that his followers should pay their taxes and obey civil laws, meaning that they should be involved in the everyday things of life. They are to live their lives as an example to others of what it means to be Christian – for example, to have high moral standards and to treat other people as they themselves would like to be treated. In the end, though, Christians have their sights set on another existence that is greater than this life – the life of heaven.

The Christian focus on the end of time has been a common theme during periods of violence, social unrest and war throughout history. One such example was at the end of the first century, when a Jewish uprising resulted in the Roman army destroying the temple in Jerusalem, expelling all Jews from the city. People at that time thought that the end of the world was near and that God would come to avenge the destruction of Israel's most holy place.

> **Task**
>
> Find examples of incidents when Christians believed that the end of the world was near and write a short paragraph on each. You might start with the prophet hen of Leeds (1806), the Millerites (1843) or the American evangelist Pat Robertson (1982).

The **Rapture** refers to the belief that, either before or at the same time as the second coming of Jesus Christ to earth, righteous Christians who have died and those still alive will be raised up to heaven.

Contemporary fundamentalist Christians tend to interpret the book of Revelation and other parts of the New Testament in a literal way. They attempt to tie its teaching, examples and images into current political events in the Middle East. For instance, the '**Rapture**', described mostly in 1 Thessalonians 4:13–18 and 1 Corinthians 15:50–54, is an event in which God will suddenly 'snatch away' all Christian believers from the earth in order to make way for his righteous judgement to be poured out during the period of tribulation for non-believers. After this, Christ will come again to reign for 1,000 years. Fundamentalists believe this to be literally true and try to see signs of the beginning of the 'end times' (such as great floods and earthquakes) in current events such as climate change.

More liberal interpreters of the Bible see the purpose of eschatological books such as Revelation as pointing to a hope of God's justice and peace being established by Christians in the world. Liberals believe that the present political order is not the hoped-for perfect world and resolve to work towards the ideal situation for all people to live in peacefully and according to the principles laid down in the Bible.

Some fundamentalist Christians see floods, earthquakes and other natural disasters as warnings of the coming of the end of the world, since all these are signs given in the Bible of the Apocalypse.

Heaven and hell

In Christian theology, beliefs about what life after death will be like are expressed in terms of **heaven** and **hell**. In the early parts of the Old Testament, there was no belief in life after death at all. People simply believed in a shadowy existence in Sheol. Sheol was thought of as a great pit under the earth, where everyone ended up after they died (regardless of their moral status). This was a logical deduction, since the dead were buried in the earth, and it seemed to make sense that there was a communal place where dead people went. Sheol was not a place where the dead had another form of life – simply a collecting ground for the bodies of people who had died. It was only towards the end of the Old Testament period that an idea developed about those Jews who had died for their faith – for instance, in war or persecution. God would reward these martyrs with everlasting life at the Day of Judgement. Most Jews came to believe in this form of life after death as a resurrection of the body. One exception was the ultra-religious Sadducee group, who adhered only to the Torah, which contained no teaching about life after death.

The early Christian communities accepted mainstream later Jewish views. Some New Testament writers suggest, however, that life after death is not just a future state but that Christians can experience it in the present. John's Gospel (5:24), for example, emphasizes that 'eternal life' can be experienced now and will continue after physical death: 'Very truly I tell you, whoever hears my word and believes him who sent me has eternal life and will not be judged but has crossed over from death to life.' In 1 Corinthians 15, St Paul also taught that Christians will be raised to a new spiritual

Heaven
describes a state after bodily death reserved for those who have lived according to God's laws.

Hell
describes a state after bodily death where those who have disobeyed God's laws spend eternity in pain.

life in a '*soma pneumatikon*' ('spiritual body'), because God had raised Jesus from the dead. For Paul, in contrast to John, eternal life is a future state, not one that exists yet in the present.

Another idea developed in the New Testament is that of rewards and punishments. Faithful Christians who have lived their life according to the will of God will be rewarded with eternal life. Those who have sinned and strayed from or disobeyed God's commandments will have only themselves to blame when they end up in eternal hell, with its fiery torments. In the Middle Ages, the Catholic Church developed the idea of **Purgatory**. This is a temporary, intermediate state after the death of the body, where those who are destined to go to heaven can first be purified of their sins. No one in Purgatory will stay there permanently or go to hell. It was believed that Christians could lessen the amount of time a deceased relative stayed in Purgatory by praying for them – which is part of Roman Catholic belief today.

> **Purgatory** describes an intermediate, temporary state after death in which a soul is prepared for entry into heaven.

ROMAN CATHOLICISM

Aquinas on life after death

The ideas of St Thomas Aquinas arising from Christian views on eschatology have had a very significant influence on Roman Catholic thought in relation to life after death. Aquinas says there are three possibilities for a person at death.

- *Hell* Hell is a permanent place where souls that have not been saved will be given a body and will suffer both physical and spiritual punishment. Aquinas says that this punishment will last forever.
- *Purgatory* Purgatory is a place where souls that have been saved will be purified to prepare them to experience the **Beatific Vision**, which can be attained only by perfect souls. Such purification will be a painful process, but one where they will learn and develop spiritually. The medieval abuse of the idea of being able to shorten the length of time a soul spent in Purgatory by paying for 'indulgences' is no longer taught by the Roman Catholic Church, though individuals may still earn indulgences in their lifetime by performing spiritual or devotional acts on behalf of others. This is a spiritual rather than a financial idea.
- *The Beatific Vision* For Aquinas, the Beatific Vision is the 'final end' in which a person attains perfect happiness. Perfect happiness cannot be achieved through any physical pleasure, worldly power or finite reality. It can be found only in something that is perfect and infinite, and this can only be God. The Beatific Vision brings direct union with the essence of God. Humans will know God directly, grasping his perfect goodness and love.

> The **Beatific Vision**, in Christianity, refers to a person's direct experience of God.

Since the end of the nineteenth century, Christian theologians have played down the idea of hell, partly because they want to emphasize the overarching love of God for all people, including sinners, and partly because a critical reading of the Bible shows that the language used about heaven and hell is poetic imagery and should not be taken literally.

Taking it further

Aquinas was heavily influenced by the philosophy of **Aristotle** (384–322 BCE), a former pupil of Plato. Aristotle believed that the soul was a 'primary substance' – it could exist on its own without a body – but it also had a 'secondary substance'. For instance, Bert is a cat: his 'catness' is his 'primary substance', and his black, brown and white fur, his long claws and his loud purr form his 'secondary substance'. His primary substance of being a cat is permanent and intrinsic to him – he would not be Bert if he did not have 'catness' – while his fur, the length of his claws, and so on, can change over time. In Aristotle's terms, the primary substance is the soul, which is eternal and unchangeable, while the body, which changes over time and eventually dies, is the secondary substance.

Aquinas, however, adapts Aristotle's view and teaches that the body and soul together make up a human being – that is, the primary and secondary substances are indistinguishable and cannot be separated from each other. He considered that a soul on its own could survive the death of the body, but it does not constitute a 'person' on its own.

The symbolism of life after death

Many Christians believe that the symbols used in accounts of death and life after death are very important, the most powerful being the cross. This is not only a reminder of the cruel and painful death that Jesus suffered and a reminder of the historical context in which he lived and died; it is also a symbol of the Incarnation, the belief that Jesus was 'God made flesh'. Jesus' death on the cross was not just another instance of a criminal execution by the Romans but the most powerful turning point of history. The cross is the symbol of the 'self-emptying' (Greek: *kenosis*) of God: God giving himself wholly for the sake of human beings, God emptying himself so that human sin could be rubbed out and the slate wiped clean. It is through the death of Jesus that human beings can achieve eternal life with God. The once-for-all sacrifice made by Jesus on the cross is the fulfilment of the idea of the **Covenant**, made first with Abraham and renewed with Moses, David and Jeremiah, for it shows that God is with Christians at every point of their existence, even at the point of death. Because Jesus suffered death, he paved the way for all Christians to go beyond death and achieve eternal life. One denominational difference in the symbolism of the cross is between the Roman Catholic 'crucifix', which shows the dead Jesus on the cross, and the Protestant cross, where Jesus has gone from it. This shows a slight difference in theological emphasis between the two denominations: Roman Catholics concentrate on the saving death of Jesus, while Protestants emphasize his resurrection.

CHRISTIANITY
ROMAN
CATHOLICISM

Kenosis
is the Christian term for the 'self-emptying' of Jesus to redeem the sins of humans.

A **covenant**
is a special, mutually binding agreement between two or more people, or between God and his people.

The cross as a symbol: on the left, an empty cross in a Protestant church emphasizes the new life of the Resurrection; on the right, a crucifix in a Roman Catholic church emphasizes the saving death of Jesus.

ISLAM

Muslim views on death and life after death

Muslim views on death

Islam has very clear ideas about the nature of life after death. Muslims believe that there are two stages of every person's existence – this life and the next – and understand death to be the gateway between the two. Death is therefore both a natural occurrence and a necessary stage through which everyone must pass.

Muslims believe that humans continue to exist after death and that the next life will take the form of both a spiritual and a physically resurrected body. Whether the resurrected person has a life of bliss in Paradise or a life of punishment in hell depends on what they have done in their earthly life. There is a direct correlation, therefore, between their conduct on earth and their life beyond death. At some point, God will gather in one place everyone who has ever lived and judge them individually. Only God knows when the Day of Judgement will be. It has many names in the Qur'an, including the Day of Reckoning, the Day of Distress, the Day of the Gathering, the Great Announcement, and The Hour. After this judgement, people will be sent to their allotted place in either Paradise or hell and stay there forever.

Muslim eschatology

Eschatology concerns the teachings about the end times and the end of the world. One of the most important beliefs in Islam is life after death and the Day of Judgement. If a Muslim were to reject belief in life after death, he or she would effectively be rejecting every other Islamic belief. Belief in life after death is what motivates Muslims to behave morally and strive to do the right thing at all times. They know that, if good people suffer, God will show justice to them and they will go to Paradise. God will also judge those who do evil acts and they will be sent to hell. In this way, God's justice will be served.

Muslims believe that, when a person dies, they enter an intermediate state between death and resurrection called Barzakh. Two angels, Munkar and Nakir, ask three questions of the newly dead in the grave. If they answer correctly, because they have lived a good life, a window opens where they can see the different levels of Paradise. For those who do not, a window will open on hell and their grave will become narrower, crushing their ribs, and they will feel the heat of the flames. These states continue until the Day of Judgement. Those who have died in **jihad** will go directly to Paradise and will not undergo Barzakh.

There is much discussion and speculation in Islamic sources, but nothing conclusive, about how long this state lasts for. There is more of a consensus, however, about the end of the world, signalled by an angel blowing a horn. The environmental events that will follow are described in surahs 81 and 82, and include the skies being cracked, the earth being flattened, the mountains turning to dust and the planets being dispersed throughout the universe. Graves will also be overturned. According to the ahadith, the end times (sometimes called the 'Last Hour') will include the return of Isa (Jesus) and also the Dajjal or the Antichrist, who will play a significant and destructive role until he is killed by Jesus. After this, Jesus will get married, have children and live for another forty-four years before being buried beside the Prophet Muhammad.

Eventually, the horn will blow a second time and the dead will rise up from their graves and be resurrected in physical form. God will gather all humans (both those who believe and those who do not) in the Great Plain of Gathering. Here, they will wait for God to give his judgement on them. The righteous will be sheltered from the unbearable heat by the shade of God's magnificent throne.

God will judge every person who has ever lived, the only exception being those Muslims who have died for their beliefs in battle, who will pass directly into Paradise. Everyone else will be handed a book that records all of their deeds in this life. Those who receive this book in their right hand will pass into Paradise, but those who receive it in their left hand will be damned and pass directly into hell.

After this judgement, both the righteous and the damned will walk over the Assirat Bridge. This bridge is very narrow and passes over hell. Three groups of people will cross this bridge easily – those who have lived a faithful life and performed works of charity; those who have been persecuted for the sake of God; and those who have fought for God. Everyone else will fall from the bridge into hell.

Muslims believe that 'Paradise' and 'hell' refer to real places and that they are eternal. The happiness and bliss of those who are in Paradise will last for ever, and the punishment of those condemned to hell will never diminish or end. The Qur'an describes Paradise as a garden of physical pleasures and spiritual delights:

> God will deliver them from the evil of that day and make their faces shine with joy. He will reward them for their steadfastness with robes of silk and the delights of paradise. Reclining there on soft couches, they will feel neither the scorching heat nor the biting cold. Trees will spread their shade around them, and the fruits will hang in clusters over

Jihad
is an Islamic term referring to the religious duty of Muslims to defend their religion. The term is Arabic for 'struggle'.

them. They will be served with silver dishes . . .. When you gaze upon that scene, you will behold a blissful and glorious kingdom. (Surah 76:11–20)

The description of hell is equally vivid but much more frightening:

For the unbelievers we have prepared fetters and chains and a blazing fire. Scalding water will be poured on their heads, melting their skin as well as what is inside their bodies. They will be beaten with rods of iron. Whenever they try to escape from hell, the angel will drag them back, saying 'Taste the torment of hell-fire!' (Surah 22:19–22)

It is very clear one's behaviour in the present life plays a crucial role in the destiny of a Muslim. God will judge each individual on the Day of Judgement on the basis of how they have lived their life on earth. God has given Muslims two guides to help them make correct decisions about living a religious and moral life:

- the Holy Qur'an and the Five Pillars
- the example of the Prophet Muhammad.

If they live according to these principles and examples, they will have no excuse when they account for themselves before God on the Day of Judgement. God will take into account what they have actually done in life but also their intentions. If these were good, they will be able to go to Paradise; if not, they will go to hell. This is explained in a hadith as follows:

If a person intends to do something wrong and does not do it, this is a good deed. If a person intends to do something wrong and does it, this is a bad deed. If a person intends to do a good deed but cannot manage to carry it out, this is a good deed. If a person intends to do a good deed and carries it out, this is equal to ten good deeds.

Muslims offer prayers for the dead that God may be merciful to them – there are a number of duas (or supplications) for the deceased.

> **Task**
>
> Summarize Muslim ideas about a) Paradise and b) hell.

Non-religious views on death and life after death

Many, if not most, non-religious philosophers do not talk about life after death as they believe it does not make sense to discuss things that do not exist.

Jean-Paul Sartre

French existentialist writers such as **Jean-Paul Sartre** (1905–1980) and **Albert Camus** (1913–1960) believed that we are alone in a material universe, with no God, meaning or purpose. Hope is built on despair – Sartre wrote that 'a man is a useless passion' because, when we confront our mortality, we are faced with the necessity of creating some purpose and meaning in our lives. We must act freely and make choices that determine who we are as opposed to simply following the crowds and fashions to achieve a false sense of security. We have a choice between 'being' (creating our own choices, choosing our authentic essence) or 'nothingness' (reducing ourselves to the level of mere objects governed by external forces). The sheer absurdity of a universe cold and indifferent to our fate leads us to despair. In our anxiety, we create a benevolent and omnipotent, omniscient creator. But this is 'bad faith'. For Sartre it is a false attempt to relieve the anxiety of death and the pointlessness of life. We are radically free: when we grasp this, 'all the guard-rails collapse'. Every person is an individual, and the choices we make in life determine who we become. We cannot be held back by fear of heaven or hell or judgement. We become the source of our values and goals in life. This freedom is too terrifying for most people to handle, so they retreat into becoming pawns of others, allowing others to make choices for them, or telling themselves myths that they are powerless, that they are victims of their past and of circumstances beyond their control. They have created these myths as facts in their minds when actually they are governed by the fear of having to choose for themselves who they want to be. According to Sartre, 'Man is fundamentally the desire to be God' – that is, we aspire to live forever, to know all things, to be all powerful, to be wholly good.

Karl Marx

Karl Marx (1818–1883) regarded religion as a pacifying influence used by the rich and powerful to keep the poor in their place within the social order. He said that religion offered the poor 'pie in the sky when you die', so that they thought they would be rewarded for their suffering in heaven. Marx was deeply suspicious of eschatology that, in his view, stressed the discontinuity between the present and the future to the exclusion of political hopes of improving the present order, leading to passivity and the view that the masses just had to put up with injustice and oppression. As a consequence of Marx's critique, capitalism in the West has seen economic growth and medical technological advances which have raised the standard of living to a level almost unimaginable fifty years ago, enhancing quality of life expectations here and now and directing aspirations to material pleasures and life *before* rather than *after* death.

Don Cupitt

Don Cupitt (b. 1934) is a life fellow and former dean of Emmanuel College, Cambridge, who in 1984 wrote and produced a BBC series called *The Sea of Faith*. Although an ordained priest in the Church of England, he believes in God not as an objective being but, rather, as a reflection of human longing. He thinks that traditionalist religious believers are holding on nostalgically or superstitiously to a God who is rather like Father Christmas. Religious people feel 'how frail the human life is, how wretched most men's lives and how threatened our happiness is by evil within and about us', so that 'for 999 people out of every thousand religion has to do with metaphysical yearnings and a desire to be reassured about God's existence and a real life after death . . .' For Cupitt, God is a symbol for reaching out beyond our egocentric selves to the transcendent – moral good, aesthetic beauty, intellectual truth. In the traditional images and practices of religious communities, humans express commitment to the ideals of peace, justice, hope, moral goodness and the **sanctity of life**. Cupitt says that this, and not God, is 'religion'. He believes in religion and sees Christian faith as a river of symbols that express our own deepest desires:

> The **sanctity of life** is the view that human life comes from God and therefore must be protected and preserved.

> We value things insofar as they turn us on, that is, heighten or stimulate the life-impulse in us. . . . We must get rid of all ideas of the substantial and the lasting, all fantasies of omnipotence and invulnerability, and accept the radical contingency, the fleetingness of our expression and transitoriness of our life. . . . Human salvation is now understood to consist in the integrity and plenitude of our expression and affirmation of life now, in this fleeting moment; it passes and we are gone. There are no more guarantees of progress or preservation. (*Sea of Faith*, 1988, p. 226)

Cupitt's is a secularized Christianity far removed from the God of classical theism. In *Life Lines*, he reinterprets Jesus crucifixion as a call to accept the inevitability of death and the fact that we will cease to exist; we will disappear, so we should abandon the belief in the indestructible self and life after death.

Task

Do you think that Cupitt would agree with this quotation from Act 5, scene 5, of Shakespeare's *Macbeth*?

'Life's but a walking shadow, a poor player that struts and frets his hour upon the stage and then is heard no more; it is a tale told by an idiot, full of sound and fury signifying nothing.'

Tasks

End of the world scenarios

There are many proposed ways by which the world might end. You may have seen films such as:

- *On the Beach* (1959)
- *Dr Strangelove* (1964)
- *The Day After* (1983)
- *The Rapture* (1992)
- *12 Monkeys* (1995)
- *28 Days Later* (2002) and *28 Weeks Later* (2007)
- *Time of the Wolf* (2003)
- *War of the Worlds* (2005)
- *This is the End* (2009)
- *2012* (2009)
- *Melancholia* (2011)
- *This is the End* (2013)

Look these up to discover the supposed threat to earth and its inhabitants. Put your results into a grid.

Some of the (non-religious) threats to the end of the world that are proposed most often are:

- global warming
- super volcanoes
- super tsunamis
- overpopulation
- pandemic threats, such as SARS or its engineered version, H5N1
- nuclear war
- bioterrorism
- misuse of nanotechnology or biotechnology
- an asteroid strike
- extra-terrestrial invasion.

Research three of these and decide which you think is the most likely reason for the possible end of the world. Give reasons for your answer.

TICK THE TOPICS

Now you should tick the relevant boxes to check what you have learned in this chapter.

Sections	Topics	Tick
	Definitions of death	
	Personal identity and life after death	
	Dualism and monism	
Immortality or resurrection?	Immortality	
	Problems with immortality	
	Resurrection	
	Problems with resurrection	
Evidence for life after death	Memories of past lives	
	Spiritualism	
Christian views on death and life after death	Apocalypse and eschatology	
	Christian views on heaven and hell	
	Aquinas on life after death	
	Symbolism of life after death	
Muslim views on death and life after death	Muslim views on death	
	Muslim eschatology	
	Muslim views on heaven and hell	
Non-religious views on death and life after death	Jean-Paul Sartre	
	Karl Marx	
	Don Cupitt	

Sample questions

AQA Religious Studies A (8062)

1 Which of the following is the name for a form of the afterlife?
   a) Cloudland b) Haven c) Hinterland d) Heaven   (1 mark)
2 Give two views of death.   (2 marks)
3 Explain two contrasting beliefs in contemporary British society about hell. (4 marks)
4 Explain two religious beliefs about life after death.   (5 marks)
5 'It is reasonable to believe in life after death.'
Evaluate this statement. In your answer, you:
   ● should give reasoned arguments in support of this statement
   ● should give reasoned arguments to support a different point of view
   ● should refer to religious arguments
   ● may refer to non-religious arguments
   ● should reach a justified conclusion.   (12 marks)

Edexcel Religious Studies B Full Course (1RB0) and Short Course (3RB0)

a) Outline three forms of existence after death according to religious beliefs. (3)
b) Explain two responses to the idea of life after death.   (4)
c) Assess the strength of religious ideas about life after death. (9)
d) 'We live then we die, that is all there is to it.'
Evaluate this statement, considering more than one point of view. (12)

Edexcel International GCSE Religious Studies (4RS0)

a) Define what is meant by 'brain death'.   (2)
b) Describe the views of one religion about what happens after death. (5)
c) Explain why non-religious people deny the possibility of life after death. (8)
d) 'Believing in life after death is like believing in fairy tales.'
Do you agree? Give reasons for your answer, showing that you have considered another
point of view.   (5)

WJEC Eduqas Religious Studies (Full Course and Short Course)

a) Giving one example, state what is meant by 'judgement'.   (2)
b) With reference to one religion you have studied, explain views about the afterlife. (5)
c) From two different religions or two religious traditions, explain views about eternal
    punishment and hell.   (8)
d) 'There is no afterlife.'
Discuss this statement, showing that you have considered more than one point of view.
(You must refer to religion and belief in your answer.)   (15)
                                                                   (SPaG + 6)

Human Nature

In this chapter, you will be studying what is probably the only thing that unites all human beings, regardless of their race, gender, religious beliefs or anything else. The question of what it is to be 'human' is central to all our ideas about how we live our lives, so it is very important that you are clear about what being 'human' actually means. You will look at different definitions of 'human nature' as well as Christian, Muslim and non-religious ideas about life.

Definitions

Many of the problems and difficulties we encounter in our everyday language arise from people having different understandings of important words, particularly differences in definitions. In this chapter, we are going to be talking about 'human nature' and, in order to do this properly, we need to have a working definition of what we mean by '**human**'.

Human describes a member of the species *homo sapiens*.

Human

For starters, here are some definitions:

- a member of the genus *Homo* and especially of the species *Homo sapiens*.
- a person
- of, relating to, or characteristic of humans
- having or showing those positive aspects of nature and character regarded as distinguishing humans from other animals
- having the form of a human.

> **Task**
>
> Read through these definitions carefully. Do you agree with them? Do they leave anything out? How would you define 'human'? Give reasons for your answer.

Person

One of the elements of many definitions of 'human' is that a human is a 'person'. Here, again, we need to start our discussion with a definition of what we mean by a 'person'. Note that the way we define this term will have huge consequences for how we think about and deal with a wide range of important issues.

Here are some definitions of 'person':

- an adult human being
- an individual human being
- a thinking, intelligent being that has reason and reflection and can consider itself the same thinking thing in different times and places (John Locke, British philosopher)
- a human being with the capacity for wishing to continue to exist
- a living soul or self-conscious being.

> **Task**
>
> Write down (without discussing it with anyone) the names of five different people you know and then
>
> - think about what they all have in common
> - write down your initial definition of 'person'
> - discuss your definition with your neighbour/group
> - amend your initial definition as appropriate
> - think about whether there are any cases where the term 'person' is not appropriate for human beings. Why might this be?

You will gather from these that defining what exactly 'person' means is no easy feat.

We said earlier that the definition of a 'person' we settle on will have huge implications for our discussion of many issues. You may already be beginning to see the importance of this. To help you with this, try to answer the next questions.

- Why is the definition of 'person' important in discussions about ethics?
- Are persons more important than other entities, such as animals? (If so, why? If not, why not?)
- How is your definition of 'person' important for the way we think about embryos, foetuses and animals?

Taking it further

Below is a passage showing one definition of a 'person'. Read it carefully and then discuss the questions that follow. The passage comes from the influential German philosopher Friedrich Nietzsche, whose *Thus Spoke Zarathustra* opened up many issues in thinking about human nature and what it is that constitutes a person.

'I am body and soul' – so speaks the child. And why should one not speak like children?
But the Awakened, the enlightened man says: I am body entirely, and nothing beside; and soul is only a word for something in the body. The Body is a great intelligence, a multiplicity with one sense, a war and a peace, a herd and a herdsman. Your little intelligence, my brother, which you call 'spirit', is also the instrument of your body, a little instrument and toy of your great intelligence. You say 'I' and are proud of this word. But greater than this – although you will not believe it – is your body and its great intelligence, which does not say 'I' but performs 'I'.

Task

How does Nietzsche think of persons? What might be his definition? What, for him, characterizes a person?

Task

Explain how your definition of 'person' might apply to someone who is blind and deaf, cannot speak, is severely mentally impaired, and needs round-the-clock care.

You should now have a reasonable understanding of what you consider to be the centrally important features of human nature. You will need to use these features as you begin to look at the religious and non-religious views of the nature of human life and how they might be applied in certain situations. You will also need to have them firmly in mind when you reach chapters 9, 10 and 11 of this book.

CHRISTIANITY
ROMAN
CATHOLICISM

Christian views on the nature of human life

Christian ideas and beliefs concerning the nature of human life come from discussion of and reflection on several passages in the Bible. The first Christian theologian, St Paul, defined the Christian view of human nature and its importance in 1 Corinthians 15, where he talks of the 'physical body' and the 'spiritual body'. This view has influenced the way Christians understand human nature as being more than just the physical body. Every human being has a spiritual dimension which is an integral part of their personality. To put this in a slightly different way, human beings are made up of two different dimensions: the physical dimension of flesh and blood and the spiritual dimension, which is non-material. These two dimensions cannot be separated; both are necessary. The 'psycho-physical reality' that makes up every human being is, according to St Paul, created by God. In all Christian discussion, therefore, human life is considered to be sacred because it has been created by God. Humans are unique, the only part of creation to have the breath of God in them. When God creates all other life in Genesis 1, he sees that it is good, but in 1:31, having created human beings, we read that 'God saw all that he had made, and it was very good.'

Christians believe that humans are made in the 'image' of God and are thus uniquely connected to their creator. Genesis 1:27 says, 'So God created man in his own image, in the image of God he created them.' Humans have a unique connection to God. Indeed, there is some evidence that humans were created as companionship for God. Genesis records that God walked through the Garden of Eden searching for Adam but could not find him. Genesis 2:18, when God says, 'It is not right that man should be alone. I will make a helper who is suitable for him', and the creation of Eve imply that humans were created as relational beings to *one another*.

Part of what it means to be made in the image of God is seen in the sixth commandment: 'You shall not commit murder' (Exodus 20:13). Indeed, many of the laws in the Torah underline the sanctity of life, as, for instance, does Leviticus 24:21: 'whoever kills an animal must make restitution, but whoever kills a man must be put to death.'

There are passages in the Old Testament which exhibit a sense of wonder at the nature of human life. For example, the Psalmist, speaking to God, says, 'I praise you because I am fearfully and wonderfully made; your works are wonderful, I know full well' (Psalm 139:14).

The sanctity of life

Many Christians believe that human life is sacred – that is, it has a unique importance in the universe because it was designed by God. On the basis of their interpretation of biblical passages, all human life is sacred. Humans were given a unique position in the created world by God; only humans have souls, only humans have a special relationship with God, only humans are made in the image and likeness of God (Genesis 1:26).

Jeremiah 1:5 and Psalm 139 talk of God's establishment of a relationship with individuals from the moment of conception.

13　For you created my inmost being;
　　you knit me together in my mother's womb.
14　I praise you because I am fearfully and wonderfully made;
　　your works are wonderful,
　　I know that full well.
15　My frame was not hidden from you
　　when I was made in the secret place.
　　When I was woven together in the depths of the earth,
16　your eyes saw my unformed body.
　　All the days ordained for me were written in your book
　　before one of them came to be.
　　(Psalm 139:13–16, New International Version [NIV])

Based on a literal interpretation of this passage, many Christians believe that the soul must be present from the moment of conception too. Those who interpret the Bible more liberally will point to other guiding principles concerning the sanctity of life. They note that the Bible does not talk of preserving human life *at all costs*. Hebrews 9:27, for instance, 'inasmuch as it is appointed for men to die once and after this comes judgement', reminds people that death is a natural part of every person's existence. Also, there was a long tradition of capital punishment in the Bible and early Christianity. (For more information on this, see chapter 13, pp. 264–6.) This was justified by reference to the command of God for the punishment of certain crimes – for example,

- Genesis 9:6, where the death penalty for murder is justified on the grounds that 'God made man in his own image', and therefore killing another human being was just like killing God.
- John 8:3–11, where Jesus discusses the case of a woman who was discovered committing adultery; the normal punishment under Jewish law was for an adulterer to be stoned to death.

For Christians, the single most important evidence for the sanctity of human life is seen in the Incarnation, when God became human in the person of Jesus. John 1:14 says, 'And the Word became flesh and dwelt amongst us, full of grace and truth.' The idea that God, the almighty creator of the universe, would humble himself to become fully human means for Christians that God designed humans to have a special relationship with God. Christian theology argues that this must mean that human life is sacred.

Imago dei is a Latin term meaning 'in the image of God'. Christians believe that all humans are created in God's image.

> ### Tasks
> - Explain what a Christian might understand by the nature of human life.
> - Try to find out more about the meaning of *'imago dei'* and its importance for Christians.
> - Research the idea of the Incarnation and explain its importance in Christianity.
> - Look up Psalm 8 and Matthew 6:25–34 in the Bible. What do these passages say about the nature of human life?

Euthanasia

Euthanasia means 'good death'. It refers to the practice of deliberately ending a very ill person's life without pain because that person wants to die. Euthanasia is currently illegal in Britain and many other countries, though it is legal in the Netherlands, Belgium, Ireland, Colombia and Luxembourg.

To see how the idea of the sanctity of life might work in more detail, we will look at the example of **euthanasia** and Christian beliefs.

Most of the arguments in favour of euthanasia are made by non-religious people or groups. One of these is that every human being should have the right to decide when they die. Some Christians, however, are also in favour of euthanasia, using Jesus' commandment to 'love your neighbour as yourself'. They argue that, if you really love someone who is terminally ill and in great pain, you would want to help that person to end their suffering. For Christians (and other religious people), death is not the end. Death should not be feared but is a much better state than a life of suffering.

Most Christian believers tend to argue against euthanasia because of the sanctity of life and emphasize that all life comes from God and that only God has the right to take life away. They also point to the fact that there are viable alternatives to euthanasia: hospices can provide a caring environment where terminally ill patients can die a dignified and painless death. According to this argument, there is no need for euthanasia. Some Christians point to biblical passages to assist them in their decision. St Paul taught that people must expect suffering in life and should not try to escape from it (1 Thessalonians 3:4), and, in parables such as 'The Sheep and the Goats' (Matthew 25: 31–46), Jesus taught that Christians will be judged by God on how they have helped the sick. Jesus always cared for the sick, and therefore euthanasia should not be an option.

The Roman Catholic Church condemns euthanasia completely. The *Declaration on Euthanasia*, issued in 1980, stated that any attempt on an innocent person's life is opposing God's love for that person. Circumstances such as long illness and old age can actually help people to face death, even though death is frightening.

The Church of England's report in 1975, *On Dying Well*, and the Methodist Conference's statement in 1974 both oppose euthanasia. They emphasize the fact that humans are God's creation and that life is sacred. Killing is therefore 'playing God' to say who should live and who should die.

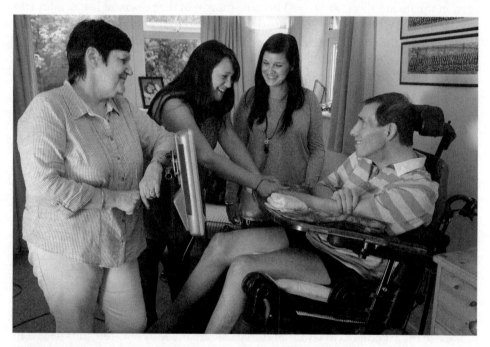

Tony Nicklinson, who was left totally paralysed following a stroke in 2005, fought for many years for the right to an assisted death and became an important voice in the campaign for legal euthanasia. His case was turned down by the High Court, and he died in 2012, aged fifty-eight.

Tasks

1 Summarize the arguments for and against euthanasia.
2 How important do you think the idea of the sanctity of life is for Christians in the case of euthanasia? Give reasons for your answer.

Muslim views on the nature of human life

The sanctity of life

Islam teaches that God created the universe and everything in it. God created the order and purpose in the universe so that everything he designed is good and works as he wishes it to. God rules over the universe with compassion and mercy. The Qur'an uses the words 'merciful' (*rahmah*) and 'compassionate' (**rahim**) many times. Both words come from the same linguistic root – '**rahma**' – which means 'forgiveness'. The phrase 'In the name of Allah, the merciful, the compassionate' appears at the beginning of each surah of the Qur'an. Muslims believe that God will show his abundant mercy to all who believe in him. The mercy and compassion of God sustains, protects and rewards all those who believe in him.

The first surah of the Qur'an reads:

> In the name of Allah, the Compassionate, the Merciful
> Praise be to Allah, Lord of the Creation,
> The Compassionate, the Merciful,
> King of Judgement Day!
> You alone we worship, and to you alone
> We pray for help.
> Guide us to the straight path
> The path of those whom you have favoured,
> Not of those who have incurred your anger
> Nor of those who have gone astray.

This surah shows how God is the creator and is in control of the universe from its beginning to its end (Judgement Day) (see chapter 7, pp. 146–8). Everything in the universe depends upon God for its existence. The purpose of all creation, including humans, is to love and serve God. Because God has created and sustains the universe, Muslims believe that God has given them a well-ordered world, in which night follows day and the seasons follow in predictable patterns, so that, for instance, humans may grow crops to feed themselves. The animals are given by God to help humans to live according to God's laws. Humans are God's stewards on the earth. The Qur'an teaches a strong respect for human life: '. . . do not take the life God has made sacred, except by right. This is what He commands you to do: Perhaps you will use your reason' (6:151).

The Prophet Muhammad cited murder as being a major sin against God and warned his followers that 'the first cases to be settled between people on the Day of Judgement will be those of bloodshed.' Muslims are also forbidden to harm animals without good reason, because the Prophet taught that 'there is reward in kindness to every living thing – animal or human.'

Islam teaches that God created humans from a lump of clay and breathed the spirit of life into them. He separated them from everything else in creation by giving them three divine gifts:

Rahim
is one of the ninety-nine names of God in Islam, meaning 'the Merciful'.

Rahma
is the Islamic concept of mercy.

- intelligence to tell the difference between truth and falsehood
- the free will to choose freely between these
- the power of speech so that they may worship God.

It is because God provided humans with these three gifts that they are superior to any other creature in the universe. The second of the three gifts, free will, means that humans can sometimes make the wrong choice because they are not perfect – only God is perfect. Humans are vulnerable to temptation and sin. They can rebel against God's will because they are proud and sometimes think that they are equal with God.

The name of the Muslim religion, Islam, reminds people of their nature and their duty to God. Islam means 'submission' or obedience to God, so Muslims must submit to the will of God and accept that Muhammad was the Prophet of God. The purpose of human beings in Islam, therefore, is to fulfil their purpose as given to them by God. Everything in the universe, including plants, animals, the weather, and the stars and planets, fulfil their purpose naturally and therefore serve and worship God. In this way, the whole universe surrenders to the will of God.

Obedience to God means that Muslims have a duty to do God's will in the world every day and are commanded to do good for others as often and in as many ways as they can. An example of one way in which this can be brought about, Muslims refer to the Prophet, who taught that God praises those who put others before themselves: 'Those who preserve themselves from their own greed shall surely prosper' (Surah 59.9). The Prophet Muhammad said: 'God constantly helps the one who helps his

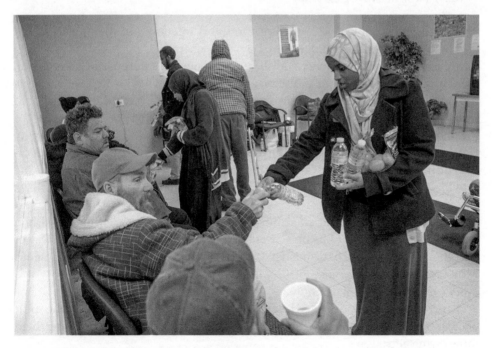

Islam teaches that Muslims should seek to help those who suffer, as shown here at a shelter for the homeless run by an American university's Muslim student union.

brother' and 'even a smile or a kind word is charity'. He taught that children must be respectful to their parents, even when the parents are in their old age: 'And your Lord has decreed that you worship none but Him, and that you be dutiful to your parents. If one of them or both of them attain old age in your life, say not to them a word of disrespect, nor shout at them but address them in terms of honour' (Qur'an 17:23). The Prophet also taught that men should show great respect for women and forbade the common practice of wife-beating and domestic abuse (Surah 4.19). He disapproved of sex outside marriage and never engaged in it himself, although it was very common at the time. He ordered men to 'provide for and protect' women, whether it was their mother, sister, wife or daughter, or even those of others, whether Muslims or not (Surah 4.34)

In Islam, there is a particular emphasis on helping those members of society who are downtrodden or cannot look after themselves, particularly orphans, the poor and needy. Muslims must strive to make their community better. Doing this will bring blessings from God and will give them peace and happiness. If Muslims live according to God's laws given in the Qur'an, they will be respected in their community, will find wealth and success, and will always choose the right thing to do. In return, God will bless them and they will be a positive example to others.

Tasks

1 Summarize Muslim beliefs on human nature.
2 Do you think it would have been better for God not to have created humans with free will?
3 Explain the importance of service to others in Islam.

Abortion

Abortion is the expulsion of a foetus from the womb.

We will look here at another example of a moral issue – **abortion** – to show how the idea of the sanctity of life is relevant for many Muslims.

Abortion is **haram** (forbidden) in Islam after 120 days of pregnancy. There is one exception to this ruling, however, which is if the mother's life would be in danger if she did not have an abortion. In Shari'a law, this is considered to be the 'lesser of two evils'. If an abortion was not allowed in this kind of case, it could result in the death of both the mother and the foetus, which would be worse than the death of the foetus alone. The Qur'an does not explicitly refer to abortion but gives advice on similar issues where the sanctity of life is involved, and this may be used to make decisions about abortion.

Islam puts great emphasis on the sanctity of life. Surah 5:32, says: 'Whoever has spared the life of a soul, it is as though he has spared the life of all people. Whoever has killed a soul, it is as though he has murdered all of mankind.' In terms of the foetus, then, Muslims argue that it has the status of a human being, so it should be given the same rights as any other human being.

One contentious area is where it is established during pregnancy that the foetus has a defect that cannot be treated and will cause premature death or a life of suffering. An example might be hydrocephalus (fluid on the brain, where the brain has not developed at all and there is only a brain stem). Some Muslim scholars would argue that it is allowable to abort the foetus as long as it falls within the 120 day limit. In this case, two medical opinions would be needed before the operation could be performed. Others disagree because they emphasize the sanctity of *all* human life. Giving birth to a disabled child provides an opportunity for the parents to show their love for the child and provide it with the best life they can.

Task

1 Summarize the arguments for and against abortion for Muslims.
2 How strong do you think these arguments are? Give reasons for your answer.

Non-religious views on human life

Physicalism

Physicalism is a philosophical position which states that everything that exists consists merely of its physical properties and that the only existing substance is physical. So, on a purely physical level, it is possible to be quite precise about what constitutes a human being. We could look at the chemicals that make up a human body and conclude that this is all that a human being is. Table 8.1 lists the chief constituents of a human body. Roughly 96 per cent of the mass of the human body is made up of only four elements: oxygen (65%), carbon (18%), hydrogen (10%) and nitrogen (3%), much of which is in the form of water. Scientists do not really know what purpose some of the other trace elements serve.

While this is a description of what constitutes a typical human body, it does not explain anything about what makes a human different to a dish containing all the elements listed here. Even physicalists must admit, however, that there is something else that is essential to a human being. They tend to concentrate on the properties of the human mind rather than the composition of the body and assert that the mind is a physical organ, just like the other organs of the body. Humans have thoughts, wishes and desires, such as hoping that the lesson you are in now will soon be over, that you can have your favourite meal tonight, and that the person you would really like to get closer to will notice you soon. Religious believers, among others, think that the cause of these thoughts, hopes and desires is the 'mind' or the 'soul'. Physicalists think that the cause is the firing of neurons in the brain and that this is a purely physical and normal activity of the brain. They believe that nothing or no one external to the brain is necessary for these processes to occur. Obviously, physicalists are not religious.

> **Physicalism** is the belief that the entirety of the world is made up of physical substances without the need for any non-physical or spiritual elements.

Table 8.1 Approximate quantities of the chemical elements present in an average 70 kg man

Element	Amount
Oxygen	43 kg
Carbon	16 kg
Hydrogen	7 kg
Nitrogen	1.8 kg
Calcium	1.0 kg
Phosphorus	780 g
Sulphur	140 g
Potassium	100 g
Sodium	96.5 g
Chlorine	95 g
Magnesium	19 g
Silicon	18 g
Iron	4.2 g
Fluorine	2.6 g
Zinc	2.3 g
Rubidium	320 mg
Strontium	320 mg
Bromine	200 mg
Lead	120 mg
Copper	72 mg
Aluminium	61 mg
Cadmium	50 mg
Boron	48 mg
Barium	22 mg
Tin	17 mg
Iodine	13 mg
Manganese	12 mg
Nickel	10 mg
Gold	10 mg
Molybdenum	9.3 mg
Chromium	1.8 mg
Caesium	1.5 mg
Cobalt	1.5 mg
Uranium	0.09 mg

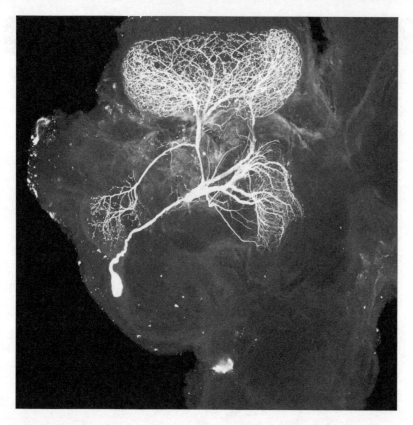

According to a physicalist understanding, human beings are made up simply of physical matter, and our personalities and emotions are best understood as an assemblage of connections and synapses in the brain.

Task

Do you think that a human person is merely a combination of chemicals? If you agree, how would you explain the different personalities that people have? If you disagree, what else is there that makes a human person?

Existentialism

Existentialism is one of many different non-religious perspectives on the nature of human life. 'Existentialism' is a term that describes a wide variety of philosophical, religious and political views, for there is no universal agreement as to its definition. Many philosophers who might be called 'existentialists' dislike this term because they think it categorizes them into a single 'school of thought', whereas each one struggles to find the most *individual* freedom for people within a society, an emphasis on the individual that is not consistent with being 'branded' as an ideology. Although there are a few religious existentialists, most are atheists.

Existentialism
is a philosophical movement that argues that humans are responsible for how their life develops, as there is no God to guide them in the choices they make.

Most existentialist thinkers agree that human life is in no way complete and fully satisfying. This is because of the suffering and loss that occur when we consider the lack of power and control we have over our life. Existentialism is the search and journey for true self and personal meaning in life.

Most importantly, what existentialists find most objectionable is when a person or society tries to impose or demand that their beliefs, values or rules be accepted and obeyed without question. Existentialists believe this destroys individualism and makes a person become whatever is wanted by those in power. This dehumanizes individuals and reduces them to the status of objects. Existentialism therefore stresses that an individual person needs to make up their own mind about what to believe and do rather than simply obeying what the state or religion tells them.

Jean-Paul Sartre helped to popularize existentialism during the 1940s and 1950s. His novels, plays and other writings were works of philosophical activism and are still influential today. Sartre's major philosophical text, *Being and Nothingness*, was composed in the winter of 1942–3, at the height of the Second World War. His philosophy focuses on the actions that a person takes, and he argues that a man's character and significance (essence) are determined by his actions, not his views, by his deeds, not his words. Ultimately, there is no reason for acting. This is mankind's dilemma: he is totally free to act, but there is no significance to his actions. There is no God to give predetermined meaning to our actions. Humankind is 'sentenced to total freedom'. The self exists only as a mind that is conscious of a series of objects. One of Sartre's

A cat hunts as a matter of instinct – it makes no sense to say that it is a 'good' or 'bad' thing. For Sartre, there is no such thing as right and wrong in the natural world, and the only difference between animals and humans is our ability to think, rather than acting purely through instinct.

most famous sayings is that 'existence precedes essence'. Humans are nothing until they act; their actions (i.e., not God or the state or parents or any other source of authority) then define who they are.

Sartre determined that human beings are unique only in their ability to think of something that is not real, of alternatives to what is actually happening, of nothingness. This is what gives us the freedom that other animals do not possess. According to Sartre, humans must accept the fact that there are no values to be found outside of humankind itself. Nature holds no evidence of good and evil. Science cannot tell us what we *ought* to do, only what we *can* do.

People often run from the responsibility of choosing by acting in bad faith or self-deception – that is, by unthinkingly accepting the values of the surrounding culture as being actually true or real. Life goes on as normal. Authentic people must create their own values *ex nihilo*, completely aware that there is nothing to guide them in their decisions. Sartre says, at the end of *Being and Nothingness*: 'All human activities are equivalent and all are on principle doomed to failure. Thus it amounts to the same thing whether one gets drunk alone or is a leader of nations.'

Tasks

- The seventeenth-century English philosopher Thomas Hobbes famously said that life in the state of nature is 'solitary, poor, nasty, brutish and short'. Do you agree with him? Give reasons for your answer.
- Explain what Sartre means by the phrase 'existence precedes essence'.
- What does Sartre mean by saying that humans are 'sentenced to total freedom'? Do you agree with him? Give reasons for your answer.
- Explain an existentialist perspective on the nature of human life.
- Find out about other existentialist thinkers – Nietzsche, Kierkegaard, Heidegger, Camus, Jaspers and Marcel – and their views on human nature.

Economics

Many people take out life insurance policies so that, if they have a serious accident that prevents them from working, or if they die, their relatives will receive money to live on. The way that the value of someone's life is determined is carried out by professionals called '**actuaries**'.

Actuaries are experts in the management of risk. They use their mathematical ability to measure the risk of future events, particularly in healthcare, pensions, insurance, banking and investments, where a single decision can have a major financial impact. What is interesting in the context of the value of a human life is the assumptions actuaries make, calculating a person's value solely on economic criteria. They take into account such things as:

An **actuary** is an expert in the management of risk, usually future risks for individuals.

- how long a person will live
- how much they are likely to earn during their lifetime.

Lifespan is often discussed in terms of life expectancy, the average length taking into account the expected mortality rates that apply to the individual. Mortality rates are estimated on the basis of such characteristics as age, gender, health status, habits such as smoking and drinking alcohol, and participation in dangerous activities. Of course the specific mortality for any individual cannot be known in advance, but a large volume of data and years of research allow the rates to be estimated with a high degree of accuracy. Mortality rates change over time, in response to changes in health care, in the environment, and in society in general.

Future earning capacity may be estimated on the basis of earnings history, age, education, health status, and published data on population income. There are numerous government and industry sources for relationships between various relevant characteristics and earnings. The economic value that a person generates also includes the value of employee benefits. (This information has been excerpted from Donald F. Behan, *Determining the Economic Value of Human Life*, www.behan.ws/lifevalue.htm?Num=3.) Actuaries, then, calculate the value of an individual's life in purely economic terms.

> **QALYs**, an abbreviation of quality-adjusted life years, is a way of determining the cost benefit of someone's life.

Taking it further

One way in which this might be explained is by studying an example. We will use the issue in healthcare of quality-adjusted life years (**QALYs**). There are some situations in medical care when a decision has to be made about balancing up the quality of a patient's life against the cost of sustaining that person's health. For instance, if an eighty-year-old man has breathing difficulties and cannot move about without pain, doctors and other health officials would have to think carefully about whether the cost of providing nursing care and the medicines he needs will actually be cost effective. That is, they have to decide whether the eighty-year-old will receive enough benefit from the money spent on his medical care. It might be that better economic value could be gained by spending the money on a younger person who needs a liver transplant, resulting in his being more likely to live for longer than the old man.

The QALY is a measure of the economic value of the outcome of any treatment provided. The example just given is a very basic case. In reality, the decision is made in a much more sophisticated way, taking many more factors into account. There are several problems with using the system of QALYs. One of these is that decisions about health and life expectancy should not be made by comparing one patient with another, as this is unfair to both. Decisions should be made on each individual person on their own merits. Following from this, financial considerations should not be put above patient health. Just because someone is old does not mean that they are of less value than a younger person. For instance, in the example above, if the eighty-year-old was a scientist who was on the verge of discovering a cure for cancer, and if the younger person was an alcoholic who had already had a liver transplant but continued to drink heavily, then a different decision might be made. We might conclude that making health decisions on purely economic grounds is not a satisfactory method.

Task

1 Explain what a QALY is.
2 Find out more about QALYs and prepare a talk for your class about their benefits and drawbacks.

Tasks

1 How helpful do you think it is to put an actuarial value on a human life?
2 What are your own views on the value of human life? Give reasons for your views.

TICK THE TOPICS

Now you should tick the relevant boxes to check what you have learned in this chapter.

Sections	Topics	Tick
Definitions	Human	
	Person	
	Christian views on the nature of human life	
Christian views	The sanctity of life	
	Euthanasia	
	Muslim views on the nature of human life	
Muslim views	The sanctity of life	
	Abortion	
Non-religious views	Physicalism	
	Existentialism	
	Economics	

Sample questions

AQA Religious Studies A (8062) and Religious Studies B (8063)

1 Which of the following is a religious idea about human nature?
   a) Mortal b) Created c) Unique d) Person   (1 mark)
2 Give two religious beliefs about the sanctity of life.   (2 marks)
3 Explain two contrasting beliefs in contemporary British society about the
   idea of 'person'.   (4 marks)
4 Explain two religious beliefs about relationships between men and women.   (5 marks)
5 'Humans are totally dependent on God.'
Evaluate this statement. In your answer, you:
   • should give reasoned arguments in support of this statement
   • should give reasoned arguments to support a different point of view
   • should refer to religious arguments
   • may refer to non-religious arguments
   • should reach a justified conclusion.   (12 marks)

Edexcel Religious Studies B (1RB0)

a) Give three ideas about human nature.   (3)
b) Explain two elements in being a human person.   (4)
c) Assess the extent to which religious ideas about human nature may be helpful
    for religious believers.   (9)
d) 'Euthanasia is the killing of a human, so it should never be allowed.'
Evaluate this statement, considering more than one point of view.   (12)

Edexcel International GCSE Religious Studies (4RS0)

a) What is meant by 'physicalism'?   (2)
b) Describe two arguments in favour of euthanasia.   (5)
c) Explain why the 'sanctity of life' is important for religious people.   (8)
d) 'Humans are the most important creatures on earth.'
Do you agree? Give reasons for your answer, showing that you have considered another
point of view.   (5)

OCR Religious Studies Full Course (J625)

a) Give three ideas about human nature.   (3)
b) Outline religious ideas about what God is like.   (6)
c) Explain why personhood is important for religious believers.
You should refer to sources of wisdom and authority in your answer.   (6)
d) 'Having an abortion is to kill a human being.'
Discuss this statement. In your answer, you should draw on your learning from across your
course of study, including reference to beliefs, teachings and practices within your chosen
religion.   (15)
                                                                            (SPaG + 3)

WJEC Eduqas Religious Studies (Full Course and Short Course)

a) State what is meant by 'human'.   (2)
b) Describe ways in which members of one religion you have studied encourage
    family life.   (5)
c) From two different religions or two religious traditions, explain views on euthanasia.   (8)
d) 'Human nature is not complete without a belief in God.'
Discuss this statement, showing that you have considered more than one point of view.
(You must refer to religion and belief in your answer.)   (15)
                                                                            (SPaG + 6)

9 Relationships and Families

CONTENTS

In this chapter, you will learn about different family structures and what families are for. For most people, families are the central social group to which they belong and have a crucially important role to play in bringing up children and teaching them moral standards and how to think and act in society. You will look at Christian and Muslim beliefs and ideas about families and then at the main issues concerning marriage and divorce, as well as issues and attitudes towards gender prejudice and discrimination.

Families

There are several different kinds of family in today's world, and you should keep this in mind as you read this chapter. Examples are given in table 9.1.

Table 9.1 Types of family	
Nuclear	Consists of mother, father and children
Extended	Where several generations live together – e.g., grandparents living with children and grandchildren
Reconstituted	Consists of a mother and her children and a father and his children in a remarriage
Single parent	Consists of one parent (usually the mother) with her children

Christian views on the nature and purpose of families

The traditional view of the family in Christianity is modelled on that given in the Bible. The idea of the family was handed down to humans at the time of creation:

> Go forth and multiply, fill the earth and subdue it. . . (Genesis 1:28)

> Therefore a man shall leave his father and his mother and hold fast to his wife, and they shall become one flesh. (Genesis 2:24)

A man and a woman leave their own families and form a new family unit, in which it is appropriate and expected that they should have children. This unit is not designed by humans on their own but created by God, so that men and women may fulfil their God-given purpose. The family, therefore, is a special union sanctified by God. Because of this, marriage is understood by Christians to be a lifelong bond; to end a marriage before the death of one of the couple would be going against the will of God.

In the New Testament, guidelines for the roles of husband and wife are seen in Ephesians 5:22–6:

> Wives, submit to your own husbands, as to the Lord. For the husband is the head of the wife even as Christ is the head of the church, his body, and is himself its Saviour. Now as the church submits to Christ, so also wives should submit in everything to their husbands. Husbands, love your wives, as Christ loved the church and gave himself up for her, that he might sanctify her, having cleansed her by the washing of water with the word.

In this traditional view, the writer makes an analogy between the relation of husband and wife and that of Christ and the Church:

Husband → Wife

Christ → Church

He explains how, as Christ is 'head' of the Church, so the husband should be 'head' of his wife. Also, just as Christians (the Church) love Christ, so a wife should love her husband and submit to his leadership. In this model, the husband has the responsibility of leading his wife (and any children) in spiritual matters, as well as making sure that the whole family lives according to biblical principles. Later in the same letter (Ephesians 6:4), fathers are instructed to bring up their children in the way Jesus taught. A father also has to provide for his family; if he does not, he is 'worse than an unbeliever' (1 Timothy 5:8). A wife too can provide for her family, but this is not her primary responsibility (Proverbs 31), which is to be her husband's helper and to bear children (Genesis 2:18–20). Children are given two responsibilities: to obey and to honour their parents (Ephesians 6:1–3).

Patriarchal is an adjective of 'patriarch' or 'father leader'. It denotes a relationship in which the man is the dominant partner. It was the norm in biblical times and is still seen today.

Many Christians, particularly fundamentalist and conservative Christians, take these teachings literally and have a **patriarchal** view of their family relationships. For example, the ultra-evangelical Christian organization Faith in the Family, founded in 1977 and based in Colorado Springs, Colorado, has a budget of $100 million to teach and disseminate its views. It specializes in family issues approached from a fundamentalist viewpoint and encourages people to live according to biblical principles. This means that a wife will obey her husband and the husband will rule the family in the same kind of patriarchal way as men did in the Bible.

For many centuries, Christians have taken the Holy Family of Jesus, Mary and Joseph as a guide to family life. This seventeenth-century Spanish painting of the Holy Family shows traditional roles for the man (Joseph is working at carpentry) and woman (Mary is sewing), while Jesus and St John the Baptist play.

Others, however, do not feel that these biblical teachings need to be taken literally. Such Christians argue that the Bible is inspired by God but was written many centuries ago, when social relationships and beliefs about the roles of men and women were vastly different from those of today. Thy say that, while biblical documents are still useful, they are time- and culturally conditioned, so have to be understood in their historical, cultural and theological contexts. This means that the biblical teachings on marriage and families should be used for guidance only. Many Christians who take the biblical documents as guiding principles say that the important thing about family life is that it should be a nurturing and supportive relationship, grounded in love. The Church of England, for example, says that:

- the family remains the most important human grouping; children thrive, grow and develop within the love and safeguarding of a family
- within the family, care for the young, the old and those with needs are important as a way of demonstrating Christian beliefs
- families should be able to offer each of their members commitment, fun, love, companionship and security.

The Church of England is aware that many families face new and challenging pressures. It works with various agencies and bodies to give practical help, for example, to people who self-harm or have eating disorders and those suffering family neglect or child abuse, as well as campaigning against increasing inequalities between families. The Church lobbies relevant government, health and social work organizations to provide more effective aid to vulnerable members of society. It is the quality of relationship that should be endorsed if the Church is to continue to offer a place of acceptance for people in need where they can find wholeness.

Tasks

1 Summarize the biblical view of the family.
2 Explain what is meant by a 'patriarchal' view of family life.
3 Design a leaflet that explains the different Christian views on the family.
4 'Wives should submit to their husbands'. Do you agree? Give reasons for your answer.

ROMAN CATHOLICISM

Roman Catholic views on the nature and purpose of families

Pope John Paul II stated that:

> All members of the family, each according to his or her own gift, have the grace and responsibility of building day by day the community of persons making a family a school of deeper humanity. This happens when there is care and love for the children, the aged and the sick; where there is a sharing of goods, of joys and of sorrows.

The Catholic Church is very active in helping its members embrace Christian teaching on the family. It does this in many ways.

- Priests preach about the moral law, which is God's plan for family life.
- Papal documents, such as Pope John Paul II's *The Role of the Christian Family in the Modern World* (*Familiaris Consortio*, 1981), state clearly the Church's view on family.
- The Church provides a clear view of the responsibilities of family members.
- It explains the potential dangers that are to be avoided and provides help to support families.
- It provides religious education for children in church schools, at both primary and secondary levels, where religious teaching is an important part of the curriculum.
- It provides classes in family planning, counselling and pastoral care, particularly in the **sacrament** of reconciliation and forgiveness.
- Most importantly, the Church provides the sacraments, through which every man, woman and child can obtain the spiritual help they need to resist temptation, to pursue virtuous living, and to grow in the worship and praise of God.

A **sacrament** is described as 'an outward sign of an inner grace', or a ceremony that imparts special gifts to the believer. Roman Catholic Christians have seven sacraments, and Protestants share two of these (baptism and the Eucharist).

Task

Explain how the sacraments can provide families with spiritual help.

Muslim views on the nature and purpose of families

The family is centrally important to all Muslims, for it is at the heart of a healthy and happy Muslim community. Each member of the family has a part to play in its integrity and proper working, and each family has a similar part to play in keeping the community a healthy one. Disagreement and discord in a Muslim community comes about only if the family does not run smoothly.

Whereas most families in the Western world are nuclear, many Muslim families are extended families. This kind of structure has many advantages, such as stability, physical and psychological support, and mutual understanding, particularly when problems arise. Muslim culture has a strong feeling of showing respect and esteem to family members, and this increases with age, so grandparents are especially respected because of their life experience. This is why it is seen as a blessing from God to look after one's parents when they become old. The Qur'an says:

> Your Lord has enjoined you to worship none but him, and to show kindness to your parents. If either or both of them attain old age in your house, show them no sign of impatience, or rebuke them; but speak to them kind words. Treat them with humility and tenderness and say: 'Lord, be merciful to them. They nursed me when I was an infant.' (Surah 17:23–4)

Mothers are especially praised, as they have a central role in producing children, bringing them up and looking after the whole family. Surah 31:14 says: 'And we have enjoined upon man to be good to his parents. With difficulty upon difficulty did his mother bear him and wean him for two years. Show gratitude to Me and to your parents; to me is your final goal!'

Mothers are especially praised in Muslim families as they work to look after the family.

In an **extended family**, several generations live together or within very close proximity to each other.

Despite all the positive elements of the **extended family** in Islam, there are also some challenges that Muslims have to face. When a marriage takes place, it is very common for the bride to move into her husband's family home. This can bring both happiness and problems, for the daughter-in-law makes the transition not only to being a married woman but also to living with a new family. There will inevitably be differences for the bride in the new home, and she will take time to get used to these. Such difficulties will be multiplied if she also has to move to a new town or part of the country, where she may not know anyone or have any friends of her own. She may feel isolated and vulnerable. In the Western world, young Muslims may be used to having lots of choice in what they do, and these may be restricted when they join a new family. There is also a growing trend in some Muslim communities for people to get married when they are older. This can mean that they are more resistant to having to learn new ways of doing things.

Tasks

1 Explain how the model of an extended family has benefits for a Muslim family.
2 'A Muslim family that is based on faith in Allah will be able to hold on to Islamic morals and manners and feel a great attachment to the mosque. No Muslim will be able to survive on his or her own without a family to give support.'
Do you agree with this statement? Give reasons for your opinion.

Marriage and sexuality

Marriage is the legal joining of two individuals in a mutually beneficial relationship. It is seen by many Christians as a sacrament.

There is a lot of controversy nationally about **marriage**. Should people get married or not? What is wrong with **cohabitation**? Does marriage make any difference to the way children develop? Discussion of the importance of marriage rarely leaves the headlines.

In 1980s Britain, it was the norm for young people not to have sex until they were married. Marriage was the social norm, and most couples got married in church by the time they were about twenty-five. Most people stayed married for life; all marriages were heterosexual (husband and wife), and most would produce children (**nuclear family**). In the generations since the 1980s, however, many attitudes have changed about marriage and the family, as summarized in table 9.2.

Cohabitation refers to a couple living together without being married.

Reasons for the changing attitudes to marriage

There are several reasons why attitudes to marriage have changed so much in recent decades, including those listed below.

A **nuclear family** is one where a married couple of a man and a woman have their own children.

- Christianity (the traditional established religion in the UK) has lost its influence on the way society thinks about moral issues, since fewer people attend church services regularly, and its teaching against sex before marriage is now seen as outdated.
- Increased availability and effectiveness of contraception for both men and women has made it easier to have safe sex without necessarily wanting to start a family.

Table 9.2 Trends in marriage, sexuality and the family since the 1980s

Sex and marriage	• Many people have sex before or outside marriage. In 1983, 28% of British people thought that premarital sex was wrong. In 2013 this figure had dropped to 11%.
	• It is socially acceptable for couples to live together (cohabit) before or instead of marriage. Between 1996 and 2012 the number of cohabiting heterosexual couples increased from 1.5 to 2.9 million.
	• Between 1983 and 2010, the marriage rate in England and Wales halved, from 52 to 22 per 1,000 for men and from 42 to 20 per 1,000 for women.
	• The average age of those who decide to get married has increased (32 for men, 30 for women).
	• Only a minority of marriages take place in church or other religious building (60% of weddings in 1970 took place in a church but only 30% in 2012).
Family forms	• More use is made of extended families, as many mothers are in employment, so make use of grandparents or other relatives to look after children.
	• Many more children are brought up by cohabiting parents.
Sexuality	• Homosexual sex between consenting adults (those over 21) became legal in 1967, and homosexual sex is now treated in the same way as heterosexual sex.
	• Civil partnerships were created in 2004. It is legal for two people of the same gender to form a union, and they have the same legal rights as heterosexual couples.
	• The Marriage (Same-Sex Couples) Act was passed in 2013. This made it legal for same-sex couples to be treated in exactly the same way as heterosexual married couples.

- There has been greater media coverage of celebrities who do not get married. This has helped to make both cohabitation and premarital and extra-marital sex more socially acceptable – even something to be aspired to.
- The presentation of sexual relationships on television and film has influenced many people in thinking that sex outside marriage is acceptable.

Religious trends

Religious people are much more conservative or traditional in their views about marriage. Around one in ten Anglicans and Roman Catholics think that sex before marriage is wrong, and just 2 per cent of non-religious people think that premarital sex is wrong. All religious groups, with the exception of non-Christians, have become more accepting of premarital sex over the last thirty years. Among Anglicans, for instance, the proportion thinking premarital sex is wrong is now a third of what it was in 1983 (10 and 31 per cent respectively); 54 per cent of Anglicans believe that people should get married before having children, compared with just 30 per cent of non-religious people.

Public attitudes have become much more accepting of gay and lesbian relationships in recent years, and there is wide public support in the UK for same-sex marriage.

Taking it further

Cohabitation

Cohabitation is when two people live in a partnership but are not married or in a civil partnership. In 2012, there were 5.9 million people cohabiting in the UK. This is double the 1996 figure. Over the same period, the percentage of people aged sixteen or over who were cohabiting increased steadily, from 6.5 per cent in 1996 to 11.7 per cent in 2012. This makes cohabitation the fastest growing basis for a family in the UK.

The main reason for the rise in cohabitation as a lifestyle choice is the diminishing influence of religion in society, especially the Christian churches. Another reason is the increase in the number of people whose marriages break down. Those involved may not wish to make another commitment for fear that a new relationship will also break down.

All religious believers, Christians and Muslims, are against cohabitation. They believe that the only appropriate basis for couples to live together is marriage.

Tasks

1 Summarize the main changes in people's attitudes towards marriage since the 1980s.
2 Explain three reasons for the changed attitudes towards marriage.

Christian teaching on marriage

Most of what Christians believe about marriage comes from the Bible, which has over 500 references to the words 'marriage', 'married', 'husband' and 'wife'. In the creation story, it says that 'God created man in his own image, in the image of God he created him, male and female he created them' (Genesis 1:27). This is considered to be the origin of marriage, and, because it goes back to the very beginning of the universe, it is seen to be fundamental to human beings. It is also believed by many Christians that marriage is a divine institution that comes from God.

The teaching of Jesus is key to the Christian understanding of marriage. Jesus had been asked what his view was on divorce, and in reply he said:

> But at the beginning of creation God 'made them male and female. For this reason a man will leave his father and mother and be united to his wife, and the two will become one flesh.' So they are no longer two, but one flesh. Therefore what God has joined together, let no one separate. (Mark 10:6–9)

This answer is both a condemnation of divorce and an affirmation of marriage. It says that marriage comes from God, that it began at creation, that in marriage two individuals (traditionally speaking, a man and a woman) become a single unit and that this union is intended to be permanent and lifelong.

In a Roman Catholic wedding ceremony, the priest binds the bride and groom's hands together with his stole (part of his priestly vestments) to bless and symbolically join the couple together for life.

St Paul's teaching on marriage

The teaching of St Paul on marriage has caused some confusion for Christians over the centuries. On one hand, he appears to be preaching a very patriarchal view of the superiority of the husband over his wife; on the other hand, he seems to be advising people not to get married at all.

In 1 Corinthians 7: 3–4, Paul writes:

> The husband must give his wife what she has the right to expect, and so too the wife to the husband. The wife has no rights over her own body; it is the husband who has them. In the same way, the husband has no rights over his body; the wife has them.

Here, Paul paints a picture of a close relationship based on mutual love and respect. This is the ideal of a Christian marriage, where husband and wife share everything and there is no selfishness. Paul talks about the qualities of Christian love in a famous passage often read at weddings:

> Love is patient; love is kind; love is not envious or boastful or arrogant or rude. It does not insist on its own way; it is not irritable or resentful; it does not rejoice in wrongdoing, but rejoices in the truth. It bears all things, believes all things, hopes all things, endures all things. Love never ends. (1 Corinthians 13:4–8)

All of what Paul teaches here shows a very positive view of marriage, and it is this view that is foremost in Christian teaching today. Paul also talks about marriage in a very different way, however, which appears to contradict the positive view above.

In I Corinthians 7:8–11, Paul says:

> To the unmarried and the widows I say that it is well for them to remain unmarried as I am. But if they are not practising self-control, they should marry. For it is better to marry than to be aflame with passion. To the married I give this command – not I but the Lord – that the wife should not separate from her husband (but if she does separate, let her remain unmarried or else be reconciled to her husband), and that the husband should not divorce his wife.

Here, it appears that Paul is saying that not being married is better than being married. Why would he say this? The answer is probably that he believed that the end of the world would happen very soon, as promised by Jesus. In Matthew 24:37, Jesus warns the disciples to be watchful, because the 'coming of the son of Man' would be sudden and could take place at any time. Paul clearly believes this and is saying to the Christians in Corinth that, because of it, there is little point in getting married. Jesus had also said that there would not be marriage in heaven (see Matthew 22:30). For Paul, this meant that single people should stay single. For those Christians who were already married, however, it would be worse for them to get divorced, because that would be to break a divinely blessed and sacred partnership. There is no real contradiction, therefore, in Paul's teaching on marriage, as he was talking in two different contexts: one where he praises the state of marriage as a sacred loving relationship between two people, the other when he is speaking about the end of the world and the place of marriage at that time.

Roman Catholic teaching on marriage

Roman Catholics agree with other Christians that marriage is a God-given state and should be a lifelong commitment by couples. They also agree that marriage is a sacrament, and they accept the Bible's teaching as the model for all Christian marriages. St Ambrose (339–397), bishop of Milan in the fourth century, was the first to write that there were no reasons why a marriage should be dissolved (other than death). He himself never married because he took a vow of celibacy. He said: 'No one is permitted to know a woman other than his wife. The marital right is given you for this reason: lest you fall into the snare and sin with a strange woman. "If you are bound to a wife do not seek a divorce"; for you are not permitted, while your wife lives, to marry another' (*Abraham* 1:7:59).

Ambrose's pupil St Augustine also taught that marriage was for life, as it was a sacrament; just as Christ was faithful to the Church, so should a husband be to his wife, and vice versa. This teaching did not find universal acceptance among Christians, however, until the twelfth century, when Pope Alexander III decreed that marriage was an unbreakable contract. Since then, the Roman Catholic Church has always held that marriage cannot be broken so long as it has been entered into voluntarily, has been properly celebrated and has been consummated – a position that has been ratified in all Church documents and teaching since then, and which can be seen especially in the document *Gaudium et Spes* ('Joy and Hope'), issued in 1965. This is considered to be one of the most important and influential documents from the Second Vatican Council, a major meeting of Roman Catholic theologians, bishops and cardinals between 1962 and 1965 to reassess and reform Roman Catholic doctrine and practice. *Gaudium et Spes* is a pastoral document discussing several ethical issues, such as abortion and contraception, that were and continue to be pressing for Catholic Christians around the world. It is the longest single document produced by the Council (around 37,000 words in its English translation). Section 48 is a long passage on the nature and state of marriage, including the following statement that shows the three reasons for marriage being a lifelong state:

> The intimate partnership of married life and love has been established by the Creator and qualified by His laws, and is rooted in the conjugal covenant of irrevocable personal consent . . .. For God Himself is the author of matrimony, endowed as it is with various benefits and purposes.
>
> Thus a man and a woman, who by their compact of conjugal love 'are no longer two, but one flesh' (Matt. 19:4–6), render mutual help and service to each other through an intimate union of their persons and of their actions. Through this union they experience the meaning of their oneness and attain to it with growing perfection day by day. As a mutual gift of two persons, this intimate union and the good of the children impose total fidelity on the spouses and argue for an unbreakable oneness between them.

Task

Read the following passage by the atheist philosopher **Bertrand Russell** (1872–1970) and discuss whether you agree with him. Give reasons for your decision.

'The Christian view of marriage and sex is an irrational system of taboo created by medieval superstition and oriental asceticism. The fact that it is embedded in Christian ethics has made Christianity, throughout its whole history, a tendency towards mental disorders and unwholesome views of life.'

ISLAM

Muslim teaching on marriage

Muslim teaching on the purpose of marriage is summed up in a short phrase from the Qur'an: 'You are a garment to them, and they are a garment for you' (Surah 2:187). The aim of marriage is to provide warmth, comfort and protection for the husband and wife. This is the right relationship in which to bring up children; a secure and supportive environment will ensure that children grow up healthy and happy and will learn about Islam. Celibacy and sex outside marriage are strongly discouraged because neither of these states leads to a wholesome society. Surah 30:21 says: 'And among his signs is that he created for you mates from among yourselves; that you may find peace with them. And he put between you love and compassion. Surely in this are signs for people who reflect.'

For Muslims, a marriage is a joining of two families, and it is quite common for it to be arranged by the parents of both the bride and the groom, though the couple to be married has to give their consent.

It is important for many Muslims to marry from within their own (Muslim) community. One aspect of this is referred to as **consanguinity**. This is where cousins marry each other. It is not uncommon in Islam and is even encouraged. In Pakistan, for example, it is estimated that about 75 per cent of Muslim marriages are consanguineous and about 50 per cent involve first cousins. This figure is an increase from the previous generation, where about 30 per cent of first cousins were married to each other.

> **Consanguinity** means being descended from the same ancestors.

Consanguinity confers several advantages for Muslims. It means that the couple probably knows each other well and so there should be fewer problems in the marriage. This is a particular advantage among families living in a minority population, as it can be much more difficult for the parents to find an appropriate partner for their child in a largely non-Muslim community. The disadvantage of consanguineous marriages is that the possibility of genetic birth defects is increased.

> **Tasks**
> 1 Summarize what is meant by 'consanguinity' as it relates to Muslim marriage.
> 2 Explain the benefits of consanguinity for Muslim families.

Marriage breakdown and divorce

> **Divorce** is the legal declaration that a marriage has ended.

In Britain, an increasing number of marriages end in **divorce**. According to official figures from 2013, about 42 per cent of all marriages break down, most of them within the first ten years. Divorce is much more socially acceptable than it was a few decades ago. As a result of the higher divorce rate, **single-parent families** are more common, as are reconstituted families formed by divorced couples getting married again.

The possible reasons for this are listed briefly here.

> A **single-parent family** consists of one parent (usually the mother) plus children.

- The Divorce Reform Act of 1969 made it quicker and cheaper for ordinary people to obtain a divorce. This led to a huge increase in the number of divorces.

- People's expectations of marriage have changed greatly. Women have more equality than before and expect to be treated on a par with men. Wives have the power to divorce their husbands if they feel that they are being treated unfairly.
- Many women are in full-time employment, so are not financially dependent on their husbands. In fact, an increasing number of women are the primary bread-winners in the family, earning more than their husbands.
- When both husband and wife have to work it adds strain to the marriage.
- Unemployment adds stress to a relationship.
- Couples often do not live near relatives, so can feel isolated.
- One partner may have an affair.
- The couple may have disagreements about whether or when to have children.
- Both partners are too young at the point they get married to realize fully the commitment required.

It is estimated that around 500,000 people in Britain each year are affected by the sorrow, stress and suffering raised by marriage breakdown and divorce.

Christian teaching on divorce

The Old Testament is rather vague about how a divorce was performed, though the procedure was probably similar to those in the other parts of the ancient Near East. Divorce was not illegal or forbidden, but it was frowned upon. Genesis 2:24 seems to convey the message that marriage was lifelong – 'I am (your) husband . . . forever' – so divorce would not necessarily be approved of. This can be seen in Malachi 2:16, which says: '"The man who hates and divorces his wife," says the Lord, the God of Israel, "does violence to the one he should protect," says the Lord Almighty. So be on your guard, and do not be unfaithful.'

In practice in the Old Testament period, divorce was probably quite rare, though a man could divorce his wife for any reason. Deuteronomy 24:1 says he could divorce because 'she does not please him' or she has done 'something objectionable'. If the husband divorced his wife for anything other than gross sexual misconduct, he had to pay back the dowry to her family – the present given by the groom to the bride's family. This would be a strong reason not to seek a divorce, as it would be a large amount of money to pay back. If a man really wanted to go through with a divorce, he had to give his wife a written statement and put it in her hand. This was to protect her from any accusation that she had committed adultery, which could carry the death penalty, and also allowed her to remarry. In this view, the essence of divorce was to allow remarriage, not to separate from the spouse.

In the New Testament (Matthew 19 and Mark 10), Jesus is questioned about divorce: 'Is it lawful for a man to divorce his wife?' Jesus' response is quite revolution-ary. He says that the Old Testament law that allowed divorce (see above) was wrong and cites Genesis 2, where God tells Adam and Eve to marry: the 'two shall become one flesh' and 'what God has joined together, let no man separate.' For Jesus, there-fore, divorce is wrong and should not be permitted, because God instituted marriage and it is forever. Mark says that Jesus opposed divorce more vigorously than the

CHRISTIANITY ROMAN CATHOLICISM

Pharisees. He emphasizes Jesus' views in Mark 10:11: 'Whoever divorces his wife and marries another commits adultery.' This is revolutionary as it puts women on the same basis as men in terms of their rights within marriage.

St Paul talks about divorce in 1 Corinthians 7:10–11, where he says: 'To the married I give this command (not I, but the Lord): A wife must not separate from her husband. But if she does, she must remain unmarried or else be reconciled to her husband. And a husband must not divorce his wife.' He refers to Jesus' view opposing divorce and agrees with it, insisting that those who divorce must stay single. In the case of a marriage between a Christian and a non-Christian, he says that the Christian can grant his or her partner a divorce if the partner asks for one. He does not mention whether the Christian may later remarry.

In the early centuries of Christianity, there were discussions about whether divorce should be allowed. Most scholars and church leaders took Jesus' opinion on the matter, arguing that neither divorce nor remarriage should be allowed. The Council of Elvira in 300 CE declared: 'Likewise, women who have left their husbands for no prior cause and have joined themselves with others may not even at death receive communion' (canon 8). This was a very strong disincentive to divorce. St Jerome said in 398 CE:

> Wherever there is fornication and a suspicion of fornication, a wife is freely dismissed. Because it is always possible that someone may calumniate [i.e., slander] the innocent and, for the sake of a second joining in marriage, act in criminal fashion against the first, it is commanded that when the first wife is dismissed a second may not be taken while the first lives. (Commentary on Matthew 3:19:9)

Most non-Catholic churches now believe that divorce is wrong because God instituted marriage and intended it to be a lifelong commitment between husband and wife. However, the churches do recognize that sometimes things go wrong in a relationship and the least painful thing is to allow a divorce. They point to statements in the Bible, such as Matthew 19:9, where Jesus allows divorce in a case of adultery. They also point out that Christians believe in the idea of forgiveness for sins committed, and that no human being is perfect, as only God is perfect. The unhappy couple must therefore be forgiven for the breakdown of their marriage and allowed to divorce so that they do not become utterly miserable. This gives them an opportunity to acknowledge that they have failed, so that they might remarry and make a greater success of their second relationship.

The Church of England accepts that marriages sometimes fail for all sorts of reasons. Since 2002, the Church has allowed divorced people to remarry in church under certain circumstances.

Tasks

1 Explain why some non-Catholic churches allow remarriage.
2 'Divorce should not be allowed, otherwise people will never learn the importance of marriage.' Do you agree? Give reasons for your answer.

Roman Catholic teaching on divorce

The Roman Catholic Church teaches that marriage is a sacrament and should be a lifelong commitment for a couple. Divorce is not recognized, and couples who obtain a civil divorce are not permitted to remarry in church. There are, however, a few circumstances within the teaching of the Church where a marriage can be brought to an end, or annulled. **Annulment** can take place only if it can be proved that the marriage is invalid, even though the ceremony took place. There are only three conditions where this may be granted:

- when some barrier exists to prevent the marriage – for example, when one of the partners is incapable of having sexual intercourse, meaning that the marriage was not consummated
- when the marriage ceremony did not take place as required by the Church – for example, if the ceremony took place in a register office
- when either of the partners did not fully understand what marriage entailed or was not free to marry.

Until very recently, the process of obtaining an annulment was deliberately slow, partly to discourage couples from trying to obtain a divorce and partly to ensure that full discussion and arbitration could take place between the partners and the Church. In some cases, the procedure could take up to ten years. In September 2014, however, Pope Francis announced a new commission to bring about changes, recognizing that many couples who wished to separate and move on with their lives were being prevented from doing so because of the intricacies and slowness of the process. The Pope wishes to improve the situation for churchgoing Christians by making annulment quicker, cheaper and easier to obtain.

> An **annulment** is a declaration in the Roman Catholic Church that a marriage never existed.

Task

'The Pope should not try to change the Church's rules about annulment.' Do you agree? Give reasons for your answer.

Muslim teaching on divorce

Divorce and remarriage are acceptable in Islam, but many Muslims are against it. They believe that marriage is for life and that divorce should be avoided. Couples should work very hard to maintain their marriage, being patient with each other, attempting to work out their difficulties, and taking advice from friends and relatives and perhaps from professional counsellors. Muslims believe that the marriage contract is sacred and that both partners should obey this. Divorce is seen as the most hateful thing that is permitted in Islam because it breaks up families, depriving children of a happy upbringing.

A husband should not divorce his wife because it will bring shame on her and will separate her from her children. If he were to divorce her out of spite, this would be seen as a form of oppression, which is forbidden in Islam. Similarly, a woman should never ask for a divorce without a very good reason, because that is 'haram' and is a major sin. The Prophet Muhammad said: 'Any woman who asks her husband to divorce her without an acceptable reason will never smell the scent of Paradise', and the Qur'an counsels against divorce when it says:

> And if you fear breach between the two of them, appoint an arbiter from his family and an arbiter from her family. If they desire to set things aright, Allah will bring about reconciliation between them; indeed, Allah is Knowing, Aware. (Surah 4:35)

Husband and wife should call on their respective families for help to reach an agreement so that their differences may be acknowledged and worked out.

If all attempts at reconciliation between husband and wife fail, then divorce may be the only option. The Qur'an (Surah 65, Divorce) sets out the terms of the period, called the **Iddah**, before either partner may remarry, which states that the couple must wait for three months after all attempts to save the marriage have failed. The reason for this is to check whether or not the wife is pregnant, so that any baby may be taken into account in the divorce settlement. It is also a final chance for the couple to get back together again. If they still wish to separate, documents are drawn up and the divorce becomes final. The man must not do anything to prevent the woman from remarrying and must make financial arrangements for the upkeep of any children from the marriage. The financial arrangements also include the repayment of the **mahr**, the mandatory payment made by the husband to his wife at the time of the marriage. This remains legally her possession.

Iddah
is the period that a woman must observe after the death of her husband or a divorce before marrying again.

Mahr
is a dowry paid by a Muslim husband to his wife as a sign of respect to her.

Tasks

1 'Divorce in Islam favours the woman. This is unfair.' Do you agree with this statement? Give reasons for your answer.
2 Explain why Muslims think divorce should only be a last resort.
3 'Just because divorce is allowed by the Qur'an does not make it right.' Do you agree with this statement? Give reasons for your answer.

Gender prejudice and discrimination

Prejudice
is 'pre-judgement', or forming an opinion without knowing all the facts.

Discrimination
is the act of putting prejudices into practice.

Gender prejudice
involves thinking that one gender is superior to another.

Prejudice is when someone forms an opinion about someone or something before becoming aware of the relevant facts. It is usually used negatively, when an unfavourable judgement is made about someone because of his or her gender, religious beliefs, social class, age, sexuality, race or language. It can also be used positively, as when a member of a minority group is favoured above someone who is equally or better qualified for a job, the intention being to make the minority group less marginalized and to give them more recognition among the majority population. This is when prejudice becomes **discrimination**, which is defined as putting prejudice into practice.

Gender prejudice is prejudice (mostly in a negative sense) against someone because of her or his gender. This becomes gender discrimination when the prejudice is put into practice.

Examples of gender prejudice

One aspect of gender prejudice and discrimination is the '**glass ceiling effect**'. This can be seen in many areas of work, including the teaching profession. Of the 365,000 teachers in England, 74 per cent are female. But there are far fewer women in senior leadership in schools, and fewer still who are headteachers. Information from the Department of Education reveals that, while 6 per cent of men were headteachers, this was the case for only 4 per cent of women. The same trend is seen when it comes to pay, with 23 per cent of men working in schools sitting in the top pay bracket compared to 19 per cent of women.

Women are discriminated against in many areas other than education. The United Nations Convention on the Elimination of All Forms of Discrimination Against Women (CEDAW) fights to ensure that women gain equal access and opportunities in political and public life, as well as in education, health and employment. This is the only human rights treaty that affirms the right of women to reproduce and to change or keep their nationality and that of their children. Countries which have ratified the convention are committed to taking appropriate measures against all forms of trafficking and exploitation of women.

Some of the areas in which women suffer discrimination are listed briefly below.

> ### Task
> When you have read the list, choose two areas and research them in more depth. Present your findings to the class or make a poster that highlights the relevant facts and issues.

- *At work* Women are often paid less than men for doing the same work. They have often been denied promotion because of their gender.
- *In politics* In some countries, women have not been allowed to vote or take part in politics. This is because their traditional role is to stay at home and bring up children. In the UK in 2015, there were 148 female MPs out of 650 in the House of Commons and 191 female members out of 790 peers in the House of Lords.
- *In marriage* Sometimes, women have no choice of whom or at what age they marry. Arranged marriage has been practised in some societies for thousands of years and remains the case in some countries. One example is the ancient 'custom' in Kazakhstan of 'bride kidnapping', where between 8,000 and 10,000 young women in the past ten years have been forced to marry men they barely knew. It was declared a 'crime' only in 2014.
- *In divorce* Women are often not treated fairly in divorce settlements. In some places, a woman's property passes to her husband on marriage, and sometimes this is not returned to her on divorce, leaving her with little or no assets.

Extreme examples of gender discrimination

Female genital mutilation

An extreme example of gender discrimination is female genital mutilation (**FGM**). This practice is also known as 'female circumcision' or 'female cutting'. The World

The **glass ceiling effect** descibes the unseen barrier that prevents some people, typically women, from attaining certain jobs or roles.

FGM is the abbreviation of female genital mutilation.

Health Organization defines it as 'all procedures that involve partial or total removal of the external female genitalia, or other injury to the female genital organs for non-medical reasons'. This procedure can cause a great deal of pain for the girls or women who experience it and it can cause ongoing problems such as cysts, infections and infertility. It is internationally condemned because it is a fundamental violation of the human rights of girls and women and is seen as an extreme form of discrimination. According to a 2013 UNICEF report, 125 million women and girls in Africa and the Middle East have experienced FGM. The highest prevalence in Africa is documented in Somalia (98% of women affected), Guinea (96%), Djibouti (93%), Egypt (91%), Eritrea (89%), Mali (89%), Sierra Leone (88%), Sudan (88%), Gambia (76%), Burkina Faso (76%), Ethiopia (74%), Mauritania (69%) and Liberia (66%).

Rape

Rape
refers to forced sexual relations with a person against that person's will.

Rape is defined as the sexual violation of a person without their consent and is per-haps the most invasive kind of discrimination against an individual. The Ministry of Justice, part of the Home Office, publishes an annual statistical bulletin which con-tains figures concerning rape. Between 2009 and 2012, there were an estimated 78,000 victims of rape in England and Wales – 69,000 females and 9,000 males. Of these, only about 15,600 were recorded by the police each year, not all of which were recorded as a crime. Of the reports that were considered as crimes, just over 3,000 were taken to court, leading to about 1,000 convictions. In 2011, the conviction rate for rape against a female was 39.7 per cent, just below the 45.2 per cent rate for rape against a male. This compares with an aggregate rate across all sexual offences of 60.3 per cent.

For those who have been raped, there can also be a secondary form of discrimina-tion. Women in particular can be rejected by their family or subjected to violence by loved ones. In some extreme cases, rape victims may be killed because they are thought to have brought their family into disrepute. This is one instance of a so-called honour killing.

Rape is often used during war as a way of showing the power of the attacking forces and of wearing down opposition. Following the official end of the war in the Demo-cratic Republic of Congo in 2003, the prevalence and intensity of all forms of sexual violence in the country led to its being described as the rape capital of the world. A 2010 report suggested that almost 40 per cent of all women in one part of the country had suffered sexual violence, while one the following year estimated that 1,000 women had been raped every day. It is also common for men to be raped. One estimate said that over 20 per cent of men in the east of the country had been exposed to sexual violence. This may be a lower figure than the actual numbers involved, as men are more reluctant to report that they have been raped. Many children, typically under the age of ten, have been raped. According to a United Nations report, over 65 per cent of all victims during the past fifteen years were children.

Male gender discrimination

In 2006, *The Guardian* newspaper reported the landmark case of a male student nurse who was discriminated against because of his gender. He was not allowed to perform certain procedures, such as cervical smears, on female patients unless he was accompanied by a female chaperone. Andrew Moyhing, a 29-year-old nurse, took a case to court because he said it was discriminatory to treat him in a different way from female nurses, who were also allowed to perform intimate procedures on male patients without being chaperoned. Over 90 per cent of nurses in Britain are female, and Mr Moyhing felt that there was an assumption in the profession that men were sexual predators. Mr Moyhing won the case but left the nursing profession.

Military discrimination

Military personnel put their lives at risk while defending their country. However, many suffer discrimination because of their sexuality. It was only in 2011 that the United States military allowed gay, lesbian and bisexual people to serve. In the previous fifteen years, over 14,000 military men and women were dismissed because of their sexual orientation. It has been estimated that approximately 150,000 transgender people have served in the US armed forces, but they have done so secretly because medical regulations label such people as mentally unstable.

In 2010, nearly 20,000 sexual assaults occurred in the military, but fewer than 14 per cent of these were reported by the victims for fear of dismissal or reprisals. Many of these people suffer from depression and stress and are more likely to become addicted to drugs.

In some countries, military service is a male-only occupation. Others use a system of conscription where men are required to join the armed forces. Women may choose to join, but it is not compulsory for them to serve. This leads to a criticism that men are discriminated against because they are being forced into a potentially dangerous or even fatal role against their will, whereas women are not. The exception to this is Israel, where both men and women are required to serve in the military for a certain amount of time.

> ### Task
> Choose one of the four topics discussed above and design a poster to display. You should highlight the most important facts and explain the ethical issues involved.

Christian teaching on gender prejudice and discrimination

The Equality Act of 2010 was an important piece of legislation for the Church of England. The Church had allowed female clergy since 1994, and there was a great deal of pressure to follow this up by appointing female bishops. The Equality Act made it unlawful for a person to engage in direct or indirect discrimination in employment, the provision of services, access to premises, and certain kinds of office holding, unless this can specifically be justified on the grounds of disability, gender reassignment, marriage and civil partnership, pregnancy and maternity, race, religion or belief, sex, and sexual orientation.

The Act defines 'direct discrimination' as where, because of a specific reason, one person is treated more or less favourably than another. 'Indirect discrimination' is where a person puts someone with a 'specific reason' at a disadvantage that cannot

CHRISTIANITY

In the Church of England, the first women were ordained as priests in 1994 and the first female bishop in 2015. The Roman Catholic Church does not permit the ordination of women as priests.

be properly justified. Essentially, this meant that the Church of England could have been accused of discrimination under the terms of the Equality Act 2010 if it did not allow women to be ordained as bishops.

Unless one of the exemptions applies, however, those responsible for selection processes will lay themselves open to legal challenge if, in any part of the process, they appear to allow a protected characteristic to be taken into account in considering a candidate's eligibility for appointment.

The first female bishop in the Church of England, the Right Reverend Libby Lane, was consecrated as bishop of Stockport at York Minster in January 2015, and the second is the Right Reverend Alison White, bishop of Hull since July 2015. There have been female bishops in other branches of the Anglican communion since 1989, the first of whom was Barbara Harris, who was appointed suffragan bishop of Massachusetts in February of that year. There are now women bishops in many (but not all) parts of the Anglican communion.

Task

Summarize non-Catholic Christian teaching on gender prejudice and discrimination.

Roman Catholic teaching on gender prejudice and discrimination

Critics of the Roman Catholic Church argue that it has been at the forefront of prejudice and discrimination against women for hundreds of years. The teaching of St Paul, which was developed by the Church Fathers and medieval theologians such as St Thomas Aquinas, preached that men were superior to women and that God had ordained this view. The Roman Catholic Church does not allow women to be priests or to play any major part in church worship.

Most Catholics, however, dispute this criticism and point to many historical and theological arguments to make their points.

- The abolition of slavery was brought about, to a large extent, by Catholic missionaries. This involved women who were held in sexual slavery.
- Deaconesses served in the early church. A deaconess was a woman who assisted a priest in church services and in the ministry, particularly in looking after sick women and in other roles also performed by male deacons.
- Women served as monastics, and there has been a very long and important history in the church of nuns, who have served God in a distinctive way.
- Women may gain salvation in just the same way as men, by living a godly life. Salvation does not depend on ordination.
- Sainthood is open to women as well as men, whether they are ordained or not. The Blessed Virgin Mary, who holds a pre-eminent position in the Church, is venerated as the 'Queen of all saints'.
- Four of the thirty-six Doctors of the Church (the leading theologians, thinkers and religious leaders in the Catholic Church) – Saints Teresa of Ávila, Catherine of Siena, Thérèse of Lisieux and Hildegard of Bingen – are women. Although they lived and were canonized much earlier, all were made Doctors of the Church after 1970.

> **Task**
>
> Debate the statement: 'The Catholic Church has been at the forefront of prejudice and discrimination against women for hundreds of years.'

Muslim teaching on gender prejudice and discrimination

Islam teaches that there should be no gender prejudice or discrimination and that, although they have different roles in life, men and women are equal in spiritual terms. The Qur'an says: 'O mankind, reverence your guardian Lord who created you from a single person created of like nature his mate and from those two scattered [like seeds] countless men and women' (Surah 4:1). This is showing that God created men and women and both have the same spiritual nature. In the account of Adam and Eve in the Qur'an (7:19–27), both bear the blame for disobeying God's command not to eat the forbidden fruit.

Men and women have the same moral and spiritual duties:

If anyone does deeds of righteousness whether they are male or female and have faith in God, they will enter Paradise and not the least injustice will be done to them. (Surah 4:124)

Those who surrender themselves to God and accept the true faith; who are devout, sincere, patient, humble, charitable and chaste; who fast and are ever mindful of God – on these, both men and women, God will bestow forgiveness and a rich reward. (Surah 33:35)

Muslims believe that it is right and proper that men and women have different roles and responsibilities in everyday life. So, traditionally, the roles of men are

- to learn a trade and go out to work to earn a living for themselves and their family
- to ensure that their children are brought up as good Muslims who understand the teachings of the Qur'an and the obligations of Islam
- to educate their sons about their religious and social responsibilities and to worship alongside them in the mosque.

The traditional roles of women in Islam are

- to have and bring up children within marriage
- to keep a good Muslim home, according to halal rules
- to worship God
- to fulfil the Five Pillars.

Islam strives to protect the rights of women and not discriminate against them. The Prophet Muhammad said: 'I command you to be kind to women.' For example, although men may have up to four wives, each wife must be treated equally; there should not be any discrimination between the wives. Women have full rights to property both before and after marriage. A married woman may keep her maiden name if

The burqa has been a controversial issue in debates about the role of women in Islam.

she wishes to do so. She is entitled to full financial support for running the household and for bringing up children, and she is not to be forced to marry a man she does not want. A woman may pursue her education and may have a career that is independent from that of her husband.

Task

Read the information below about the controversy over the wearing of the burqa, then prepare a speech either for or against the motion: 'This house believes that the burqa should be banned in public places.' You may need to research some of the points to get more information to use in the debate.

1 A burqa is a garment worn by some Muslim women to cover their bodies in public. It obscures their face either completely or so that only the eyes are visible. In this it is different from various forms of head covering, such as the hijab, dupatta scarf or niqab. You should consider whether *all* forms of head covering should be banned.

2 The Qur'an does not require women to cover either their faces or their full bodies, but different Muslim communities have interpreted the relevant qur'anic verse differently.

3 Qur'an 33:59 says 'O Prophet! Tell your wives, daughters and women of the believers to lower [or possibly draw upon themselves] their garments. That is better so that they will not be known and molested. And God is forgiving and merciful.'

4 The word 'face' does not appear in this verse.

5 A hadith requires both men and women to dress and behave modestly while in public places.

6 Generally in the Muslim world, it is seen as a virtue (*namus*) to prevent a woman from being seen in public. Namus is an ethical idea that applies only to women and has to do with respect, attention, honour and modesty.

7 Wearing a burqa is either required for Muslim women or strongly encouraged in some Muslim-majority countries, but not in all.

8 In Britain in 2006, the Labour MP Jack Straw caused a controversy when he called for Muslim women in his Blackburn constituency – then 30 per cent Muslim – not to veil their faces when meeting him. The controversy led to the Face Coverings (Prohibition) Bill 2013–14 being put before Parliament; however, this did not become law because it ran out of parliamentary time.

9 In several European countries, face coverings have been made illegal on the grounds of security. France passed a law in 2014 which was ratified by the European Court of Human Rights that same year. A similar law was passed in Belgium in 2011.

10 An Australian Muslim woman, Semaa Abdulwali, said in 2014: 'The niqab makes me feel liberated, and no law will stop me wearing it.'

TICK THE TOPICS

Now you should tick the relevant boxes to check what you have learned in this chapter.

Sections	Topics	Tick
Nature and purpose of families	Christian views	
	Roman Catholic views	
	Muslim views	
Sex and marriage	Changing attitudes and the reasons for them	
	Christian teaching on marriage	
	Roman Catholic teaching on marriage	
	Muslim teaching on marriage	
Marriage breakdown and divorce	Christian teaching on divorce	
	Roman Catholic teaching on divorce	
	Muslim teaching on divorce	
Gender prejudice and discrimination	Definitions	
	Examples of gender prejudice and discrimination	
	Christian teaching on gender prejudice and discrimination	
	Roman Catholic teaching on gender prejudice and discrimination	
	Muslim teaching on gender prejudice and discrimination	

Sample questions

AQA Religious Studies A (8062), Religious Studies B (8063) and Religious Studies Short Course (8061)

1 Which of the following best expresses the religious ideal of family life?
   a) Dysfunctional b) Compulsory c) Coping d) Loving   (1 mark)
2 Give two religious beliefs about children.   (2 marks)
3 Explain two contrasting beliefs in contemporary British society about divorce. (4 marks)
4 Explain religious beliefs about family life.   (5 marks)
5 'Divorce should not be allowed under any circumstances.'
Evaluate this statement. In your answer, you:
   • should give reasoned arguments in support of this statement
   • should give reasoned arguments to support a different point of view

- should refer to religious arguments
- may refer to non-religious arguments
- should reach a justified conclusion.   (12 marks)

Edexcel Religious Studies A (1RA0), Religious Studies B (1RB0) and Religious Studies B Short Course (3RB0)

a) Give three types of relationship.   (3)
b) Explain what is meant by 'nuclear' and 'extended' families.   (4)
c) Assess whether religious views of the family are of any relevance today. (9)
d) 'Men and women should be treated equally.'
Evaluate this statement, considering more than one point of view.   (12)

Edexcel International GCSE Religious Studies (4RS0)

a) What is meant by 'nuclear family'?   (2)
b) Outline reasons why some religious people are against divorce.   (5)
c) Explain why religious people are against prejudice and discrimination.   (8)
d) 'A religious view of the family is out of touch with reality today.'
Do you agree? Give reasons for your answer, showing that you have considered another
point of view.   (5)

OCR Religious Studies Full Course (J625) and Short Course (J125)

a) Give three reasons why a religious couple might consider getting married. (3)
b) Outline different religious attitudes to divorce.   (6)
c) Explain religious beliefs and teachings about the roles of men and women.
You should refer to sources of wisdom and authority in your answer.   (6)
d) 'Same-sex marriage should be accepted by religious believers.'
Discuss this statement. In your answer, you should draw on your learning from across
your course of study, including reference to beliefs, teachings and practices within your
chosen religion.   (15)
                                                                   (SPaG + 3)

WJEC Eduqas Religious Studies (Full Course and Short Course)

a) Giving one example, state what is meant by 'marriage'.   (2)
b) With reference to one religion you have studied, explain views about divorce. (5)
c) From two different religions or two religious traditions, explain views on gender
    prejudice and discrimination.   (8)
d) 'Same-sex marriage should be recognized by religions.'
Discuss this statement, showing that you have considered more than one point of view.
(You must refer to religion and belief in your answer.)   (15)
                                                                   (SPaG + 6)

10 Religion, Human Rights and Social Justice

CONTENTS

In this chapter, you will be studying three very important issues that affect all human beings in one way or another: equality and the freedom of religion or belief; issues of prejudice and discrimination in religion and belief; and human rights.

Equality and freedom of religion or belief

Freedom of religion or belief is a fundamentally important idea in international law and is guaranteed in many human rights treaties, including the United Nations Declaration of Human Rights. It is something that cannot be taken away, even in times of war or other national emergency. Freedom of religion or belief relates to individuals, not to the religion itself: religions are protected in society because the human rights of individual people are guaranteed, not the other way round. This means that not all 'religions' may be accepted.

> The word **'religion'** is usually associated with belief in a transcendent deity or deities, so Christians refer to 'God', and Muslims refer to 'God' or 'Allah'. The term **'belief'** does not necessarily involve a divine being but, rather, relates to a certain set of ideas that are important to an individual or group. Not all beliefs are covered by human rights legislation. For example, if, like Wallace and Gromit, you believed that the moon was made of Wensleydale cheese, you would probably not be protected in your belief by any law. In general, however, most belief systems used in most societies are covered.

Having the freedom of religion and belief means that any person has the right

- to hold personal thoughts and convictions
- to display these on their own or with other people in private or in public
- to choose between differing schools of thought within a religion and to be able to change their religion
- not to be forced to change their religion or belief
- to express their beliefs and to criticize the beliefs of others in a non-violent manner
- to worship or assemble in connection with a religion or belief, and to establish and maintain places for these purposes
- to establish and maintain appropriate charitable or humanitarian institutions

Most international airports have special rooms allocated for use for prayer and religious purposes, consistent with a commitment to freedom of religious practice and belief.

and to make, acquire and use to an adequate extent the necessary articles and materials related to the rites or customs of a religion or belief

- to write, issue and disseminate relevant publications in these areas
- to teach a religion or belief in places suitable for these purposes
- to solicit and receive voluntary financial and other contributions from individuals and institutions
- to train, appoint, elect or designate by succession appropriate leaders called for by the requirements and standards of any religion or belief
- to observe days of rest and to celebrate holidays and ceremonies in accordance with the precepts of their religion or belief
- to establish and maintain communications with individuals and communities in matters of religion and belief at the national and international levels.

Task

Which of the following do you think would fulfil the definition of a 'religion' or suitable 'belief'? Give reasons for your answers.

- Worship of a teapot
- Worship of a sports personality
- Worship of mathematics
- A religion based on the idea that you are the only person in the universe
- A religion that teaches that having children is forbidden and that abortion is compulsory
- A belief that euthanasia and cannibalism are morally acceptable
- A belief in extra-terrestrial beings
- A belief that teddy bears have souls
- A belief that mobile phones are the work of the devil

Respect means treating people as individuals who have feelings, desires and rights.

Proselytism means attempting to convert people to a particular religious view.

One of the most important principles in how to apply the legislation on human rights as it relates to the freedom of religion and beliefs is **respect**. Respect here means taking heed of the needs and rights of everyone concerned in a case, issue or controversial incident. The first such case that came before the Court of Human Rights was of a member of the Christian Jehovah's Witnesses in Greece who had been convicted of the crime of **proselytism** – the attempt by an individual to convert someone to their beliefs or way of doing things. This case showed that there can often be a conflict between the beliefs and practices of one person or group and those of another (in this case, the state). The court decided that it is sometimes necessary to place restrictions on the freedom of religion and belief in order to ensure that everyone's beliefs may be upheld and respected. The principle of respect, therefore, is more important that the rights of any one individual or group in ensuring the smooth running of a society. It is the rights of individuals, not the beliefs themselves, that are important.

Task

Look at the example below of a case when the rights of an individual came into conflict with the rights of an organization. In pairs, decide what the important issue is and whether you agree with how it was resolved. Report your findings to the class.

A Muslim schoolgirl was prevented from attending school because she refused to wear the school's shalwar kameez uniform, preferring instead to wear a more modest jilbab. She argued that this breached her rights under Article 9 to manifest her religion. The House of Lords found that there was no breach of her right to manifest her religion because she could have attended other schools in her catchment area that permitted students to wear the jilbab. Moreover, the school had worked hard to develop a uniform policy that took into account the beliefs of its Muslim students and had devised the policy in an inclusive way. In these circumstances it was inappropriate for the courts to disturb the decision of the school that was better placed to assess this sensitive situation. (Summary provided by the British Institute of Human Rights)

Issues of prejudice and discrimination in religion and belief

Racial prejudice is having a negative opinion or attitude towards a person of a different race, regardless of the nature or character of the person in question. This kind of prejudice usually comes about as the result of ignorance and lack of knowledge of the individual's customs and traditions. Racial prejudice is therefore irrational and can be based on such superficial things as differences in the way people dress, the colour of their skin, their names or even their choice of music. For example, some British people are racially prejudiced against the Irish because they have different accents, traditions and names.

> **Racial prejudice** means thinking that someone is of less value because of their race.

Racial prejudice can sometimes spill over into **racial discrimination**. This is where actions are taken against members of a particular racial group on the basis of their differences. One example of this occurred after the terrorist attacks on the Twin Towers in New York on 11 September 2001, when hate crimes were carried out against Muslim Americans or those thought to be Muslims. Americans of Arab descent were treated differently at airports, having to undergo stricter security checks than other passengers.

> **Racial discrimination** means treating someone differently because of their race.

International issues

Freedom Declared is the name of the all-party parliamentary group, which exists both to raise awareness and the profile of international freedom of religion or belief as a human right among parliamentarians, media, government and the general public in the UK and to increase the effectiveness of the UK's contribution to international institutions charged with enforcing this human right. According to its website (www.freedomdeclared.org):

> There has been a dramatic increase in religious persecution worldwide in the past six years. 5.3 billion people (76% of the world's population) live in countries with a high or very high level of restrictions on religion. An official US government report states 'religious freedom abuses occur daily around the world for people of all faiths and none.'
>
> A 2014 study by the Pew Research Center examined the years 2007–12 and concluded

that religious hostilities had increased in every major region of the world except the Americas. The sharpest increase was in the Middle East and North Africa, impacted by the Arab Spring.

- 29% of all countries had a high or very high level of government restrictions
- 39% of countries had seen violence, or the threat of violence, used to compel people to adhere to religious norms
- 32% of countries experienced harassment of women over religious dress
- 25% of countries witnessed mob violence related to religion
- 20% of countries experienced religion-related terrorist violence.

The study also reported an increase in the level of harassment or intimidation of particular religious groups. Two of the seven major religious groups monitored by the study – Muslims and Jews – experienced six-year highs in the number of countries in which they were harassed by national, provincial or local governments, or by individuals or groups in society. As in previous years, Christians and Muslims – who together make up more than half of the global population – were harassed in the largest number of countries (110 and 109, respectively).

Islamophobia – discrimination against Muslims – can be a problem in many Western countries, including the UK. As this mural explains, people should not allow their fears of terrorists acting in the name of Islam to give them false ideas about what Muslims believe.

An estimated 76 per cent of the world's population live in countries with high levels of government restrictions on freedom of religion or belief, or where they face high-level hostility due to their religious affiliations, and this figure is rising. That's why I initiated this APPG – it's time to act, and for Parliamentarians to take a lead. (Baroness Berridge of the Vale of Catmose)

The all party parliamentary group tries to influence people and groups both in Britain and abroad to work for change, so that citizens of many countries no longer suffer discrimination on the basis of their religious beliefs.

At work

Many people may be discriminated against at their place of work because their religious beliefs conflict with demands made by their employer. Discrimination at work because of a person's religion or belief could include:

- advertising for job applicants of one religion only
- requiring employees to dress in a certain way – for example, requiring all women to wear a short skirt, which would not be acceptable for women of several different religions
- making a person work at times that conflict with their religion
- bullying at work because of a person's religion.

People are protected from discrimination at work because of their religion or belief for a number of reasons, among them belonging to an organized religion such as Christianity, Judaism or Islam, having a profound belief which affects their way of life or view of the world, such as **humanism**, or taking part in collective worship. If they belong to a smaller religion or sect, such as Scientology or Rastafarianism, they would also be covered by the legislation, as would be the case if someone discriminates against them because they think they are of a certain religion when they are not. For example, it is against the law to discriminate against somone for wearing a headscarf on the supposition that they are Muslim, even if they are not actually Muslim. Humanists and atheists are also protected by this legislation.

Humanism is a non-religious set of beliefs that promotes certain values, such as reason, to make decisions about how humans should live, without the need for God.

Christian attitudes

Based on their reading of the creation stories in Genesis 1 and 2, Christians believe that God created all humans and that he created them equal. Humans were created in God's image, meaning that they are sacred and valuable in the sight of God.

This idea of equality is shown in Jesus' parable of the Good Samaritan (Luke 10:25–37), where a Jewish man was travelling between Jerusalem and Jericho when he was attacked, beaten, robbed and left seriously injured. A Jewish priest passed by on the other side of the road ignoring the man. So did a Levite. Then a Samaritan saw him, stopped, bandaged up his wounds, put him on his own donkey, took him to an inn and took care of him. The next day, he paid for the innkeeper to care for the man

CHRISTIANITY ROMAN CATHOLICISM

while he continued his own journey. Jesus asked which of the three was a neighbour to the victim. The answer was (obviously) the Samaritan. Jesus told his listeners to go and do likewise. The message of the parable of the Good Samaritan for Christians is that help should be given to anyone in need, not just to those with whom you are friendly or to people you know.

Taking it further

To understand the significance this story fully, it is important to know a little of the background:

- The road between Jerusalem and Jericho was notorious for robbers, who were able to mug travellers on the many bends in the road. What happened to the man would not have been an uncommon occurrence.
- Samaritans, originally Jews from Samaria, were hated by most Jews because they disobeyed the tradition in Judaism of not marrying gentiles (non-Jews). For most orthodox Jews, this was a great sin and they would have nothing to do with the Samaritans. The Samaritan would have been the least likely person to help the victim.
- The Jewish priest did not help the victim, even though he was Jewish, because to have done so would be to break the strict laws of ritual purity. This meant that they could not touch anyone who had blood on them. To have done so would have rendered them ritually unclean so that they could not perform their duties at the Jerusalem temple. While there was an exception in the Torah that would have allowed him to help the victim, he chose not to do so, and even crossed the road to avoid him.
- The Levite was an expert in Jewish law and should have known that it was allowable to help someone in need but, again, this religious man chose not to do so.

In Mark 12:31, in answer to a 'teacher of the Law' (a Pharisee) who was impressed by his teaching and asked Jesus which was the greatest commandment, Jesus taught that people should 'love your neighbour as yourself', where a 'neighbour' meant anyone with whom you come into contact, including strangers or those of a different culture or nationality. Famously, St Paul wrote, in Galatians 3:28, 'There is neither Jew nor Greek, slave nor free, male nor female, for you are all one in Christ Jesus.' All Christians, therefore, are against any form of prejudice or discrimination, and all people should be treated equally.

Tasks

1. Make your own summary of the story of the Good Samaritan.
2. Explain Jesus' teaching in this story about being a good neighbour.
3. Would you help someone who is lying on the ground bleeding if you had never seen them before? Give reasons for your answer.
4. Explain how St Paul's statement in Galatians 3:28 relates to prejudice and discrimination.

Church of England

The Church of England takes prejudice and discrimination very seriously and tries to uphold all relevant legal regulations. One aspect of this was seen in 1994, when the Church of England allowed women to be ordained as priests on the same basis as men. This was a ground-breaking moment for the Church and caused a lot of tension in some parishes that did not want to have a female as their priest. Since the 1990s, however, most members of the Church of England accept women priests. A further change took place in 2014, when the General Synod passed a bill to allow women to be bishops. The first woman bishop was the Right Reverend Libby Lane, who was consecrated bishop of Stockport at York Minster in January 2015.

As of 2015, in the Church of England, there are:
- 7,798 full-time priests
- 1,781 of which are women
- 100 male bishops
- 8 women bishops.

There are thirty-one women bishops in the Anglican Church worldwide.

In 2004, the General Synod of the Church of England passed a motion

That this Synod, noting the recent success of the British National Party in local elections in parts of Lancashire:

a. believe that any political movement that seeks to divide our communities on the basis of ethnicity is an affront to the nature of God revealed in creation and scripture and is a grave danger to harmonious community relationships; consequently voting for and/or supporting a political party that offers racist policies is incompatible with Christian discipleship;

b. call on all Christians in England to nurture a loathing of the sin of racism and to model the teaching of Christ in loving all our neighbours; and

c. commit the Church of England to work in partnership with our ecumenical partners, other faith groups, voluntary and statutory organisations, mainstream political parties and all people of good will, in building cohesive communities and affirming our multi-ethnic, culturally and religiously diverse society.

This statement clearly shows that the Church is strongly against any form of racism or discrimination.

Task

Find and summarize four reasons given in this passage as to why the Church of England is against racism.

The Archbishop of York, John Sentamu, was born in Uganda, where he was a lawyer and judge. He was forced to leave Uganda in 1975, when President Idi Amin initiated a reign of terror in the country. Archbishop Sentamu has worked tirelessly in England to raise awareness of racism within British society and the Church of England.

John Sentamu, Archbishop of York, has worked to raise awareness of racism and racial discrimination in the UK.

The Roman Catholic Church

The Catechism of the Catholic Church affirms its hatred of prejudice and discrimination:

> **1931** Respect for the human person proceeds by way of respect for the principle that 'everyone should look upon his neighbour (without any exception) as "another self," above all bearing in mind his life and the means necessary for living it with dignity.' No legislation could by itself do away with the fears, prejudices, and attitudes of pride and selfishness which obstruct the establishment of truly fraternal societies. Such behaviour will cease only through the charity that finds in every man a 'neighbour,' a brother.

> **1935** The equality of men rests essentially on their dignity as persons and the rights that flow from it: Every form of social or cultural discrimination in fundamental personal rights on the grounds of sex, race, colour, social conditions, language, or religion must be curbed and eradicated as incompatible with God's design.

These statements show that Roman Catholics support the equality of all people regardless of their gender, race or social status. One contentious issue within the Roman Catholic Church is the refusal to ordain women priests. The Church argues that men and women have equal roles in life and equal rights in society and the same educational, social and political rights. The only area in life not open to women is the ordained ministry, although they may teach at theological colleges. Church authorities cite three reasons for refusing to allow women to be deacons, priests or bishops.

1   Jesus and his closest Apostles were men. Because priests and bishops are considered to be the successors of the Apostles, women cannot fill these roles.

2   Priests represent Jesus in the Mass; since Jesus was a man, only men may be priests.
3   The Catechism of the Catholic Church (1577) says 'The Lord Jesus chose men from the college of the Twelve Apostles, and the Apostles did the same when they chose collaborators to succeed them in their ministry . . .. For this reason, the ordination of women is impossible.'

There are several arguments against these points. Some of these are made by the Catholic Women's Ordination (CWO), an organization set up in 1993 in the UK:

- God created men and women together (Genesis 1:27), so women should have the same rights as men in *all* things, including ordination to the priesthood
- many women feel that they are called by God to be priests in the Roman Catholic Church, but they cannot fulfil that calling
- if they could be ordained, the Church community would benefit positively from women's experience and their strengths in the ministerial priesthood
- 80 per cent of the pastoral workers in the Church are women, and it is unfair to exclude this large majority from being priests
- just because Jesus was a man does not mean that only men can be priests; Jesus was carried in a woman's womb and born in the normal way, and several women followed him during his ministry
- at Jesus' crucifixion, the (male) disciples ran away because they were afraid of being caught, while the women stayed at the foot of the cross, prepared his body for burial and were the first to hear of his resurrection; surely these points show that women were just as important as men in Jesus' life.

Taking it further

The Roman Catholic Church has experienced discrimination at first hand: after the Reformation in the sixteenth century, when the Church of England was established under Henry VIII, various laws were passed discriminating against Catholics.

- They were treated as traitors because their first allegiance was to the Pope, not the king of England.
- Catholics were hanged and burnt at the stake during the reign of Elizabeth I.
- Further laws were passed against Catholics under Charles II.
- During the reign of William and Mary, laws were passed restricting the rights and power of Catholics.
- Catholics were allowed to join the British armed forces without vowing their allegiance to the Church of England only in 1778.
- Catholics were allowed to vote only from 1793, but until 1829 they could vote only for Anglican candidates.

Task

'Women should not be priests.' Do you agree? Give reasons for your answer.

Muslim attitudes

Some non-Muslims believe that Muslim women do not have the same rights as men and are therefore discriminated against. Islam argues against this, however, that, because men and women have different but complementary roles in life and in religion, so they should have different rights. In Islam, there is no difference between men and women in the sight of God. The Qur'an says: 'The rights of women over men are similar to those of men over women' (Surah 2:228).

Women have souls just as men do and will enter Paradise so long as their life is lived in accordance with the Qur'an: 'Whoever does that which is right and believes, whether male or female, we will hasten him or her to happy life' (Surah 16:97). The Qur'an tells men to 'Live with them [women] on a footing of kindness and equity' (Surah 4:19). The Prophet Muhammad believed that men and women were made from the same soul and said, 'Women are the twin halves of men.'

Women are not discriminated against in Islam. In fact, the role of women is just as important as that of men, if not more so. Many Muslims believe that the main role of women is to have children and to bring them up according to the faith. In Islam, the role of a mother is so important that they are said to be the individuals most worthy of love and respect and are described as a gift from God. Mothers are given the responsibility of teaching their children the basics of the faith. In return, the husband has to provide for all her needs and treat her with great respect. In practice, however, some Muslim women are treated differently. In those countries governed by Shari'a law, women have fewer rights than men. The wearing of the **burqa**, for instance, is compulsory in Afghanistan, and women are not allowed to be educated or to have a career. Women are expected to obey their husband in everything and are punished if they do not do so.

The **burqa** is a style of clothing covering the body and face worn by many Muslim women.

Taking it further

Amnesty International has highlighted a number of areas where Muslims are being discriminated against on religious grounds, for example:

- women are denied jobs and girls are prevented from attending school because they wear traditional head-coverings
- in Switzerland, since 2010, mosques are forbidden to have minarets
- in the Catalonian region of Spain, new mosques are not being permitted because they are incompatible with Catalonian traditions and culture. Because the existing mosques are too small to accommodate all the worshippers, this means that some people must pray outside.

Tasks

1 Summarize what the Qur'an says about the relationship between men and women.
2 Find out more about the specific duties of women in the Muslim home.
3 'It is the duty of Muslim men to support their wives.' Do you agree? Give reasons for your answer.

Human rights

What are human rights?

A '**human right**' is based on the principle that all people should be treated fairly and have the same basic entitlements and freedoms. Sadly, in many parts of the world, many people do not enjoy these basic human rights. For example, individuals have

- been tortured or abused in at least eighty-one countries
- faced unfair trials in at least fifty-four countries
- had their freedom of speech restricted or taken away in at least seventy-seven countries.

Article 3 of the **Universal Declaration of Human Rights (UDHR)** states that 'Everyone has the right to life, liberty and security of person.' Figures show, however, that

- in Brazil in 2007, 1,260 individuals were killed by the police. Each of these was officially recorded as an 'act of resistance' and was not investigated.
- in Uganda, approximately 1,500 people die every week in camps for internally displaced people. According to the World Health Organization, more than 500,000 have died in these camps.
- in Vietnam, at least 75,000 drug addicts and prostitutes have been put into over-populated 'rehabilitation' camps, but they do not receive any treatment.

Article 4 of the UDHR states: 'No one shall be held in slavery or servitude; slavery and the slave trade shall be prohibited in all their forms.'

- In Asia, Japan is the major destination country for trafficked women, especially women from the Philippines and Thailand. Estimates say that there are 60,000 child prostitutes in the Philippines.
- In northern Uganda, the Lord's Resistance Army guerrillas have kidnapped 20,000 children over the last twenty years and forced them to serve as soldiers or sexual slaves for the army.

Article 5 of the UDHR states that 'No one shall be subjected to torture or to cruel, inhuman or degrading treatment or punishment.'

- The US government held 270 prisoners in Guantánamo Bay, Cuba, without charge or trial, and subjected them to 'water-boarding' (a torture that simulates drowning). Former President George W. Bush authorized the CIA to continue this secret detention and interrogation despite its violation of international law.
- In Darfur, violence, atrocities and abductions are very common and outside aid is almost cut off. Women are the usual victims of violent assault, with more than 200 rapes being recorded in one camp within a five-week period. The authorities made no attempt to punish those responsible, despite knowing who they were.

(Information edited from www.humanrights.com/what-are-human-rights/
violations-of-human-rights/article-3.html)

> **Human rights** are those rights that people have by virtue of being members of the human race, such as rights to life, freedom of belief and religion.

> The **Universal Declaration of Human Rights** was the declaration of the United Nations in 1948 that clarified basic human rights.

The Universal Declaration of Human Rights

Violations of human rights throughout history, particularly the trauma of the Second World War (1939–45), eventually led to the development of the Universal Declaration of Human Rights (UDHR) – a milestone document in the history of human rights. Drafted by representatives with different legal and cultural backgrounds from all regions of the world, it was proclaimed by the United Nations General Assembly in Paris on 10 December 1948 and sets a common standard for the fundamental human rights that have to be protected for all peoples and all nations around the world. The basic principle behind the declaration is stated in Article 1: 'All human beings are born free and equal in dignity and rights. They are endowed with reason and conscience and should act towards one another in a spirit of brotherhood.'

The principles of the UDHR inspired the European Convention on Human Rights (1953), the key components of which are the right to liberty and legal equality, together with freedom of religion, speech and opinion. These were reinforced in UK law in 1998 by the **Human Rights Act**, which means that individuals can defend their rights in the UK courts and that public organizations (including the government, the police and local councils) must treat everyone equally, with fairness, dignity and respect. The Human Rights Act protects every person who lives in the UK – young and old, rich and poor – regardless of whether they are British citizens or foreign nationals. Prisoners are also able to call on it.

> The **Human Rights Act** is a legal document that protects the rights of all humans.

The Human Rights Act covers many fundamental rights and freedoms.

- *The right to life* The state is required to investigate suspicious deaths and deaths in custody and to take steps to prevent such things as infanticide.
- *The prohibition of torture and inhuman treatment* No one should ever be tortured or treated in an inhuman or degrading way, no matter what the situation.
- *Protection against slavery and forced labour* No one should be treated like a slave or subjected to forced labour.
- *The right to liberty and freedom* All people have the right to be free, and the state can imprison a person only if they have very good reason – for example, if that person has committed a crime.
- *Respect for privacy and family life and the right to marry* This protects against unnecessary surveillance or intrusion into people's lives and guarantees the right to marry and raise a family.
- *Freedom of thought, religion and belief* A person can believe whatever they like and practise their religion or beliefs.
- *Free speech and peaceful protest* Everyone has a right to speak freely, and join with others peacefully, to express their views.
- *No discrimination* No one should be treated unfairly because, for example, of their gender, race, sexuality, religion or age.
- *Protection of property, the right to an education and the right to free elections* This protects against state interference in relation to an individual's possessions, means that no child can be denied an education, and states that elections must be free and fair.

Tasks

1 Define the term 'human rights'.
2 Explain why having human rights is so important for individuals.
3 'Freedom of religion is the most important human right.' Do you agree? Give reasons for your answer.

Many religious leaders, such as the Archbishop of Canterbury, have publicly spoken out about the need for the UK to help migrants and refugees from North Africa and the Middle East who are suffering in their attempts to reach safety in European countries.

Christianity and human rights

Most Christians will look to the Bible for help in thinking about human rights issues. They acknowledge that, when humans were created by God in his image (Genesis 1:27), they were endowed with dignity and a sense of morality. Christians have a strong belief that human beings are very important in the eyes of God and that human rights must therefore be taken very seriously indeed. If an individual killed another person, for example, the punishment was the loss of the killer's life (Genesis 9:6).

The Ten Commandments emphasize that human rights should be upheld – there are prohibitions against murder, theft, covetousness, adultery and bearing false witness (in court). Elsewhere in the Torah, there are commands to treat immigrants well (Exodus 22:21), to provide for the poor (Leviticus 19:10) and to release all servants every fifty years (Leviticus 25:39–41).

The New Testament states that God treats every person the same (Acts 10:34) because everyone is a unique creation of God. Christians should not discriminate on

CHRISTIANITY
ROMAN
CATHOLICISM

the basis of race, gender or social status (Galatians 3:28; Colossians 3:11). The Gospel of Luke tells Christians to be kind to everyone (Luke 6:35–6) and to help all who are in need (Matthew 5:42; Luke 10:30–37).

Torture is mentioned several times in the Bible – for example:

- Jeremiah 20:2 – the prophet Jeremiah was tortured by being beaten and put in the stocks
- Matthew 18:34 – Jesus mentions a servant who was 'turned over to the jailers to be tortured'.

However, in every case where torture is mentioned, the religious people are the victims, never the ones who inflict it on others.

Torture
is the act of deliberately inflicting physical or psychological pain on someone for the benefit of the torturer.

Task

Torture can be defined as 'inflicting severe mental or physical pain on a person in order to gain useful information'. It is a denial of human rights. Look at the following examples and decide which of them might be called torture, and why. Add any other examples that you think count as torture.

- Causing pain to someone (of any kind or degree)
- Sleep deprivation
- Enforced change of diet (e.g., for someone who is very overweight)
- Refusal to talk to someone
- Shouting loudly at someone continuously
- Using persuasive techniques to sell you something

Look at the following examples and decide whether there may be cases when it might be morally justifiable to use torture. Discuss your findings with the class.

1 A prisoner is withholding vital information about a kidnapped child.
2 A captured enemy soldier has information that could save the lives of 100, 1,000 or 10,000 innocent civilians.
3 A pupil continually bullies another pupil.
4 A teacher continually picks on a particular pupil.
5 An MP refuses to vote for his political party in an important motion on child cruelty.

Islam on human rights

ISLAM

Islam, like most other religions, supports human rights and teaches that all its members must put these rights into practice. We will look here briefly at three of the most important human rights and their justification in Islam.

Justice
refers to people gaining what is fair or right.

- *Justice* Sur'ah 42:15 says: 'Call men to the true faith and follow the straight path as you are taught. Do not be led by their desires, but say "I believe in all the scriptures that God has revealed. I am commanded to exercise justice among you."' All Muslims, therefore, are commanded to exercise justice with others, regardless of whether they believe in the same things or not.

- **Compassion** One of the most important phrases in Islam is 'In the name of God, the Compassionate, the Merciful', which emphasizes the importance of 'compassion'. This phrase occurs over 300 times in the Qur'an. Muslims attempt to live their lives according to God's commands. Compassion, which includes giving full retspect to other people's human rights in everyday life, is centrally important to this.

- **Prohibition of terrorism** Islam forbids the bloodshed of innocent human beings, as this is a sin against all humanity and equivalent to killing the whole human race. Surah 5:32 says: 'whoever kills a person – unless it is for murder or for spreading mischief in the land – it would be as if he has killed the whole of humankind, and whoever saves the life of a person it is as if he has saved the life of the whole of humankind. Our Messengers have already come to them with the clear signs; then many of them thereafter commit excesses in the earth.' Even during war, the Prophet Muhammad gave strict instructions against killing civilians. 'Fight in the name of God, but do not kill old men, children and women . . .' (Hadith of al-Bukhari).

> **Compassion** means showing a caring attitude towards someone.

> **Terrorism** is the unauthorized use of violence and intimidation against ordinary people in order to achieve political objectives.

Many religious leaders – Muslim as well as Christian – have come together to condemn terrorism and the actions of so-called Islamic State.

Tasks

1 Define what is meant by 'human rights'.
2 Explain why human rights are important for every individual.
3 Outline the work of one organization that promotes human rights.
4 Explain the teachings of one religion on human rights.
5 'Torture is sometimes the right thing to do.' Do you agree? Give reasons for your answer.

Non-religious views on human rights

The **British Humanist Association** states: 'In all our work, we strive to embody our values by –

- engaging in debate rationally, intelligently and with attention to evidence
- recognizing the dignity of individuals and treating them with fairness and respect
- respecting and promoting freedom, democracy, human rights and the rule of law
- being cooperative, working with others of different beliefs for the common good
- celebrating human achievement, progress and potential.'

Another non-religious organization is **Amnesty International**. This was founded in London in 1961, after two Portuguese students were imprisoned for seven years for raising a toast to freedom. A British lawyer, Peter Benenson, wrote an article for *The Observer* calling for an international campaign entitled 'Appeal for Amnesty 1961' for people everywhere to protest against the imprisonment of men and women for their political or religious beliefs – 'prisoners of conscience'. Amnesty is now the world's largest grassroots human rights organization with a membership of over 7 million. It investigates and exposes abuses, educates and mobilizes the public, and helps to transform societies to create a safer, more just world. Amnesty was awarded the Nobel Peace Prize in 1977 for its 'campaign against torture'. In particular it seeks to influence governments – for example, in the UK, by talking directly to ministers, civil servants and members of parliament, and also indirectly by talking to ordinary people. Amnesty issues public reports and stories on the government's human rights record. It lobbies MPs, it engages in consultation, sharing its reports and having discussions with various individuals and bodies.

Task

Find out more about the work of Amnesty International UK and make a poster for display, highlighting some of the organization's activities that you think are particularly important or impressive.

Task

Copy out the grid below and fill in definitions of the words (not all of them are given in the chapter).

Term	Definition
Prejudice	
Discrimination	
Racial discrimination	
Racial prejudice	
Equality	
Persecution	

TICK THE TOPICS

Now you should tick the relevant boxes to check what you have learned in this chapter.

Sections	Topics	Tick
Equality and freedom of religious rights		
Issues of prejudice and discrimination in religion or belief	International issues	
	At work	
	Christian attitudes	
	– Church of England	
	– Roman Catholic Church	
	Muslim attitudes	
Human rights	What are human rights?	
	Universal Declaration of Human Rights	
	Christianity on human rights	
	Islam on human rights	
	Non-religious views on human rights	

Sample questions

AQA Religious Studies A (8062) and Religious Studies B (8063)

1   Which of the following best expresses the religious ideal that everyone may worship freely?
    a) Respect b) Belief c) Hopeful d) Impossible   (1 mark)
2   Give two examples of what religious believers may see as prejudice.   (2 marks)
3   Explain two contrasting beliefs in contemporary British society about discrimination.   (4 marks)
4   Explain two religious beliefs about human rights.   (5 marks)
5   'Discrimination of any sort should not be allowed.'
    Evaluate this statement. In your answer, you:
    • should give reasoned arguments in support of this statement
    • should give reasoned arguments to support a different point of view
    • should refer to religious arguments
    • may refer to non-religious arguments
    • should reach a justified conclusion.   (12 marks)

Edexcel Religious Studies B (1RB0)

a) Give three human rights. (3)

b) Explain two reasons in favour of freedom of religion and belief. (4)

c) Assess whether women should be allowed to hold positions of authority in religious organizations. (9)

d) 'Religious symbols should never be allowed in public.'

Evaluate this statement, considering more than one point of view. (12)

Edexcel International GCSE Religious Studies (4RS0)

a) What are 'human rights'? (2)

b) Describe how racial prejudice may affect a person. (5)

c) Explain why freedom of religion is important for religious believers. (8)

d) 'Discrimination is sometimes justifiable.'

Do you agree? Give reasons for your answer, showing that you have considered another point of view. (5)

OCR Religious Studies Full Course (J625)

a) Give three examples of human rights. (3)

b) Outline what religion teaches about equality. (6)

c) Explain religious teaching about social justice.

You should refer to sources of wisdom and authority in your answer. (6)

d) 'Human rights are more important than belief in God.'

Discuss this statement. In your answer, you should draw on your learning from across your course of study, including reference to beliefs, teachings and practices within your chosen religion. (15)

(SPaG + 3)

WJEC Eduqas Religious Studies (Full Course)

a) Giving one example, state what is meant by the 'dignity of human life'. (2)

b) With reference to one religion you have studied, explain views about equality. (5)

c) From two different religions or two religious traditions, explain views on the freedom of religious expression. (8)

d) 'Religious extremism should be made illegal.'

Discuss this statement, showing that you have considered more than one point of view. (You must refer to religion and belief in your answer.) (15)

(SPaG + 6)

11 Global Relationships

CONTENTS	
The environment	**World poverty**
Case study	Causes of poverty
Threats to the planet	Christianity and poverty
Non-religious responses to the threats	Modern Christian responses to poverty
Christian responses	Muslim responses
Muslim responses	

In this chapter, you will learn about two major issues that affect almost every person in the world: the environment and world poverty. The environment topic will include discussion of the causes and problems of global warming and pollution, together with some possible solutions. The relationship between the first world and the third or developing world will be examined, and responses will be considered from Christian, Muslim and non-religious points of view.

The problem of poverty will be investigated, using relevant examples and discussing responses to the needs of the millions of poor people. We will look at biblical teaching, the meaning and morality of 'charity', how people use their disposable income, and whether people in one part of the world have any moral responsibility towards those living elsewhere.

The environment

We will begin this chapter with a case study.

Case study

The Belo Monte hydro-electric dam in the Para region of Brazil is due to open in 2019, when it will be the fourth largest dam in the world, flooding an area of 258 square miles, and costing an estimated $18 billion. Its creation has caused a lot of controversy both in Brazil and internationally. The protestors argue that:

- the dam would flood a large area of land, dry up certain parts of the Xingu River, cause devastation to the rainforest, and reduce fish stocks on which the tribespeople who live in the area depend for their survival;
- construction would attract large numbers of migrant workers and colonists who are likely to bring diseases to the area, putting the lives of the tribespeople at risk;
- the livelihoods of thousands of tribal people who depend on the forest and river for food and water would be destroyed;
- the tribes have not been properly consulted, which is against both Brazilian and international law;
- the many tribespeople who have not been contacted about the plan are at high risk, as they have no resistance to diseases brought in by workers;
- approximately 40,000 people will have to be moved from their ancient homelands and relocated, and they may not be able to find employment in their new area;
- more dams are planned for this area further upstream in the future, multiplying the problems for the inhabitants.

Cacique Raoni Metuktire – pictured here at a press conference in the European Parliament – is a chief of the Kayapo people of Brazil whose community is threatened by the Belo Monte dam.

Supporters of the dam argue that it will bring huge benefits: it will supply the region's energy needs far into the future and enable the growth of aluminium and metallurgy industries. This in turn will help Brazil to grow economically and bring greater prosperity to its citizens. Over $1 billion has been set aside to help the native people to be relocated.

Task

Find out more information on the Belo Monte dam. Do you think the Brazilian government is right to build it?
What issues does the building of this dam raise for the environment?

Extension task

Find out about the Three Gorges project in China and compare the issues there with those at Belo Monte.

Threats to the planet

There are many threats to the health and safety of the planet we live on. Some of the most important are discussed briefly below.

- *Ozone layer depletion* The **ozone layer** surrounds the whole earth and is in the stratosphere, between 6 and 25 miles above the earth (this is where aeroplanes fly). The UV-B radiation produced by the sun is partially absorbed by the ozone layer, so that the amount of ozone that reaches the earth is much reduced. As the ozone layer degrades because of human activity, more of the harmful UV-B radiation reaches the earth, and this increases the risk of skin cancers, cataracts and damage to people's immune systems. It can also cause damage to plant life, single-cell organisms and aquatic ecosystems.

- *Climate change and global warming* During the last 150 years or so, since the industrial revolution, humans have burnt huge amounts of fossil fuels – coal, gas and oil – to heat homes and power factories. This has changed the natural balance of the carbon cycle – the way in which nature processes the carbon in the environment. Because there is now so much more carbon, nature is finding it very difficult to process it all. The extra carbon dioxide in the atmosphere traps more of the sun's heat, and this causes temperatures to rise. The World Wide Fund for Nature (WWF) estimates that a rise in the world temperature would result in

  - severe storms and floods in some countries and droughts in others
  - seas becoming more acidic, resulting in coral and krill death, which will destroy aquatic food chains
  - little or no summer sea ice in the Arctic, which will mean disaster for polar bears but also that the world's climate will become hotter more quickly.

  If the temperature rises higher still, the environmental results will be even more catastrophic: rainforests will die and the ice sheets of Greenland and Antarctica will melt, causing sea levels to rise and people and animals to suffer greatly.

- *Deforestation* Approximately half of the world's forests have been cut down since 1945, and an area the size of England is lost every year. Forests cover only 6 per cent of the earth's surface but contain 50 per cent of all species and plants, some of which are a vital source of medicines. Forests provide food, shelter and a

The **ozone layer** is a 'shield' of gas in the stratosphere that absorbs most of the sun's harmful UV radiation.

Climate change is an environmental concern affecting many countries and refers to changes in weather and climate patterns, including global warming, reduced rainfall and increased tidal floods.

Deforestation refers to the deliberate policy of destroying large areas of forest, using the land for other purposes despite the dangers to the environment.

Deforestation is one of the largest environmental issues of the twenty-first century.

Pollution refers to the introduction into the environment of contaminants that have a harmful or dangerous effect on humans or the natural world.

Population pressure refers to the reduced ability of the environment to sustain the number of people, resulting in migration, decline or extinction of the population.

source of income for 1 billion people. Importantly, they also regulate the climate and water cycle and prevent soil erosion. Wildlife is suffering because of deforestation. In the Amazon rainforest in Brazil, for instance – the largest forest in the world (6.7 million square kilometres – almost half the size of South America) – there are over 400 mammal species, 1,300 types of birds, nearly 400 reptile species, at least 3,000 types of fish and over 400 species of amphibians. If deforestation continues at its present rate, many of these will become extinct.

- *Pollution and waste* Acid rain is a real problem. This is where the rain possesses a much higher level of hydrogen ions than normal, and it can have harmful effects on plants, aquatic animals and the natural environment. **Pollution** and acid gases produced by factories, vehicles and homes can be carried across large areas, so that pollution emanating from Britain can end up falling in acid rain in Norway, Sweden and Denmark. Sweden spends millions of euros each year on adding lime to its lakes to counteract the influx of acid rain and pollution. In the 1980s the Statue of Liberty in New York had to be given a facelift costing more than $35 million because its copper construction had been seriously damaged by pollution and acid rain.

- *Population pressure* The dramatic increase in the world's population in the last century – from 2.5 billion to almost 8 billion today – means greater pressure on the world's resources. Most of the increase has been, and will continue to be, in developing countries, which have traditionally had low levels of education and health standards and suffered widespread poverty, political instability (often leading to war), and the depletion of natural resources. With all of these problems to contend with, the governments of such countries have little time to think seriously about population control measures.

The higher the population of a country, the more resources they will consume. Many of these resources, such as fossil fuels, are not replaceable. Others, such as fisheries and forests, are renewable but take many years to replenish themselves, and humans are currently using them up more quickly than they can be replaced.

Many governments became aware of rapidly rising population in developing countries in the 1950s. So, several Western governments and international aid agencies launched family planning schemes. The first of these was in India in 1951 and was followed by many countries, particularly in Asia. For example, in 1971 Thailand adopted a successful national population policy, which resulted in a quite dramatic reduction over the next fifteen years, from a growth rate of 3.2 per cent to 1.6 per cent. This was the result of government strongly encouraging the use of contraceptives by married couples (which rose from 15 to 70 per cent) and was followed by another decade of a continued fall in the birth rate, so that by 1997 it had dropped to 1.1 per cent, where it remains today.

One of the most controversial population control programmes was in China, which introduced its 'one child' policy in 1979. It was contentious because of the methods that were allegedly used in its enforcement, including compulsory abortion and sterilization. Forced sterilization also took place in India in the 1970s. There was a particular emphasis in both India and China on producing male babies, since boys were valued more highly by society than girls and were thought to make better and more productive workers.

- *Urban explosion* Cities in industrialized countries around the world are doubling or trebling in size every twelve years, which means that open countryside ('greenfield' sites) is disappearing. This has a negative influence on the environment through increased pollution and leads to an increase in urban problems such as drug abuse, crime and violence.

- *Food and fresh water shortages* 1 billion people around the world are chronically hungry, having little or no access to sufficient food and clean water. It is estimated that the world's population will continue to rise for at least another fifty years, so the problem of poverty and starvation will continue to get worse, probably leading to more war and violence.

> **Task**
>
> Study the list above and decide which are the most serious threats to the environment. Put them in rank order, from 1 (most serious) to 7 (least serious), and give reasons for your choice. Compare them with the choices of your classmates.

Non-religious responses to the threats

The **Gaia Hypothesis** is one of the most important and influential ideas relating to how humans can mitigate some of the ecological problems facing the earth. The

The **Gaia Hypothesis** is James Lovelock's idea that the earth heals itself.

English scientist **James Lovelock** (b. 1919) published his ideas in 1979 in a book called *Gaia*. This is the name for the Greek earth goddess, and Lovelock chose it because of what it symbolized. Throughout history, the idea of 'Mother Earth' has been both well known and important for showing how, just as mothers give birth to new life, so the earth creates and sustains new life. For Lovelock, the earth is *alive*. Both living and inorganic material are part of a dynamic system that shapes the earth's biosphere. The earth is a self-regulating system; each part works to keep the environment hospitable for life.

Lovelock believes that the earth will eventually recover from the damage caused by pollution and climate change. In his view, however, this will take over 1,000 years. Even if deforestation and pollution were to stop today, climate change cannot be avoided, as it is already happening. All humans can do is to develop ways of preventing the problem from getting worse.

One response to the problems of the environment comes from the ecology movement. The Norwegian philosopher **Arne Naess** (1912–2009) developed what he called **deep ecology**, a movement which recognizes that all living things have their own value, that they are valuable in their own right, not just because they have a use or function. Naess believed, for instance, that humans should respect trees for what they are, not just cut them down to make buildings or fuel. He was once arrested when protesting against a plan to interfere with a 'sacred' mountain. Nature, in his view, needs protection from 'the destruction of billions of humans'. Naess set out certain principles that needed to be put in place by governments if the environment was to survive, such as that non-human life forms contribute to the health of the earth and so should be respected; humans have no right to reduce the richness of the earth's natural resources and they should treat the environment with great respect. He said that humans were taking too much from the earth and there need to be changes in their view of nature. Policies were necessary to protect nature. These should include population reduction as well as economic and technological changes. In the words of Naess, humans should 'live lightly on the earth'.

> **Deep ecology** is a movement that encourages a commitment to respect the intrinsic values of nature and the interconnectedness of all species.

> **Stewardship** is the belief that humans have the responsibility to look after the created world.

> **Task**
>
> Make a list of practical things you could do to 'live more lightly on the earth'. You might include such things as making sure lights are switched off when you leave a room, turning down your central heating by a degree or two, or writing to your local council to encourage them to improve their recycling facilities.

Christian responses

All Christians believe that their holy book, the Bible, has passages that are relevant to the debate about the environment. One of the key ideas in the Bible in this regard is the idea of **stewardship**. God gave the world as a gift to humans and commanded them to look after it (Genesis 2:15). Humans are stewards (or caretakers) of the earth and are responsible to God for how they use the world and its resources. This means that humans must recognize the impact of their actions. Adam was told to 'till the

CHRISTIANITY
ROMAN
CATHOLICISM

Christian tradition sees humans as custodians and caretakers of planet earth, just as God put Adam in charge of the Garden of Eden to look after creation. This places responsibility on humans to take care of the earth and the environment.

earth' so that he could provide food for himself and Eve, meaning that it is permissible to consume the earth's resources. However, humans must learn to balance *consumption* with *conservation* of resources. Genesis 1–3 also argues that, because humans are made 'in the image of God', who created the universe, they have no right to ruin what God has created.

Taking it further

The same point was made in a statement published by the World Council of Churches in 1988:

> The drive to have 'mastery' over creation has resulted in the senseless exploitation of natural resources and the alienation of the land from people and the destruction of indigenous cultures . . .. Creation came into being by the will and love of the triune God, and as such it possesses an inner cohesion and goodness. Though human eyes may not always discern it, every creature and the whole creation in chorus bear witness to the glorious unity and harmony with which creation is endowed. And when our human eyes are opened and our tongues unloosed, we too learn to praise and participate in the life, love, power and freedom that is God's continuing gift and grace.

Many other biblical passages confirm this view of the creation.

- 'The earth is the Lord's and everything in it.' (Psalm 24:1)
- 'The heavens declare the glory of the Lord.' (Psalm 19:1)
- 'When I consider your heavens, the work of your hands, the moon and the stars, which you have set in place, what is man that you are mindful of him? . . . You made him ruler over the works of your hands.' (Psalm 8:3–6)

These passages say that:

- the world is created solely by God
- humans are special to God because they are his stewards
- stewards do not abuse God's creation but care for it
- God loves not only humans, but his other creatures too.

There are examples of what good stewardship means in the Old Testament.

- *Genesis 9*: After the Flood, God saves not only Noah and his family but all the animals as well. God makes a **covenant** (binding agreement) not just with humans but with all living beings.
- *Deuteronomy 5:12–14*: In this version of the Ten Commandments, all animals, not just humans, are to be rested for one day per week.
- *Leviticus 25:4*: Even the land is to be rested every seven years to ensure its health and fertility.
- *Deuteronomy 24:19–22*: The law concerning the harvesting of crops states that any grain that had fallen on the ground or had been missed by the harvest was to be left for the poor or for travellers, who would be allowed to glean (collect) it for their own use. This reminds believers not to be selfish and take everything for themselves, but to leave some produce for those who are less fortunate.

Task

Look up the following passages in the New Testament and note what they have to say about good stewardship:

- Matthew 6:26–9
- Luke 12:6–7
- Colossians 1:20
- Acts 4:32–5.

Taking it further

Read the passage below and write a paragraph to explain what you think it means:
 'You will go out in joy and be led forth in peace; the mountains and hills will burst into song before you, and all the trees of the field will clap their hands. . . . This will be for you the Lord's renown, for an everlasting sign, which will not be destroyed.' (Isaiah 55:12–13)

Taking it further

When the World Council of Churches (WCC) met in 1990, it issued a statement affirming that God loves his creation:

> We affirm that the world, as God's handiwork, has its own inherent integrity; that land, waters, air, forests, mountains, and all creatures, including humanity, are 'good' in God's sight. The integration of creation has a social aspect which we recognize as peace with justice, and an ecological aspect which we recognize in the self-renewing, sustainable character of natural ecosystems.
>
> We will resist the claim that anything in creation is merely a resource for human exploitation. We will resist species extinction for human benefit; consumerism and harmful mass production; pollution of land, air and waters; all human activities that are now leading to probable rapid climate change; and the policies and plans which contribute to the disintegration of creation. (Affirmation VII)

This statement recognizes that human beings are the cause of the death of many animal species and the destruction of a great deal of the natural environment. Humans are selfish and have put themselves and their own needs above those of any other living thing on earth. They have abused the rest of God's creation, putting their own wants and needs before anything else. The WCC calls on Christians to repent of their selfish attitudes and behaviour towards the created world before it is too late.

Task

1 Find out more about the World Council of Churches and how it tries to influence Christians around the world.
2 Do you think it is possible for Christians to stop being selfish towards the environment? Can you think of specific things they could do that would help restore the environment and halt species extinction?

Roman Catholic responses

In his inaugural speech after his election (19 March 2013), Pope Francis said:

> I would like to ask all those who have positions of responsibility in economic, political and social life, and all men and women of goodwill: let us be protectors of creation, protectors of God's plan inscribed in nature, protectors of one another and of the environment.

This clearly sends a signal to all Roman Catholics that the Church is serious about protecting the environment and asks them to play their part in attempting to make the world a better place in which to live for all people, present and future.

The Roman Catholic Church has developed several high-profile practical schemes that highlight environmental problems and help individuals to live more ecologically. The Catholic Bishops Conference in England and Wales provides practical information on environmental matters, such as:

- materials for environmental **liturgy**
- how to audit energy use and use less
- the mapping of activities in parishes to give others inspiring ideas
- plans for a Creation Sunday.

ROMAN CATHOLICISM

The **liturgy** is the set order in which a Christian service of worship is conducted.

In the United States, the Church has developed a seven-year plan for change in a number of areas, including encouraging churches and schools to take action on becoming 'greener' by reducing energy costs, particularly in older buildings. There are many other ideas on a specially developed website, where stories and news of Catholic action on the environment are reported each month. There is also a 'Green Pilgrimage Network' for Catholics making pilgrimages to religious sites around the world, encouraging them to reduce the amount of plastic waste, to eat environmentally friendly food en route, to use eco-friendly transport and accommodation, and to be careful with natural resources and wildlife.

> ### Task
>
> Read the following extract from a letter from Pope Francis to the Peruvian minister of the environment on 27 November 2014 and summarize the main points he makes about the urgency of taking action on the environment.
>
> The consequences of environmental changes, which are already being dramatically felt in many countries, especially the insular states of the Pacific, remind us of the gravity of neglect and inaction. The time to find global solutions is running out. We can find appropriate solutions only if we act together and in agreement. There is therefore a clear, definitive and urgent ethical imperative to act.
>
> An effective fight against global warming will be possible only through a responsible collective action, which overcomes particular interests and behaviours and develops unfettered by political and economic pressures. A collective response which is also capable of overcoming mistrust and of fostering a culture of solidarity, of encounter and of dialogue; capable of demonstrating responsibility to protect the planet and the human family.

Muslim responses

ISLAM

Muslims believe that the world is in such danger of pollution that it cannot be saved, and that all humans must do everything they can to help to bring the environment back to health. Because God made them, humans are the most intelligent beings on earth, and yet they have caused almost all the damage to the planet. The Qur'an says that God is the creator of the universe and that humans have the responsibility to look after the world properly for God and for future generations. A hadith says:

> The Earth is green and beautiful, and Allah has appointed you his stewards over it. The whole earth has been created a place of worship, pure and clean. Whoever plants a tree and diligently looks after it until it matures and bears fruit is rewarded. If a Muslim plants a tree or sows a field and humans and beasts and birds eat from it, all of it is love on his part.

This thought is also seen in the Qur'an (Surah 55:1–12), where Muslims are told to protect the environment because God has created it 'with all its fruits and blossom-bearing palm, chaff-covered grain and scented herbs'.

> ### Task
>
> Look up Surah 30:30 and explain how it relates to Muslims' responsibility to look after creation. What do you think the phrase 'There is no altering the creation of Allah' means?

In the Assisi Declarations (discussions in 1986 among the five major world religions on their faiths' responsibility towards the natural world), the Muslim statement made the following points.

The central concept of Islam is **Tawhid** or the Unity of God. Allah is Unity, and his Unity is also shown in how humans cooperate with one another and with nature. Muslims are responsible for maintaining the integrity of the earth, its flora and fauna, its wildlife and natural environment. The Prophet Muhammad said: 'Whoever plants a tree and diligently looks after it until it matures and bears fruit is rewarded.' This applies to all aspects of the natural world.

Islam has a long tradition of **shari'a law**. Part of this relates to the care of the environment, and Muslims use the closely related concepts of **harim** and **hima**.

Harim has to do with the preservation of natural environments, usually by creating a zone of land that cannot be used for housing development or any other purpose. In the harim zone, there will be wells, natural springs, underground water channels and rivers which provide natural ways of preserving whatever vegetation might grow in the area. Legal protection will be given to make sure that no misuse or pollution is caused, and pure fresh water will enable cultivation and improve the natural health and livelihood of an area.

Hima has to do with the ways in which natural resources are managed in a community in order to bring about sustainable livelihood for the inhabitants. This idea goes back the days of the Prophet himself, who perfected the system in the Arabian

Shari'a law
is the legal system derived from Muslim religious principles. It is practised in several Islamic countries.

A harim
is an area or zone set aside for special purpose. One such use is the part of a house reserved for female members of the family. It can also refer to areas of the environment set aside for specific purposes.

Hima
is the Muslim ecological practice of keeping a certain amount of land free from particular human and farming use.

The Children's Eco Village in the Mkurunga district of Tanzania, founded by the humanitarian organization Islamic Help.

peninsula. Hima is widely used in West Asia and North Africa, as well as in India and Indonesia, where Islam has had an important impact. People in a community will share their resources, making sure that animals have enough land to graze on and ensuring that everyone has a say in decisions that affect them, such as the use made of rare resources and conservation.

One example of the ideas of harim and hima may be seen in the Children's Eco Village, located in the Mkurunga district, just outside Dar es Salaam in Tanzania. This project, organized by the Islamic Help charity, started in March 2012. Set in 30 acres of lush green landscape, the Eco Village has started to provide a healthy and flourishing environment for more than 160 orphans to live in, learn and grow. When the village reaches completion, it will have sixteen homes, a sports ground, an eco-mosque, a community centre, a library and a permaculture farm. Over 30,000 trees were planted before 2014, and the target is to plant 100,000 trees, which will provide fruit as well as protect the environment.

World poverty

The facts of **poverty** in the world are startling.

Poverty can be defined as 'not having the minimum income to obtain the necessities of life'. The 'necessities of life' would include food, clean water and shelter. Poverty also means not having the opportunity of an education, access to healthcare or human rights.

- Approximately 1.4 billion people still subsist on less than $1.25 a day, the international poverty line defined by the World Bank.
- Approximately 1 billion people suffer from hunger.
- Almost 9 million children die each year before they reach their fifth birthday.
- Hundreds of thousands of women die every year as a result of complications in pregnancy or childbirth.
- About 69 million school-age children are not in school. Almost half of these (31 million) are in sub-Saharan Africa, and more than a quarter (18 million) are in Southern Asia.

Causes of poverty

There are many reasons why people find themselves in poverty, and some are interconnected.

Population explosion is a major cause of poverty, particularly in many countries in the developing world, which is home to an estimated 84 per cent (nearly 6 billion people) of the world's population. Many people want to have as many children as they can because they know that not all of them will survive into adulthood and because those that do survive can work and improve the family's standard of living.

Malnutrition means not having enough nourishment to develop properly.

Malnutrition is a major cause of poverty. The developing world produces only about 30 per cent of the world's food grain but has 84 per cent of the world's population. Consequently, many people are malnourished and not healthy enough to work. Without the right kind of food, children's health suffers, leading to physical underdevelopment and sometimes to learning difficulties that prevents them from working in later life.

It may seem odd that education should be mentioned in this context but, without education, it is extremely difficult to escape poverty. Poor families cannot afford to send their children to school because they are needed to work on the land to produce food or income. Even if they live near a school, and if the school is free, they cannot afford books. Sometimes the parents cannot read or write so cannot help their children to learn to do so.

Disease leads directly to poverty. People who are undernourished, especially children, are more likely to become ill than those who are well fed. Many children die early because of disease, meaning that the family cannot produce as much food or other goods for sale. Some diseases do not kill but cause serious injury, such as deformity, which means the sufferer cannot work. The average life expectancy of a person in the developing world is about fifty, while in the developed world it is about seventy.

Task

Copy out and complete the grid below. When you have done this, find two other statistics that you think highlight the difference between the developed and the developing world.

Developed world	Developing world
	84 per cent of world population
70 per cent of food grain	
Right to an education	
	Life expectancy of fifty years

Christianity and poverty

The Bible

The Bible has many things to say about poverty, mostly in the context of showing **compassion** to others. Deuteronomy 15:7–8 says: 'If there is a poor man among your brothers in any of the towns of the land that the LORD your God is giving you, do not be hardhearted or tightfisted toward your poor brother. Rather be openhanded and freely lend him whatever he needs.' Just after this (15:11), the author makes the statement that 'there will always be poor people in the land', and commands the people to be 'openhanded toward your brothers and toward the poor and needy in your land.'

Interestingly, it is stated in 1 Samuel 2:7–8 that God is responsible for some people being poor and others being wealthy: 'The LORD sends poverty and wealth; he humbles and he exalts. He raises the poor from the dust and lifts the needy from the ash heap; he seats them with princes and has them inherit a throne of honour.' The message here seems to be that God will provide for people who are in need by showing his compassion for them.

Task

Draw a grid like the one below and fill in the biblical passage, then write what you think it teaches Christians about poverty.

Biblical reference	Biblical text	Teaching for Christians
Psalm 82:3–4		
Psalm 109:31		
Proverbs 14:20–21		
Proverbs 31:8–9		
Isaiah 1:17		
Jeremiah 22:3		

The teaching of Jesus is central to how Christians respond to poverty, and the Gospel of Luke has a number of accounts of Jesus' teaching on wealth and poverty. It is important to note that Jesus came from a humble background, his father Joseph apparently having been a carpenter. He lived simply, with few possessions, as he moved from village to village preaching the message of God to whoever would listen to him. His disciples gave up their homes to follow him, and at his death his only possessions were the clothes he was wearing. Jesus' attitude to wealth seems to have been quite relaxed:

> I tell you, do not worry about your life, what you will eat or about your body, what you will wear. Life is more than food and the body more than clothes. Consider the ravens, how they do not sow or reap, they have no storeroom or barn; yet God feeds them. And how much more valuable are you than birds! (Luke 12: 22–4)

Jesus was well known for going against the prevailing mood of the time. He seems to have actively taught that wealth was worth nothing. In the parable of the Rich Farmer, Jesus taught that wealth was only temporary and would eventually be worthless. The rich farmer, on the basis of a bumper crop one year, decided to pull down his old barns and build much bigger ones. He could afford to take things easy – 'eat, drink and be merry'. Unknown to the rich farmer, however, God had other plans for him: 'But God said to him, "You fool! This very night your life will be demanded from you. Then who will get what you have prepared for yourself?"' (Luke 12:20). The rich farmer's accumulation of wealth was of no ultimate value. As the old saying states, 'You can't take it with you!' Jesus points out that wealth may be useful for some things but it is not valuable in itself – there is no point in having excess amounts of money just to be able to say that you have it.

Taking it further

Luke 18:18–25 states that it would be difficult for a rich man to get into the Kingdom of God – it would be easier for a camel to get through the eye of a needle than for a rich man to get into heaven. (The eye of a needle here refers to a very small gate in Jerusalem, where traders with camels loaded up with goods to sell would have to declare their merchandise to the tax officials!). A rich man had asked Jesus what he needed to do in order to gain eternal life. Jesus told him to keep all the commandments. When the man replied that he already did this, Jesus tested his faith by asking him to do the one thing that Jesus knew the man would find the most difficult – give up his wealth.

Task

Do you think that Jesus should have asked the man to give up his wealth? Give reasons for your answer.

Another story told by Jesus about the relationship between poverty and wealth concerns a rich man and Lazarus (Luke 16:19–31). The rich man was ostentatious – that is, he dressed in clothes of fine linen and in purple (both very expensive). Lazarus was a beggar covered in sores who sat at the rich man's door, begging for scraps. Even the dogs came and licked his sores. Both men died; Lazarus went to heaven, the rich man to hell.

Task

Read the story of the rich man and Lazarus then have a class discussion about what it teaches concerning the value of money.

St Francis of Assisi

Born into a wealthy family in Assisi in 1182, Francis had a religious experience that changed his life. When he was twenty years old, he was on his way to fight a battle, dressed in armour and riding a war horse, when he saw a leper in the road. As he passed the man, he thought he saw the face of Christ in him, and this sight changed Francis's life for ever. He gave up his life of luxury, sold most of his possessions, and began a life of poverty, taking literally the passage in Mark's Gospel where Jesus sends out his disciples to preach the 'good news': 'Take nothing for the journey except a staff – no bread, no bag, no money in your belts. Wear sandals but not an extra tunic' (Mark 6:8–9).

Francis made the decision to be poor. For the next eighteen years he travelled from town to town as Jesus had done, preaching the gospel. He gathered over 3,000 followers before he died at the age of forty-four. His legacy is the Franciscan order of monks, who live according to the principles of poverty he laid down. Francis was made a saint in 1228, just two years after his death, by Pope Gregory IX.

St Francis of Assisi (1182–1226), who was an Italian friar, is now one of the most popular saints among Roman Catholics. He abandoned his family's wealth to live a life of poverty, founding the Franciscan order of monks. He is also patron saint of the natural world.

> **Task**
>
> Find out more about Francis of Assisi – especially how he became committed to the cause of poverty and the difficulties he faced from his family and others.

Modern Christian responses to poverty

As we have seen, Christians have tried to follow the teaching on poverty and wealth in the Bible and the example of Jesus and other well-known Christians. Christians today also follow this teaching and attempt to put their beliefs into action. Some examples of the practical ways in which Christians may help to alleviate poverty are:

- to work with the poor in a developing country, perhaps as a nurse or aid worker
- to perform voluntary service overseas (VSO) in a developing country
- to spend a few hours a week working in a charity shop or participate in collections as part of Christian Aid Week
- to take part in fund-raising activities, such as sponsored events

- to buy Fair Trade products and avoid goods from companies that exploit the poor
- to live a simple lifestyle, buying only what you need; excess money could be donated to charity
- to use a bank that shows concern for developing countries
- to pray regularly for those who work for charities supporting poor people.

One of the ideas listed here is Christian Aid. Christian Aid was founded in 1945 and is the official aid organization for over 140 different Christian denominations and affiliated organizations, originally in the UK and Ireland. It is now a worldwide agency that works to alleviate poverty and respond to humanitarian needs, focusing on two areas: emergency relief and long-term development.

1 *Emergency relief* Christian Aid works with a number of agencies in many countries around the world where there are emergencies, such as floods, natural disasters, earthquakes or famine. For example, in April 2015, there was a devastating earthquake in Nepal that killed more than 8,000 people and injured another 19,000. Many villages were flattened and hundreds of thousands of people were made homeless. On 12 May, a further major aftershock occurred in the same region, killing another 117 people and injuring 2,500 more. In total, over 6 million people were affected. Christian Aid sent £50,000 immediately and assisted other agencies with the coordination of emergency supplies at a government-run camp to provide temporary shelter for homeless people. It appealed to the British public for donations, then sent practical aid such as 100,000 sets of water purification kits, along with food, blankets and tents.

2 *Long-term development* Christian Aid also tackles the causes of poverty and injustice. Rather than waiting for a crisis to occur, it works to change people's lives in the long term. For example, the organization:

- educates people and teaches them skills so that they may be self-reliant rather than being dependent on charity
- teaches people to improve farming methods so that food yields improve
- campaigns for fair pay for workers and for fair working conditions
- provides medicines and sets up health, education and immunization programmes, training local people to become nurses and midwives
- provides education for children, adults and especially women, who are taught skills and crafts so that they can produce goods to sell to support their families. Christian Aid supports women because they are often left alone to bring up children when their husbands are killed in war or by terrorists.

Taking it further

Two examples of the long-term development offered by Christian Aid come from their 2015 fund-raising campaign.

- *Ebola* Pate Bana Marank, a village in northern Sierra Leone, was a peaceful farming village until it became one of the first places in the country to be hit by Ebola. Ebola is a deadly disease spread by physical contact. In this village, it is the custom to touch, wash and prepare a dead person prior to burial. Ten women who did this were unaware that the woman they were dealing with had died of Ebola; they all contracted symptoms and died six days later. The son of this woman also contracted Ebola because he helped to prepare her for burial, as did his father. The boy (John) became an orphan (one of 10,000 orphaned by this disease in Sierra Leone). Thanks to the work of Christian Aid, he was treated and survived, and his education and welfare needs were funded so that he could rebuild his life.

- *Help for Women* For Christian Aid Week in 2015, the story of an Ethiopian woman called Loko was highlighted. She had to forage for firewood in order to raise enough money to feed her child just one meal every day. To do this, she had to walk for miles and carry the wood on her back. She desperately wanted to buy a cow, which would both provide milk for her child and generate money by allowing her to sell the excess milk. The capital she raised could help her to set up a business which would give her a voice in her community. Although she had not had much formal education, she would be able to speak up for the rights of women, challenge domestic violence and put an end to discrimination. Because she was trapped in poverty, she would never have been able to fulfil her dream and help other women in her community had it not been for the donation from Christian Aid.

Roman Catholic responses

In 1987, Pope John Paul II published an encyclical called *Solicitudo Rei Socialis* ('Social Concern'), which raised the following issues.

1 World markets work in favour of the rich, and profits are not shared equally.
2 International debt has crippled poorer economies.
3 There has been too much attention on war and not enough on world poverty. Wars have also caused refugee problems.
4 Problems have been caused because of the rise in the world's population.

The Pope's conclusion was that all the long-term problems of poverty in today's world are *avoidable*. Christian *thinking* is wrong, as people have been concerned only with profit and not with morality. Roman Catholics make two other points: first, that Christians have a duty to inform themselves about the problems of poverty and to pray, think and act to protect the poor (the Church calls this 'having an option for the poor'); and, second, that the Mass is a sharing meal at which people share with one another and God and is the inspiration for Roman Catholics as they think about social questions.

Something that every Roman Catholic can do is support the work of CAFOD – the Catholic Fund for Overseas Development – which was set up in 1962. It has no members as such, as every Catholic is a part of the organization. It makes particular use of the practice of fasting to raise money as well as prayer and education – not only in the developing world but also in the developed world – to raise the awareness among relatively wealthy people about the problems of poverty. CAFOD is involved with a wide variety of issues that concern disadvantaged people in the UK and abroad. Some examples of their interests are:

- campaigning on behalf of poor and elderly people so that they receive the benefits to which they are entitled
- lobbying MPs about local and national issues, such as tax evasion by the wealthy
- organizing petitions about climate change
- producing fact sheets concerning many issues, such as social reforms
- helping victims of a cyclone in Burma
- supporting priests in South America.

CAFOD is also involved in raising money for support work in emergencies, such as the Nepal earthquake mentioned above. It affirms more general Roman Catholic views on the relationship between poverty and wealth, and it agrees that the root cause of poverty is human sin. Humans disobey God's laws and spend more time thinking about politics, power and money than about morality, human rights, justice and fairness. The world is in the state it is because of human greed and selfishness. CAFOD believes that, if humans are the cause of poverty, it is not enough simply to pray about the situation.

Tasks

Compile a fact file on Archbishop Oscar Romero, who spent most of his life helping poor communities in violence-ridden El Salvador in South America.

Read the statement below and decide whether you agree with it or not. You might organize a class debate on this topic.
  'The Christian Church is one of the richest organizations in the world. It should sell all its churches and ornaments and give the money to the poor.'

Muslim responses

The community (**Ummah**) is central to Islam, so Muslims are very concerned about the issues of poverty. The concept of brotherhood means that they wish to help their fellow Muslims who get into financial difficulties. Islam teaches that all wealth comes from God.

Zakah, which teaches that giving to charity is a command from God, is one of the Five Pillars of Islam. Surah 2:110 says: 'Be steadfast in prayer and regular in charity. Whatever good you forward for yourselves, you will find it for God, for God sees what you do.' Zakah is central to the Ummah. Performing Zakah is an obligation for all Muslims: those who can afford to do so should give 2.5 per cent of their income after they have provided for their family. Those who can afford to give more will do so. Those who are very poor do not pay anything but will receive benefit from the donations of others. This benefit may come in terms of what is necessary – food, clothing or whatever is needed.

Ummah
is the Arabic word for people or community and refers to the worldwide Muslim community.

Zakah
is the Muslim belief in giving to charity, which is one of the Five Pillars.

Another aspect of the community in Islam is the giving of Sadaqah, or charitable donations. Such donations should be given by individuals privately, so that the act is known only to God. The poor who benefit from Zakah see it not as charity but as genuine assistance to help them get out of their situation. God purifies those who receive such donations, and they are thought to be helping the wealthy because God blesses those who are able to give Zakah.

Muslim Aid

One Muslim organization that works with poverty-stricken people worldwide is Muslim Aid, which has a presence in more than seventy countries in Africa, Asia and Europe. It strives to help the poor overcome suffering caused by natural disasters and the lack of life's basic necessities, such as clean drinking water and basic food. Muslim Aid responds to international emergencies, such as the 2015 Nepal earthquake, where it worked with partner organizations in the area to set up a camp providing accommodation with shower and toilet facilities, food and medical assistance. There was also a classroom were schoolchildren could continue their education. A spokesperson said: 'Muslim Aid is committed to providing support to the victims of the disaster during this time of great difficulty. We have chosen to set up a camp as this can provide long-term support for those affected by the disaster, and provide some comfort and shelter from the elements for many people who have been made homeless.'

Muslim Aid also works on longer-term strategic programmes to eliminate poverty. These focus on:

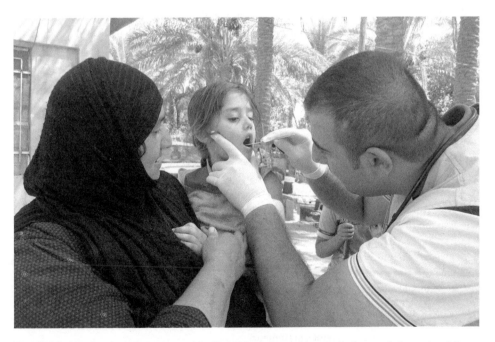

The charitable development agency Muslim Aid carries out humanitarian work throughout the world. Here an aid worker is shown providing healthcare to children in Iraq.

- education
- skills training
- provision of clean water
- healthcare
- income generation projects.

Projects such as these ensure that individuals have access to basic necessities as well as to the skills to make an income so that they are not permanently dependent on aid agencies for food and shelter.

TICK THE TOPICS

You should now tick the relevant boxes to check what you have learned in this chapter.

Sections	Topics	Tick
The environment	Threats to the planet	
	Non-religious responses	
	Christian responses	
	Roman Catholic responses	
	Muslim responses	
World poverty	The facts and causes of poverty	
	Christianity and poverty	
	Christian responses	
	Muslim responses	

Sample questions

AQA Religious Studies A (8062) and Religious Studies B (8063)

1   Which of the following best expresses the religious view of the creation of the world?
    a) Unstable b) Incomplete c) Perfect d) Imperfect   (1 mark)
2   Give two examples of what religious believers would see as threats to the planet. (2 marks)
3   Explain two contrasting beliefs in contemporary British society about ecology.   (4 marks)
4   Explain two religious beliefs about world poverty.   (5 marks)
5   'Ornate religious buildings should be sold to help the poor.'
Evaluate this statement. In your answer, you:
- should give reasoned arguments in support of this statement
- should give reasoned arguments to support a different point of view
- should refer to religious arguments
- may refer to non-religious arguments
- should reach a justified conclusion.   (12 marks)

Edexcel Religious Studies B (1RB0)

a) Give three problems with the environment. (3)
b) Explain two types of ecology. (4)
c) Assess the extent to which religious believers can contribute to solving problems of
   poverty. (9)
d) 'Rich people should pay a special tax to help get rid of poverty.'
Evaluate this statement, considering more than one point of view. (12)

Edexcel International GCSE Religious Studies (4RS0)

a) What is meant by 'malnutrition'? (2)
b) Describe the work of one non-religious organization in combating poverty. (5)
c) Explain how religions can promote the development of multi-faith society. (8)
d) 'Religious people should be as concerned to help the environment as they are to
   help other people.'
Do you agree? Give reasons for your answer, showing that you have considered another
point of view. (5)

WJEC Eduqas Religious Studies (Full Course)

a) Giving one example, state what is meant by 'poverty'. (2)
b) With reference to one religion you have studied, explain how religious humanitarian
   organizations help to address poverty. (5)
c) From two different religions or two religious traditions, explain views on how to
   respond to poverty. (8)
d) 'There is nothing that religious people can do to solve problems of global poverty.'
Discuss this statement, showing that you have considered more than one point of view.
(You must refer to religion and belief in your answer.) (15)
                                                         (SPaG + 6)

12 War and Peace

In this chapter you will be studying the topics of war and peace. First we will need to define what is meant by both terms, whether war is sometimes the only option, how it is legitimated or justified (the state, God), the concepts of holy war and just war, the morality of 'intelligent warfare', attitudes to violence of any kind, pacifism, terrorism, and non-violent protest.

Introducing war

A simple definition of **war** is 'a state of armed conflict between different countries or different groups within a country'. 'War' is an umbrella term, a general term. There are several other names used to describe wars which are essentially subsets of war: conflict, insurgence, battle, rebellion, uprising, invasion, skirmish, intifada and border dispute. If you read or research anything on war, you will probably come across additional terms.

A **war** is when nations take military action against each other.

The statistics of war are frightening. Between 1945 (the end of the Second World War) and 2015, there were at least 273 wars, of which at least thirty-three are ongoing. In 1950, there were an estimated 596,000 deaths from war; in 1990, the number was 72,000, while in 2013 this had dropped to 31,000. Some wars are very well known: the Second World War, the Vietnam War, the Northern Ireland 'Troubles', the Falklands War, the Iraq War, the Kosovo War and the Libyan Civil War. Others are perhaps less well known: the Indo-China War, the Six-Day War, the Gulf War, the Rwandan Civil War or the Algerian War.

Task

Make a grid, list all the wars mentioned above and find out some basic details about each one – when, where, who and why. You should use different colours to record each type of information and then display it in your classroom (teacher permitting!)

The costs of war

Wars are very costly, not just in terms of the amount of money but in many other ways too.

- Fighting a war costs a great deal of money. The Iraq War (2001–14) cost the USA $4.4 trillion. This means that it cost every American taxpayer about $150 per month.
- The human cost of war is the death of or serious injury to many people. Table 12.1 shows the approximate number of deaths resulting from the wars in Afghanistan, Iraq and Pakistan between 2001 and 2015.

Table 12.1   Deaths in Afghanistan, Iraq and Pakistan wars, 2001–2015

	Afghanistan	Pakistan	Iraq	Total
US military	2,357		4,489	6,846
US contractors	3,401	88	3,481	6,970
National military and police	23,470	6,212	12,000	41,682
Other allied troops	1,114		319	1,433
Civilians	26,000	21,500	137,000–165,000	184,000–212,500
Opposition fighters	35,000	29,000	36,400	100,400
Journalists/media workers	25	58	221	304
Humanitarian workers	331	91	62	484
TOTAL (to nearest 1,000)	92,000	57,000	194,000–222,000	343,000–371,000

Source: www.costsofwar.org

Task

Look at these figures carefully, then discuss the points that arise. You will want to compare the number of military deaths with those of civilians, for instance, and you might wish to ask why there were no military deaths in the Pakistan war. Are the deaths of the humanitarian workers more regrettable than those of the opposition fighters? Could the deaths of the journalists have been prevented? Should journalists be present in war zones at all? Try to come up with your own questions and points of view.

- Another cost of war is the destruction of buildings or whole cities. In March 2015, it was reported that the Islamist terrorist group known as ISIS had blown up and bulldozed the ancient city of Nimrud, 30 kilometres south of the Iraqi city of Mosul. Nimrud had been the capital of the Assyrian Empire more than 3,000 years ago and was the home of the famous King Asurnasipal II. Many of the fabulous sculptures and statues and the major buildings in the city were destroyed in a show of ISIS's power. Some of the artefacts from Nimrud had been excavated and saved in the 1840s by a British archaeologist, A. H. Layard, and later by others, many of which are housed in the British Museum in London and the Metropolitan Museum in New York.

  The destruction of cities is not a new phenomenon. In the Bible, it is recorded how Joshua was commanded by God to destroy the city of Jericho (Joshua 6). For more detail on this, see the section below on holy war.

The destruction of war can be seen clearly in this image of Homs in Syria, almost completely destroyed in the ongoing civil war.

Taking it further

'Destroy the past, and you control the future.' How do you think this statement relates to the destruction of Nimrud?

Find out how the Nazis and the Khmer Rouge tried to destroy many treasures.

Reasons for war

It is unusual for there to be just one reason for any particular war, and there is generally a combination of several reasons, such as:

- *to help other nations*: Britain is part of the United Nations and contributes money and soldiers to assist in peacekeeping operations. An example of this would be the Korean War of 1950–53, where Britain went into North Korea to help South Korea as part of a United Nations force. Another example would be the coalition to assist Kuwait in the First Gulf War.
- *to gain extra land or natural resources and therefore to gain wealth*: In the eighteenth and nineteenth centuries, Britain had an empire and fought many wars to gain more natural resources, an example being the Second Boer War of 1899–1902, where Britain was keen to control the diamond and gold mines that were being developed by the Boer republics in the Transvaal. Another example would be Hitler's invasion of the USSR in 1941 in order to seize land.
- *to gain power*: Many wars have been fought to gain power through control of the government. The most famous would be the Wars of the Roses between 1455 and 1487, when the houses of York and Lancaster, both of which were direct descendants of Edward III, fought each other in a series of bloody battles to control the English crown. Another example would be Genghis Khan who, with the Mongol horde, conquered an empire that included most of central Asia and northern China.
- *for freedom*: Boudicca's war in southern Britain in 61 CE was to free the Iceni from Roman administrative control and cultural influence. Another example would be the West's justification of the Cold War.
- *for pride and prestige*: The war of Jenkins' Ear, fought between 1739 and 1742 between England and Spain, gained its name from the activities in 1731 of Spanish coastguards, who boarded an English ship suspected of smuggling and cut off the ear of the captain, Robert Jenkins. Jenkins was brought before the House of Commons in 1738 to give his account, when he apparently showed the MPs his ear (kept in a box); this affront to British honour caused the outbreak of hostilities. In fact, there was a deeper cause of tension between Spain and England, which was the right of the England to sell African slaves in the Central American Empire, ruled by Spain. Another example would be Henry VIII's wars against France. Prestige was a major factor here, though he also wanted land and wealth.
- *for defence*: The war of the Spanish Armada in 1588 was fought in defence of England against the attempt by King Philip II of Spain to invade and to take control of the country.
- *because of oppression*: The War of Magna Carta was fought by barons against King John between 1215 and 1217 because the king refused to abide by the Magna Carta which reduced his power, and on which he had been forced to place his seal. Another example would be the English Civil War (against royal 'tyranny').

- *for religious reasons*: The best examples of this are the crusades that occurred in Europe between 1095 and 1487. Large numbers of English knights followed Richard the Lionheart during the Third Crusade (1189–93) to recapture Jerusalem from Saladin and to return the fragment of the True Cross, captured at the great defeat of the Christian army at Hattin in 1187, to Christian hands. Another example would be the French Wars of Religion of the late sixteenth century between Catholics and Huguenots.

> **Just war theory** attempts to show that some wars are necessary in order to defend justice.

CHRISTIANITY ROMAN CATHOLICISM

Christian attitudes to war

Just war theory

Just war theory is a doctrine to ensure that war is justifiable and sets down a number of conditions that have to be met, or limits to its extent, if war is to be considered 'just' or legally and morally reasonable. The development of the theory is the outcome of many centuries of warring tribes or nations agreeing a code of behaviour to prevent war being totally devastating to either side. So, for instance, the treatment of prisoners or non-combatants such as women and children would be agreed upon before the war began.

Taking it further

In the ancient world, the virtue of 'honour' would be used as a benchmark of whether a war could be justified. This is one of the main themes in Homer's *Iliad*. The concept of honour was central to the Greeks' understanding of their personal and national identity and was seen on different levels:

- *arete*: the honourable man would pursue excellence throughout his life;
- *nobility*: men had to treat each other properly on a personal level – personal regard and honour from one's peers was essential to the proper functioning of society;
- *valour* was obtained by a warrior for his struggles and successes in battle;
- *eternity*: a soldier could gain everlasting fame and glory for his accomplishments in life.

Task

Try to find a modern example of someone who has displayed one or more of these virtues. For instance, you might argue that Winston Churchill displayed the virtue of *arete*. Discuss your findings with your classmates.

There are a few elements of just war theory in the Bible, particularly in the New Testament. Jesus taught in the 'great Commandment' that people should love others as they love themselves (Matthew 22:39). This implies that Christians must try to avoid conflict with others but should defend their own life if threatened by an aggressor. If protecting his or her own life comes at the cost of the aggressor's death, then that is morally justified.

Just war theory was first stated by **St Augustine** (354–430) and most fully developed by **St Thomas Aquinas** (1225–1274). The rules they developed are still used by Christians today.

St Augustine lived at a time when Christianity was the official religion of the Roman Empire. The empire was failing to maintain its control of such a large and complex area and had to fight wars in many places. There was thus a need to establish the most appropriate way to wage war in order to maintain control over the many races in the empire. Augustine came up with two important principles that the political and military leaders put into practice:

Ius ad bellum
describes a set of criteria to show that embarking on war is morally justified.

- the right to go to war (***ius ad bellum***)
- the correct conduct during war (***ius in bello***).

The right to go to war concerns the reasons for believing a nation has a moral right to wage war on another nation. For a war to be 'just', Augustine taught that it should be in defence of others rather than of one's own country and that it must be a last resort, aimed at establishing peace, declared by a legitimate authority and undertaken with honourable aims.

Ius in bello
describes a set of criteria to be used to ensure that war is conducted in a 'just' manner.

St Thomas Aquinas, who developed and expanded on Augustine's thought, took up these principles 800 years later. He argued that there are six principles for a war to be called 'just': the first four are the '*ius ad bellum*' – the reasons why a nation might go to war – while the final two are the '*ius in bello*' – concerning the way in which the war is fought.

1 *Just authority* – the decision to go to war must have been based on a legitimate political and legal process.
2 *Just cause* – a wrong must have been committed so that war is the only appropriate response.
3 *Right intention* – the response must be proportional to the cause – that is, the war must be limited to correcting the wrong done and nothing further.
4 *Last resort* – every other means of righting the wrong must have been tried, so that going to war is the final step.
5 *Reasonable chance of success* – there must be at least a reasonable chance of success in war, otherwise the damage, death and destruction caused would not be morally justifiable.
6 *Not harm innocent people* – civilians should not be involved in the war, and soldiers should not kill or commit crimes against civilians.

Task

Find an example from a war that you know about to illustrate each of the principles above.

Taking it further

Francisco de Vitoria (c.1483–1546) added a further principle about what should happen after a war ends. This is called '*ius post bellum*' and says that the victorious nation must think carefully about how it deals with the damage done during the war. Proper organization of the defeated nation should be a priority, so that its citizens (who should not have been involved in the fighting) will be able to resume their daily lives in safety and health. Things such as local government, transport, supplies of food and water, and so on, must be sorted out by the victors because the defeated people would not be able to do this on their own.

Holy war

A **holy war** is one that is fought for a 'holy' or religious cause. In some ways, the idea that war could be started or sanctioned by a religion seems inconsistent. Religion is generally thought to be about creating a peaceful and harmonious society, whereas war is the opposite of this. There is no formal tradition of holy war in Christianity, but there are some examples of wars that are initiated by God.

In the Bible, the 'wars of Yahweh' (God) are mentioned in Numbers 21:14. Although the term 'holy war' is not used, this is what is meant (the term itself was coined in 1901 by the German scholar Friedrich Schwally). Both these and other wars in the Old Testament were battles dedicated to God's plans for his people, which God not

Ius post bellum describes a set of criteria used to show that justice is maintained after the end of a war.

A **holy war** is a war fought for a religious purpose and is thought to be sanctioned by God.

A nineteenth-century woodcut showing the biblical story of the destruction of Jericho in the Book of Joshua. The walls of Jericho can be seen falling as the Israelites blow horns, and the Ark of the Covenant (containing the tablets of the Ten Commandments) is being carried on the left.

only controlled and directed but in which he was also an active participant. This is illustrated in the account of a battle with the Amalekites in Exodus 17:8–16, where the Amalekites attacked the Israelites as they escaped from slavery in Egypt. The Israelites understood this as an attack on God's goodness, guidance and glory. Moses took the rod of God (a symbol of God's presence and power) to the top of a hill: when he held it in the air, the Israelites had the upper hand'; when he lowered it, the Amalekites began to win. Moses' brother Aaron and his companion Hur helped to hold the rod high, and by the end of the day the Israelites had won the battle. The victory was dedicated to God and was recorded in a special scroll.

The most famous example of a holy war in the Old Testament is the account of the destruction of Jericho (Joshua 6).

Jericho was the first strategic target for the Israelites when they crossed the River

> **Task**
>
> Before you proceed any further in this chapter, read carefully the story of Joshua and Jericho in Joshua 6 and answer the following questions.
>
> - Who initiates the war?
> - How many times do the Israelites march round the city? Why is this number important?
> - Which musical instrument is used? Why this one?
> - Who leads the people as they march round the city?
> - What command is given when the walls collapse? Who issues the command?
> - What happens at the end of the account?

Jordan into the land that they believed God had promised them hundreds of years previously. It was part of the covenant God had made with Abraham. If the Israelites were to fulfil this covenant, they had to start by destroying Jericho. Because God is with them on this journey, it is God who issues the commands through Joshua. They have only to follow these commands to the letter.

The first point to note about Jericho is that God commissioned and authorized the war. He commanded Joshua by a special revelation and told him what to do. God says that he has already delivered Jericho to the Israelites (6:2). Emphasizing that this is a holy war, Joshua commands the priests to carry the Ark of the Covenant round the city at the head of the procession.

The second point about Jericho is that God not only declares the war but also is the primary combatant. The ordinary means of warfare such as battering rams or ladders were not used – only silent marching round the city. The only noise was the blowing of the shofars – special 'trumpets made from rams' horns'. The shofar was a musical instrument that was played in many important events in the Old Testament and is connected in particular with the story of the sacrifice of Isaac in Genesis 22, where Abraham sacrifices a ram instead of his son. A ram was a kosher animal, and the shofar was used to introduce the festivals of Yom Kippur and Rosh Hashanah as well as other festivals. Just as God was with Abraham when he was about to sacrifice Isaac and actively saved him from doing so, so God was with the Israelites at Jericho and made sure that they were victorious.

The third point about Jericho is that its destruction was total and immediate. As soon as Joshua told the people to shout, the walls fell down: 'When the trumpets sounded, the people shouted, and at the sound of the trumpet, when the people gave a loud shout, the walls collapsed; so every man charged straight in, and they took the city' (Joshua 6:20). The repetition of what happened is deliberate and is meant to show the immediate success of God's plan and the power that God had invested in the people to bring this about. The events are stated very simply – the people shouted, the walls fell down, they took the city. There was no long military campaign of attrition, wearing down the inhabitants of Jericho, no bargaining, no lives lost. God made it all happen immediately, and destruction was total.

The final point about Jericho is that the inhabitants were all killed and the treasures of the city were devoted to God. This is the idea of herem, which is very important in the development of holy war. It means 'devoted' or 'set apart' for God. The Israelites thought of God as their king, so, as the victor of a battle, it was his right to claim all the treasures in the city. These treasures then became the personal property of God. This meant that the people were not to take any of the treasure for their own use. If they did, it would be a crime punishable by death. One of the Israelites made this mistake and met this fate (see Joshua 7 for the story of Achan and the consequences of his theft on himself, his family and the Israelites).

One of the questions raised by the story of Jericho is why all the inhabitants of the city had to be killed. We will discuss this question when we look at the issue of mass murder below.

There is no tradition of holy war in the New Testament. The teaching of Jesus was not intended for the Jews alone but for all people of any race or religion. The early Christians believed that Jesus did not believe in violence. While preaching the Sermon on the Mount, Jesus told his disciples:

> You have heard that it was said: 'An eye for an eye, a tooth for a tooth.' But I tell you, do not resist an evil person. If someone strikes you on the right cheek, turn to him the other also. (Matthew 5:38–9)

> Love your enemies, do good to those who hate you, bless those who curse you, pray for those who mistreat you. (Matthew 5:43–4)

> Blessed are the peacemakers, for they shall be called the sons of God. (Matthew 5:9)

When Jesus was being arrested in the Garden of Gethsemane, Peter drew his sword and was about to attack one of the people arresting Jesus, when Jesus said: 'Put your sword back in its place . . . for all who draw the sword shall die by the sword' (Matthew 26:52).

Based on Jesus' teaching, most of the early Christian thinkers taught a form of strict pacifism, and there is little teaching about holy war until around the beginning of the eleventh century. In 1095, Pope Urban II began the First Crusade when he initiated a holy war to recapture Palestine from the Muslims. The promise of forgiveness of any sins committed in war and an automatic place in heaven after death brought many thousands of Christian soldiers to fight on behalf of God's command. They took Galilee and Jerusalem – the most holy places, where Jesus had lived, taught, died and come back to life. The Muslims recaptured Jerusalem in 1144, and a series of battles and campaigns followed until 1261. By this time, the idea of a holy war had become less popular and many people had come to think of the Crusades simply as wars to gain territory that could be used for trade purposes.

Many Christians continued to think that war was acceptable if its purpose was to defend the rights of humans, but that a war fought for God was not compatible with the traditional view of God as loving, caring and forgiving. The idea of holy war has since disappeared from Christian thought and belief.

> **Task**
>
> Summarize early Christian views about holy war.

Later Christian views on war

During the first two centuries CE, Christians would not join the army because they believed the teaching of Jesus, including the quotes we saw above, indicated that it was wrong to kill. Jesus had been killed by the Romans, and Christians saw this as a gross injustice because he was the Son of God who preached agape (unselfish love) towards every person, regardless of their race, religion, gender or social status. To join the army would necessarily mean killing others, and this would go directly against the teaching and person of Jesus. So the early Christians were strictly pacifist.

When Christianity became the official religion of the Roman Empire in the early fourth century, many Christians believed that, as citizens, they ought to defend the empire from outside attackers. So the belief that war could be justified became more acceptable and has remained the view of most Christians until the present day.

> **Taking it further**
>
> ## British army chaplains
>
> The British army has had Christian chaplains since 1796, but it was not until the Crimean War in 1854 that they were deployed in battle. The bravery of the Reverend Henry Press Wright there brought about the financing of more chaplains, and, by the end of the war, sixty chaplains had ministered to the soldiers and twelve had died. The first chaplain to win the Victoria Cross, the highest military honour, was the Reverend James William Adams. In 1836, the Anglican clergy chaplains were joined by Roman Catholics, followed by Presbyterians in 1858, Wesleyans (Methodists) in 1881 and Jews in 1892. Chaplains served with British forces during the First and the Second World War, bringing care, compassion and comfort to the soldiers, even in the most dangerous of battle situations; 179 chaplains died in the first war and ninety-six British and thirty-eight Commonwealth chaplains in the second. Since 1945, chaplains have continued to serve wherever British troops are sent, including Korea, Northern Ireland, the Falklands, Iraq and Afghanistan.

Army chaplains are professionally qualified officers who have been ordained as clergy and chosen to hold a commission in the army. They wear uniforms and exercise leadership but are not in command. They do not bear arms and take no part in fighting. Their main role is to minister to soldiers and their families in three key areas:

- to give spiritual support, both publicly and privately, at every level of the army
- to provide pastoral care at home and abroad
- to offer moral guidance through formal teaching, counsel and pastoral example.

The chaplains minister to every soldier and their family regardless of whether they are members of a religion or not. There is also an imam to the armed forces who offers spiritual support, pastoral care and moral guidance and a Defence Islamic adviser who advises those in charge of the UK armed forces on all Islamic matters. The UK currently has approximately 650 Muslim soldiers, who are able to practise their faith and balance this with the demands of life in the army. For instance, they may wear a full beard as long as this does not conflict with operational needs, such as having to wear breathing apparatus, and female Muslim soldiers may wear trousers and shirts with the sleeves rolled down, so that their arms and legs are covered. Subject to safety and operational considerations – for example, when a helmet is required during operations – a hijab may be worn. Halal food is available. Unless operational requirements mean that this is not possible, Muslims soldiers may pray five times a day and fast during Ramadan.

Task

1 Summarize the role of an army chaplain.
2 Find out about two famous army chaplains: 'Woodbine Willy' and 'Happy Harry Thorpe'. Write a paragraph on each of these, outlining their life and explaining how their faith was shown in their ministry to the soldiers.

Muslim attitudes to war

The word 'Islam' means 'submission', which includes within it the idea of peace, and the greeting that Muslims give to other people is '**Salaam aleikhum**' – 'Peace be with you' – to which the response is 'Aleikhum salaam' – 'Peace be with you too'. One of the ninety-nine names of God is 'Al Salam', which means that God is the source of peace.

Islam is a peaceful religion and is not in favour of violence or war. Surah *al Baqarah* says that Islam is against killing anyone except in a case of self-defence: 'shed no blood amongst you, nor turn out your own people from your homes: and this ye solemnly ratified, and to this ye can bear witness' (2:84). Also, according to Surah *al Anfal*, 'if the enemy incline towards peace, do thou [also] incline towards peace, and trust in God: for He is One that heareth and knows [all things]' (8:61). It is clear, then, that Muslims should trust in God and live peaceful lives. Violence and war should be only a last resort.

ISLAM

Salaam Aleikhum is an Arabic greeting, meaning 'peace be with you'.

A monument to the seventh-century Battle of Badr, one of the few battles led by the Prophet Muhammad mentioned in the Qur'an.

Even though the Prophet Muhammad preached peaceful coexistence with his fellow humans, he was forced to fight against opposition to his teachings. In his early days, he had to fight two battles, each of which lasted only a single day, at Badr and Uhud. Through the rest of his life he had to fight sporadic battles, though the total amount of time involved added up to only a few months. As a result of the Prophet's experience, later Muslims built up rules for how war should be conducted and for the treatment of prisoners that came to be known as jihad.

Jihad

Jihad
Jihad is an Islamic term referring to the religious duty of Muslims to defend their religion. The term is Arabic for 'struggle'.

The word '**jihad**' means 'struggle' or 'effort' and can signify different things depending on the context.

- A Muslim may 'struggle' to live a good life according to the principles of Islam.
- Muslims may have to make a great deal of 'effort' to build up and maintain a society based on Islamic ideals.
- Jihad can also mean a 'holy war'. Muslims understand this in the sense of a war that aims to defend Islam.

The first two of these examples may be called the 'greater jihad', while the last would be called the 'lesser jihad'. Not all people use these terms, however, because some Muslims think of the greater jihad as referring to holy war. The majority probably believe that the greater jihad is the internal personal struggle to live as well as possible according to Islamic principles. Examples might include:

- memorizing the entire Qur'an
- following the Five Pillars as strictly as possible
- doing everything possible to help other people
- overcoming selfish desires
- going on the Hajj.

The lesser jihad is probably better known today by non-Muslims, as it is often used to describe a holy war. In this sense, a jihad is permissible in Islamic law only as a defensive war. There are strict rules about how such a war should be fought.

1 *The war must only be fought in self-defence*, so a war that was waged in order to conquer another country would not be a jihad.
2 *The war must strengthen Islam*, so it should be declared by a religious leader, not a political one.
3 *The war must be fought to protect the right of Muslims to practise their faith*, so fighting a dictator could be justified if he was not allowing Muslims to worship.
4 *The war must only be fought until the enemy lays down its arms*, so enemy prisoners must be treated humanely.
5 *The war must not involve women, children, elderly or ill people.*
6 *Trees and crops must not be damaged.*

A jihad can never be fought legitimately to force anyone to convert to Islam, to settle disputes, or to colonize another nation.

Task

Read the following excerpts from the Qur'an and explain how they support the idea of jihad.

If two sides quarrel, make peace between them. But if one trespasses beyond bounds against the other, then fight against the one that transgresses until it complies with the law of God; and when it complies, then make peace between them with justice, and be fair. (Surah 49:9)

Goodness and evil cannot be equal. Repay evil with what is better, then he who was your enemy will become your intimate friend. (Surah 41:34)

Fight in the cause of God against those who fight you, but do not transgress limits. God does not love a transgressor. (Surah 2:190)

Task

According to Islam, an act of terrorism can never be justified as a jihad. Organize a class discussion concerning the reasons behind this ruling and whether members of the so-called Islamic State can actually call themselves Muslims.

Pacifism

Pacifism
is the view that it is always wrong to use violence against another person or nation.

The word '**pacifism**' comes from the Latin words *pax*, meaning peace, and *ficus*, meaning 'making'. Pacifism, then, means making a commitment to a peaceful life and opposing war. There are two main types, which may be called 'absolute' or 'principled' pacifism and 'qualified' or 'conditional' pacifism.

Absolute pacifists are, as the name suggests, against war in absolutely any circumstances. They believe that any form of war is wrong because it necessarily results in the loss of human life. All humans have a duty to preserve human life, and going to war conflicts with this duty. Qualified pacifists take the view that war is to be avoided unless it is really the last option available. They believe that war rarely, if ever, brings any benefits to anyone. Innocent people – civilians and children – will inevitably suffer or die, so any government should take that possibility very seriously before committing to a war.

A **conscientious objector**
is someone who refuses to fight in a war because of their pacifist beliefs.

Pacifists (of either type) have often been treated harshly by people in times of war. Even their families and friends can turn against them because they refuse to fight or if they campaign against the war. During the First World War, many pacifists, known as **conscientious objectors**, were imprisoned because they would not join the armed forces. One such person was the famous philosopher and mathematician **Bertrand Russell**, who spent nine months in prison and was fined £100. Some pacifists offered their help in other ways, such as assisting injured soldiers in ambulance units in France or working in factories in Britain. As the war dragged on, there was more and more opposition to 'conshies', and many were shunned by their families.

Christianity and pacifism

CHRISTIANITY ROMAN CATHOLICISM

Many conscientious objectors were opposed to war because they held Christian beliefs: Jesus had been a pacifist, so all Christians should follow his example. Probably the most famous use of pacifism is in the Sermon on the Mount in Matthew 5, where Jesus says 'Blessed are the peacemakers'. While pacifism has traditionally been a specifically Christian belief, there are now pacifists who belong to other religions and to none. There were and still are several Christian pacifist organizations. Two that are well known are the **Quakers**, or Religious Society of Friends, and the Roman Catholic group **Pax Christi International**.

Quakers

The Quakers or Religious Society of Friends is a Christian group that was founded in reaction to the militarism of the English revolution. In 1650, George Fox, the founder, preached that something of God could be found in every person, and he spent his life working for peace and justice through non-violent means. By 1660, the Quakers had produced a 'Peace Declaration', which has become the most famous Christian declaration against war:

> We utterly deny all outward wars and strife; and fightings with outward weapons, for any end or under any pretence whatsoever. And this is our testimony to the whole world. The Spirit of Christ, by which we are guided, is not changeable, so as to command us from a

The Quakers – also known as the Religious Society of Friends – is a pacifist Christian denomination.

thing as evil and again to move us into it. And we do certainly know, and so testify to the world, that the Spirit of Christ, which leads us into all truth, will never move us to fight and war against any man with outward weapons, neither for the Kingdom of Christ nor for kingdoms of this world.

Quakers believe that non-violence challenges war, violence and injustice by focusing on the reasons why people are violent or governments argue for war. They say that violence is an oppressive use of power, leading to fear. The Quaker view attempts to create alternative approaches so that conflict may be resolved peacefully.

Pax Christi International

'Pax Christi' is Latin for 'the peace of Christ'. This is an international Roman Catholic organization whose mission is 'to transform a world shaken by violence, terrorism, deepening inequalities, and global insecurity'. It began in France at the end of the Second World War, when its founders, Marthe Dortel-Cluzdot and Bishop Pierre-Marie Théas, wanted to bring about reconciliation between the French (who had suffered greatly under the Nazi regime) and the Germans (who had killed many French people). Today, it is a global organization represented in more than fifty countries and across five continents with NGO status at the United Nations. Its key belief is that peace across the world is possible and that cycles of violence and injustice can be broken. It pays special attention to both the positive and the negative impact of religion in trying to resolve conflicts. Pax Christi operates in two different areas:

ROMAN CATHOLICISM

- it responds to requests for help from local peace groups in regions experiencing conflict;
- it supports international initiatives on important and urgent issues such as banning landmines, cutting down trade in weapons, establishing an international court and abolishing nuclear weapons.

'The mission of reconciliation which motivated our founders continues to inspire and drive our commitment to work for a more just and peaceful world.' (www.paxchristi.net)

> **Task**
>
> Find out about the Anglican Pacifist Fellowship and World Peace Day (a Roman Catholic feast day) and write a brief paragraph on each, showing what their aims are and how they help to promote peace.

Islam and pacifism

The **Muslim Peace Fellowship**, founded in 1994 and based in New York, is dedicated to the theory and practice of non-violence. It is made up of Muslims of all backgrounds and works peacefully to bring about social change in the spirit of the Prophet's teachings.

The Sufi branch of Islam is sometimes called pacifist because its members value a peaceful lifestyle and outlook. Sufis aim to live according to an inner, spiritual life, to purify themselves so as to achieve union with God through direct religious experience. In this respect, some Sufis are non-violent and could therefore be called pacifists. On the other hand, the history of Sufism shows that some of their leaders led armed uprisings during the Ottoman Empire, while others led rebellions against British, French and Libyan colonial powers. Given this information, then, it would be wrong to say that all Sufis are pacifists, but it could be argued that their lifestyle of spiritual development is one that promotes a non-violent outlook.

Non-religious pacifism

The **International Day of Peace** is a non-religious observance of the ideal of peace around the world that is organized by the United Nations and has been celebrated on 21 September each year since 1982. It is dedicated to world peace, particularly the ending of war and violence, and the idea is to encourage all warring nations to hold a ceasefire on this day. A different theme is taken every year. In 2013, it was peace education, which is seen as the best way to reduce war in the long term. In 2014, the theme was the Right to Peace, restating the UN's commitment to the right of all people to be able to live in peace. Peace is vital if people are to enjoy their human rights.

Task

Look up the UN website (www.un.org) and search for the latest information about International Peace Day. How appropriate do you think the theme for the year is? Why? You should also look at the 'Day of Peace' DVD to gain a better understanding of this topic.

TICK THE TOPICS

Now you should tick the relevant boxes to check what you have learned in this chapter.

Sections	Topics	Tick
War	Definitions and statistics of war	
	Costs of war	
	Reasons for war	
Christian attitudes to war	Just war theory and holy war	
	Later Christian views on war	
Muslim attitudes to war	Jihad	
Pacifism	Quakers	
	Pax Christi International	
	Islam and pacifism	
	International Day of Peace	

Sample questions

AQA Religious Studies A (8062), Religious Studies B (8063) and Religious Studies B Short Course (3RB0)

1 Which of the following best expresses the religious ideal that there should be no war?
   a) Deterrence b) Defence c) Peace d) Justice   (1 mark)
2 Give two ways in which religious believers can help victims of crime.   (2 marks)
3 Explain two contrasting beliefs in contemporary British society about asylum
   seekers.   (4 marks)
4 Explain two religious beliefs about war.   (5 marks)
5 'There can be no such thing as a holy war.'
Evaluate this statement. In your answer, you:
   ● should give reasoned arguments in support of this statement
   ● should give reasoned arguments to support a different point of view
   ● should refer to religious arguments
   ● may refer to non-religious arguments
   ● should reach a justified conclusion.   (12 marks)

Edexcel Religious Studies B Full Course (1RB0) and Short Course (3RB0)

a) Give three kinds of war.   (3)
b) Explain two reasons why countries go to war.   (4)
c) Assess whether religions are responsible for many wars.   (9)
d) 'Religions should be more active about ending wars.'
Evaluate this statement, considering more than one point of view.   (12)

Edexcel International GCSE Religious Studies (4RS0)

a) What is a 'just war'?   (2)
b) Describe the work of one religious organization in promoting peace.   (5)
c) Explain why religious believers might go to war.   (8)
d) 'All religious believers should be pacifists.'
Do you agree? Give reasons for your answer, showing that you have considered another
point of view.   (5)

OCR Religious Studies Full Course (J625) and Short Course (J125)

a) Give three forms of violence.   (3)
b) Outline a religious response to terrorism.   (6)
c) Explain why war is a severe challenge for some religious believers.
You should refer to sources of wisdom and authority in your answer.   (6)
d) 'Religious believers should only fight in a holy war.'
Discuss this statement. In your answer, you should draw on your learning from across
your course of study, including reference to beliefs, teachings and practices within your
chosen religion.   (15)
                                                                         (SPaG + 3)

13 Crime and Punishment

In this chapter, you will be studying the important social issue of crime and punishment. First, you will be deciding what counts as a crime and whether all crimes ought to be punished or if there are some where there are good reasons for not inflicting a punishment. Then you will look at the different aims of punishment and at both religious and non-religious views of what punishment is for. Finally you will focus on the very contentious issue of capital punishment – whether there are good reasons for arguing that some crimes, such as murder, are so serious that the only appropriate punishment is the death of the criminal.

Introducing crime

A **crime** is an act that someone does, or fails to do, that breaks a public law – a violation of some public right or duty agreed upon by a whole community. The offender who commits a crime is punishable by the law that he or she has broken.

> A **crime**
> is an action that
> breaks a law.

The term 'crime' is used in various ways, most often in its legal sense, but sometimes when it has to do with morality. According to the Office for National Statistics, in 2014:

- there were an estimated 6.9 million crimes against households and people aged sixteen and over in England and Wales (this figure covers a broad range of victim-based crimes and includes those that do not come to the attention of the police).
- while the estimate of all crime was lower than in the previous year, the apparent fall was not statistically significant compared with the previous year; the only

major category to show a statistically significant fall was theft offences, which decreased by 7 per cent.

- there was a 2 per cent increase in police recorded crime compared with 2013, with 3.8 million offences recorded in the year ending December 2014. This increase is probably due to a changed policy by the police to record more reported crimes.
- crimes of violence against the person were up by 21 per cent and public order offences were up by 14 per cent.
- the total number of sexual offences rose by 32 per cent, with the numbers of rapes (26,703) and other sexual offences (53,559) being at the highest level ever recorded since 2002–3; this is probably explained by improvements in how this type of crime is recorded and on account of a greater willingness of victims to come forward.
- fraud offences increased by 9 per cent.

Task

Look at the list below and decide which ones should be called crimes. Give reasons for your answers.

1 Someone drives at 45 mph in a 30 mph zone.
2 Someone drives at 45 mph in a 30 mph zone because they are rushing their child to hospital in an emergency.
3 Someone drives at 31 mph in a 30 mph zone.
4 Someone drives on a public road when they do not have a licence to drive.
5 Someone takes a chocolate bar from a shop without paying for it.
6 A businessman does not declare all his income on his annual tax form.
7 A group of thirteen-year-old girls play a ball game on a piece of public land that is signed 'No Ball Games'.
8 A group of thirteen-year-old boys shout abuse at a man who tells them off for throwing stones at cars.
9 A homeowner stabs and kills a burglar who has broken into his house.
10 A man, who can swim, watches as someone he does not like drowns in the sea.

Task

Look at the following figures on illegal drug use in Britain. The figures relate to 2013–14. Are you surprised by these figures? Do you think that any/some/all of the illegal drugs mentioned should remain illegal? Do you think these drugs should be illegal in the first place? Give reasons for your answer.

Around one in eleven adults aged sixteen to fifty-nine – 8.8 per cent – had taken an illegal drug in the past year. However, this proportion more than doubled, to 18.9 per cent, when looking at the age subgroup of sixteen- to 24-year-olds. Levels of drug use in 2013–14 were higher than in 2012–13, when 8.1 per cent of sixteen- to 59-year-olds and 16.2 per cent of sixteen- to 24-year-olds had taken an illegal drug. However, these figures were both lower than those in 1996.

Cocaine, ecstasy, LSD and ketamine use increased between 2012–13 and 2013–14. However, there were no statistically significant decreases in the use of any individual drug types among sixteen- to 59-year olds between 2012–13 and 2013–14. Around one-third of adults had taken drugs at some point during their lifetime. Of sixteen- to 59-year olds, 35.6 per cent had reported ever using drugs.

Should crimes always be prosecuted?

When a crime has been reported and investigated, the police have to make a decision whether to prosecute the offender (i.e., charge them and take them to court). For some people, this should be a straightforward decision – if someone commits a crime, they should be prosecuted. Another view is that the decision to prosecute depends on several things, so that the person who commits a crime may or may not be prosecuted.

The decision to charge someone for a crime is generally based on two factors:

- whether there is enough evidence to give a realistic prospect that the person will be found guilty
- whether the prosecution is in the 'public interest'.

The question as to evidence is up to the professional judgement of the police officers involved. They will only prosecute if they think the evidence is very strong; the

A statue of Justice, traditionally portrayed blindfold (i.e., not prejudiced) and holding a sword (to deal out punishment) and scales (to weigh evidence). However, the ethics of right and wrong, crime and punishment, are not straightforward.

risk that the case might fail could cause embarrassment to the police and would be a waste of public money (the courts are funded by the public purse).

If a person is to be charged, many things have to be taken into consideration, such as:

- if he was a ringleader in the crime
- if he was in a position of public trust (a teacher or a politician, for example)
- if he had previous convictions
- if he committed the crime while under a court order.

The type of offence committed is also taken into account, and the offender is more likely to be taken to court if the crime:

- was premeditated
- was carried out by a group
- was committed in front of a child
- was motivated by discrimination of any sort (racism or disability, for example)
- is widespread in the area (alcohol-related crimes or youth anti-social behaviour, for example).

One of the things the police have to do is to reinforce what is considered to be acceptable behaviour in society, and this will have an effect on whether an offender is charged with a crime. For instance, it is usually considered inappropriate for people to walk naked in public or to carry openly racist placards. On the other hand, there may be circumstances that lead the police to decide not to prosecute someone who has committed a crime – for example:

- if the person is already serving a sentence and prosecution is unlikely to lead to an increased sentence
- if the person is elderly or is suffering from mental or physical ill health, prosecution may not be in the public interest.

One example that illustrates how the police deal with a case is the following.

A mother and father helped their 23-year-old severely paralysed son to travel to Switzerland to the Dignitas clinic to die by euthanasia. Later, the parents were questioned by the police. Although there was sufficient strong evidence to prosecute them for assisted suicide, it was decided that this would not be in the public interest. The parents had acted in the best interests of their son, who wanted to die because of his disabilities, and to have taken them to court would have led to their further suffering. Prosecution would have meant great expense to the public for little or no benefit to society.

Tasks

1 Do you agree with the police decision in this particular case?
2 Do you agree that the principles of evidence and public benefit are the best ones in all cases?
3 Are there other principles that the police should use in dealing with crimes? Give your reasons.

Taking it further

What is justice?

Justice is defined as the quality of being fair and reasonable to everyone, regardless of their social position. Words such as impartiality, unbiased, neutral, unprejudiced and open-mindedness are all used in the context of justice. There is a long history of philosophical discussion about justice, starting with Plato and continuing to present-day philosophers such as John Rawls and Michael Sandel. Here, we will discuss briefly three important theories about the nature of justice that you might wish to investigate further.

The first of these theories is **divine command theory**, which argues that justice is commanded by God (or, for Plato, the gods). Murder would be morally wrong, for example, because God commands that that is the case, and for no other reason. Plato questioned this idea in the **Euthyphro dilemma**, where he asked if what is morally good is good because God commands it to be so or whether God commands it to be good because it is already morally good?

Plato is implying one of two things. The first is that justice is willed by God, who is the source of morality. Humans act morally when they obey God's commands. This means that God is separate and above moral commands – but what if God changes his mind about a moral command? For instance, at one time, God might rule that capital punishment is morally right, but at another that it is morally wrong. God would appear to be arbitrary in his judgements and commands. This would not be consistent with the usual view of God's nature. Plato's second suggestion is that morality and justice are not established by God's commands. Rather, God simply confirms moral values that exist independently of him. This would mean that God is limited and therefore not in control of morality and justice.

Scholars have debated this dilemma since Plato's time, and most agree that it is a false dilemma – that is, an either/or answer cannot be given. Most Christians, for instance, will say that moral goodness is part of the nature of God and that this is necessarily shown in his moral commands. Our idea of good and justice, therefore, is justified because we know that God is good by nature and he would not command anything that went against this.

The second theory of justice is that of distributive justice. One form of this comes from the modern philosopher **John Rawls** (1921–2002), who argued that 'fairness' was the most important concept in justice. If a society is to exist peacefully and successfully, justice must be distributed impartially among the citizens. Every citizen must have equal rights, and this means that those who are disadvantaged should have access to equal opportunities for employment and benefits that society offers. The justice system must operate in a purely fair and needs-blind way. Everyone should receive what they deserve.

The third theory of justice is that of retributive justice. This focuses on issues of punishment for wrongdoing. One version of this is seen in the Old Testament, where justice is believed to come from and is exercised by God. For instance, God gave

Divine command theory is the belief that what is right is commanded by God.

The **Euthyphro dilemma** is a problem in ethics as to whether things are good because God says so, or if God says things are good because they are already good.

Moses the Ten Commandments and other laws of the Torah to show the Israelites the correct way to govern their society. The Torah was, and still is, the standard by which all Jews were to live in their society. God is praised because 'Righteousness and justice are the foundation of your throne; love and faithfulness go before you' (Psalm 89:14).

God's justice is shown in the Torah by the set of rules given by God. As long as these are obeyed by the people, God will remain happy and the Jews will benefit from his love and mercy. If they break his laws, God will punish them. One example of retributive justice in action occurs at Exodus 32, the incident of the Gold Calf, where some of the Israelites build a false god to worship while Moses is talking to God on Mount Sinai. Worship of other gods is strictly forbidden by God, and the punishment (God's retribution) is death. So that justice is seen to be done, Moses is commanded to kill the 3,000 Israelites for their disobedience and lack of faith.

Punishment refers to the actions taken against criminals (or those who have done wrong) as a consequence of their crime.

Retribution describes a type of punishment which seeks to inflict the same kind of suffering on a criminal as the criminal inflicted on their victim.

Restitution describes a type of punishment that focuses on the criminal making up for the damages or harm they have done.

Deterrence is a strategy to dissuade someone from doing something, such as attempting to stop a person from committing a crime.

Purposes of punishment

It generally goes without saying that those who have done something wrong should be punished. It is important that those who impose the **punishment** on criminals have a good reason for so doing. People disagree about the purpose of punishment, however, and we need to look at the main reasons that are put forward. There are five possible reasons to consider.

1 *Retribution* Because the criminal has harmed a person or society, society has the right to harm the criminal.
2 *Protection* Society has the right to be protected from criminals, so criminals must be put in prison to make sure that they do not harm innocent people.
3 *Restitution* The victims of crime have a right to receive some compensation for having been harmed. This is provided by the punishment of the criminal.
4 *Deterrence* If people know that they will be punished, they might think twice about committing a crime.
5 *Reform* The punishment changes the criminal into a useful, law-abiding member of society.

It is necessary for at least one of these reasons to be present if a punishment of a person is to be justified. The first three have to do with the needs of society, particularly the victims of crime, while the other two concentrate on the needs of the criminal.

Retribution and protection sometimes go together as reasons for punishment, because they seem to help members of the public cope with the emotions raised by very serious crimes against children, the disabled, the elderly, the weak and the vulnerable in society. It is argued that all sections of society need to be protected from serial killers or those who prey on vulnerable people. They should not only be locked up in prison but forced to live a miserable life while there.

Others argue that imprisoning offenders is not a long-term solution to the problems of crime. Criminals must be reformed. Prison must teach them that they have

What is the purpose of imprisonment? To protect society from dangerous criminals? To punish those who have committed a crime? Or to rehabilitate people so that they can become law-abiding members of society?

done wrong, and they must be led to a position where they recognize this and then start to think more positively about how they can repay society when they are eventually released from prison. This is where they can become rehabilitated into society.

> **Task**
>
> Which of the purposes of punishment do you think is most appropriate? Why?

Forgiveness is a process by which a victim changes their negative emotions about something that happened to them into positive ones and pardons those who have hurt them.

Christian views on punishment

Neither the Roman Catholic Church nor the Protestant denominations have an 'official' opinion on the general issues surrounding punishment. As you will see below, they do have views on capital punishment. All Christians look to the Bible as their main source of authority for the general principles to be used when it comes to punishing wrongdoers. There are two important general principles to be borne in mind: justice and **forgiveness**.

The first mention of punishment in the Bible is when Adam and Eve are told by God not to eat the fruit of the tree of the knowledge of good and evil: 'But of the tree of the knowledge of good and evil you shall not eat, for in the day that you eat of it you shall surely die' (Genesis 2:17). Until this point, Adam and Eve were immortal, so the threatened punishment for eating the fruit – death – was very severe. Their death

CHRISTIANITY
ROMAN
CATHOLICISM

was not immediate, of course; they lived for many years and had a family. The punishment for disobeying God's command was deserved and just.

There are many other passages in the Bible that show elements of God's justice in punishing people. Here are some examples.

> Behold, all souls are mine; the soul of the father as well as the soul of the son is mine: the soul who sins shall die. (Ezekiel 18:4)

> The soul who sins shall die. The son shall not suffer for the iniquity of the father, nor the father suffer for the iniquity of the son. The righteousness of the righteous shall be upon himself, and the wickedness of the wicked shall be upon himself. (Ezekiel 18:20)

> Repent therefore, and turn again, that your sins may be blotted out. (Acts 3:19)

> Therefore, just as sin came into the world through one man, and death through sin, and so death spread to all men because all sinned. (Romans 5:12)

> Do not be deceived: God is not mocked, for whatever one sows, that will he also reap. (Galatians 6:7)

> For we must all appear before the judgement seat of Christ, so that each one may receive what is due for what he has done in the body, whether good or evil. (2 Corinthians 5:10)

> For our sake he made him to be sin who knew no sin, so that in him we might become the righteousness of God. (2 Corinthians 5:21)

> Then desire when it has conceived gives birth to sin, and sin when it is fully grown brings forth death. (James 1:15)

> Then Death and Hades were thrown into the lake of fire. This is the second death, the lake of fire. (Revelation 20:14)

One thing to note here is the use of the term 'sin'. In the Bible, sin is a very serious matter. It means that a person has broken one of God's laws but also that, in doing so, they have made an attack on God himself. Exodus 20:5 says: 'I the Lord your God am a jealous God, visiting the iniquity of the fathers upon the children to the third and fourth generation of those who hate me.' God's punishment for sinful behaviour will affect not only the person who commits the sin but also the children, the grandchildren and the great-grandchildren of the sinner. This would have served as a very serious deterrent to anyone in the ancient world, as families were seen as a blessing from God, and no one would want to inflict suffering on them if that could be avoided.

In the New Testament, there is a continuation of the theme of punishment for sin but there is also a lot of teaching about God's forgiveness. This new emphasis comes into Christianity through the teaching and example of Jesus. Jesus died to bring an end to the sins of humanity and forgiveness from God. **Forgiveness** is one of the most important themes in the teaching of Jesus.

- As he was dying on the cross, Jesus asks God to 'Forgive them, they do not know what they are doing' (Luke 23:34).
- When Peter asked Jesus how often he should forgive others, Jesus replied 'Not seven times, but I tell you, seventy-seven times' (Matthew 18:22).
- A woman who had been caught in adultery (for which the Torah's punishment would be stoning to death) was brought to Jesus (John 8:1–11). He told the crowd

that whichever of them had never sinned should throw the first stone. Obviously, no one could, so the woman was set free and the crowd disappeared. Jesus told the woman, 'I do not condemn you. Now go and leave your life of sin.'

Jesus taught that forgiveness for sin requires repentance by the sinner. The word he uses here – *metanoia* – has the idea of making a complete turnaround and doing the opposite thing. It is an active word, so the sinner has to 'do' something that takes them away from their sin and moves them towards something better and more Godlike. Christians who sin must actively work to stop sinning and start being authentically Christian.

The sacrament of reconciliation, involving confession and absolution (forgiveness) of sins, is a central part of Roman Catholic religious practice.

Tasks

1 Write a sentence on the difference between 'crime' and 'sin'.
2 Explain how a Christian might use the principle of justice in a case of theft.
3 Explain how a Christian might use the principle of forgiveness in a case of physical assault.
4 Look up the stories of Joseph and how he forgave his brothers (Genesis 37–50) and the story of the Prodigal Son and how the father forgave his son (Luke 15). Write a summary of each story, showing why the forgiveness was needed and how Joseph and the father forgave their family members.

ISLAM

Muslim views on punishment

Surah 16:90 says: 'God orders justice and good conduct and giving to relatives and forbids immorality and bad conduct and oppression. He admonishes you that perhaps you will be reminded.' The concept of **justice** is very important in Islam. The Arabic term **al-adl**, one of the ninety-nine beautiful names of God (Surah 6:115), means putting things in their correct place, so that, when God created the universe, he put everything in its correct place in order that all would function as he intended. Justice also has the idea of being in the middle of two extremes, so that a 'just' society is one that allows its citizens to live their lives as they wish, but which also has laws that regulate their behaviour. For example, giving **Zakah**, one of the Five Pillars of Islam, puts justice into action because Muslims want to eliminate the injustices associated with poverty.

> **Al-Adl**
> is one of the ninety-nine names of God in Islam, meaning 'the Just'.

This idea of justice relates to punishment because 'fair treatment' (= justice) has to be applied both to law-abiding citizens who want to live their lives free of trouble and crime and to criminals who want to abuse the laws. Justice is the way that good Muslims can live according to the laws of God. In Islam, the way that criminals are punished focuses on the protection of society rather than on the punishment of the criminal.

The basis of the Islamic justice system is **Shari'a law**. Muslims believe that this came down from God into Islamic practice through the Prophet Muhammad. Muslim society is regulated by a certain number of laws such as the Five Pillars of faith, and Shari'a interprets these so that the most appropriate punishment can be meted out to wrongdoers. There are four main reasons for punishment in Islam:

1   to protect society, so that everyone can live according to Islamic principles and develop both personally and spiritually in society;
2   to make restitution, so that members of society feel that they can live safely and that criminals have been punished appropriately for what they have done;
3   to deter those who might be tempted to commit a crime;
4   to reform the criminal, so that they can become law-abiding members of society.

The Islamic justice system is based on five general areas of life which have to do with how Muslims should conduct their lives. The example given for 'reason' below shows how, if someone drinks alcohol, they can lose their ability to think properly. If they cannot think properly, they may do something that puts them or others in danger.

- Life   example: murder
- Religion   example: apostasy (leaving the religion, then criticizing it)
- Reason   example: drinking alcohol
- Family   example: fornication, adultery
- Property   example: theft

> **Hadd**
> is a punishment fixed in the Qur'an for sins against the rights of God.

Muslims think that protecting these five areas of life is essential to the welfare of society.

Under Shari'a law, a number of punishments are laid down by the Qur'an that must be applied to certain crimes. These are called **hadd** (singular) or **hudud** (plural) and include public lashing, public stoning to death, amputation of hands or feet, and public execution. Surah 5:33 says:

> the punishment of those who wage war against Allah and His Messenger, and strive with might and main for mischief through the land is: execution or crucifixion, or the cutting off of hands and feet from opposite sides or exile from the land.

The way that these punishments are applied differs between Islamic countries, with public stoning and executions taking place only in Saudi Arabia and Iran, which practise the strictest interpretation of Shari'a.

Capital punishment

Capital punishment is where a person is legally put to death for the crime they have committed by an executioner who is the agent of the state or a legitimate authority. Capital punishment has been illegal in Britain since 1965, and the last person to be executed was Ruth Ellis, in 1955, for shooting dead her violent lover, David Blakely. There were many public debates about the Ellis case, and strongly held views on both sides of the argument about capital punishment.

> **Capital punishment** is the sentencing to death and execution of someone for very serious crimes, such as murder.

Arguments in favour of capital punishment

- It is the ultimate retribution for the most serious crimes, such as murder. For some people, this is an instance of natural justice – a life for a life.
- It is the ultimate protection of society, as the criminal cannot harm anyone else.
- It is a strong deterrent to anyone contemplating murder or another very serious crime.
- It helps the victim's family to come to terms with their loved one's murder.

Arguments against capital punishment

- There have been many mistakes where innocent people have been executed. Since the abolition of the death penalty in the UK, there have been a number of people who have been pardoned and released from prison many years after the crime they allegedly committed. If the death penalty had still been legal, they would have been dead. It is not possible to bring the dead back to life.
- There is something contradictory about a legalized death penalty. On the one hand, the state says 'murder is wrong' but, on the other hand, it effectively murders people and says 'murder is right'.
- Sometimes, the executed person can become a martyr and a figurehead, becoming even more important to their cause after their death.
- There is almost always a long time between someone being sentenced to death and the actual execution. There are hundreds of convicts on America's 'Death Row' who have been there for years. This is a serious punishment in its own right and has a real psychological effect on the prisoner and his family.

- There have been many cases in the USA where executions have gone wrong: the deadly drugs have not been administered correctly and the prisoner has suffered in agony before death. This seems a barbaric and uncivilized way to end anyone's life.

Tasks

1 Research the case of Ruth Ellis. Write a brief summary of the case and decide whether or not you agree that she should have been hanged.

2 Ellis's executioner was Albert Pierrepoint, who executed over 400 people but who, in his autobiography, wrote that he was against capital punishment, arguing that it achieved nothing. Research his life and discuss what affect executing people had on him.

3 Find out about the case of teenager Derek Bentley, who was hanged in 1953 for the murder of a policeman. He was pardoned forty-five years after his death.

4 Having read the arguments for and against capital punishment, what is your own view on the issue? Give reasons for your opinion.

5 Do you think it is possible to reform a murderer? Give reasons for your answer.

6 Should a child who commits murder be treated in the same way as an adult murderer? Give reasons for your answer.

Church of England views on capital punishment

Article 37 of the Thirty-Nine Articles of the Church of England (1563) states that 'the Laws of the Realm may punish Christian men with death, for heinous and grievous offences' – that is, it was the case in the sixteenth century that Church of England ministers officially agreed with capital punishment. Anglican priests today, however, are not bound by the Thirty-Nine Articles.

There were many debates on capital punishment before the death penalty was abolished in Britain in 1965. In a debate in the House of Lords in 1948, only one bishop, George Bell of Chichester, voted for abolition, on the basis that capital punishment was against the teaching of the Bible. By 1956, the year after Ruth Ellis was hanged, eight bishops voted for abolition and one against, while, in 1969 (the year the 1965 Act was made permanent), nineteen bishops voted for abolition and only one against. However, this vote went against the feeling of the general public, 85 per cent of whom wanted to retain capital punishment.

The General Synod of the Church of England debated capital punishment in July 1983 and the following motion was carried: 'That this Synod would deplore the reintroduction of capital punishment into the United Kingdom sentencing policy.' The subject has not been debated by Synod since 1983.

Roman Catholic views on capital punishment

Until the Middle Ages, all Christians believed that capital punishment was part of God's plan of salvation. St Thomas Aquinas was in agreement, as was **Pope Innocent III** (1161–1216), who stated that 'The secular power can, without mortal sin, exercise judgement of blood, provided that it punishes with justice, not out of hatred, with

CHRISTIANITY

ROMAN CATHOLICISM

prudence, not precipitation.' Indeed, in medieval times the papacy handed heretics to the civil authorities for execution.

In 1566 the Council of Trent reaffirmed the morality of the death penalty: 'The just use of this power [capital punishment], far from involving the crime of murder, is an act of paramount obedience to [the Fifth] Commandment which prohibits murder.'

Until 1969, it was a capital offence to attempt to kill the Pope.

During the twentieth century, attitudes towards capital punishment began to change. In 1980, the National Conference of Catholic Bishops in the USA approved a statement that criticized the death penalty. While it was approved by a majority of the bishops at the meeting, it did not achieve the two-thirds majority of the whole conference. Pope John Paul II argued in 1995 that execution should be used only 'in cases of absolute necessity' and maintained that, because of the progress in penal systems, 'such cases are very rare, if not practically nonexistent.' Following this statement, in 1997, the Vatican announced changes to the Catholic Catechism, thus making it more in line with John Paul II's 1995 encyclical *Evangelium Vitae* ('The Gospel of Life'). Paragraph 56 of this document concerns capital punishment:

> Assuming that the guilty party's identity and responsibility have been fully determined, the traditional teaching of the Church does not exclude recourse to the death penalty, if this is the only possible way of effectively defending human lives against the unjust aggressor.
>
> If, however, non-lethal means are sufficient to defend and protect people's safety from the aggressor, authority will limit itself to such means, as these are more in keeping with the concrete conditions of the common good and more in conformity with the dignity of the human person.
>
> Today, in fact, as a consequence of the possibilities which the state has for effectively preventing crime, by rendering one who has committed an offence incapable of doing harm – without definitively taking away from him the possibility of redeeming himself – the cases in which the execution of the offender is an absolute necessity are rare, if not practically non-existent.

The Pope is here stressing that all possible ways of resolving a suitable punishment for a criminal, which protects the public from further harm, should be attempted. Capital punishment should be used only as a last resort.

As head of the worldwide Catholic communion, the Pope must take great care not to alienate or upset his followers. Many Catholics live in countries and areas of the world where capital punishment is still used mainly in Asia, Africa and the Middle East, but also some states in the USA.

Among Christian groups who work for the abolition of capital punishment is the American-based **Catholic Mobilizing Network**, whose aim is to end the use of the death penalty. It works closely with the United States Conference of Catholic Bishops, preaches the Church's pro-life teaching, and informs Catholics about issues to do with the death penalty. It also publishes a range of resources for different age groups and runs workshops to 'educate, advocate and inspire' Catholics in the USA and abroad to argue for the end to the death penalty and a return to retributive justice.

ISLAM

Muslim views on capital punishment

Most Muslims accept capital punishment as an appropriate form of punishment for the most serious crimes: '. . . take not life, which God has made sacred, except by way of justice and law' (Surah 6:151). The method of execution in Islamic states varies from country to country, but includes beheading, use of a firing squad, hanging and stoning.

In Islamic law, the death penalty is a suitable punishment for two sorts of crime.

- *Intentional murder* In these cases, it is not the court which makes the decision but the victim's family, who are given the option whether to insist on the perpetrator's death or to receive money in compensation. Surah 2:178 says: 'If any remission is made to anyone by his [aggrieved] brother, then prosecution [for the murder] should be made according to usage, and payment should be made to him in a good manner; this is an alleviation from your Lord and a mercy.'

> **Fasad fil-ardh** is a Muslim concept meaning 'spreading mischief in the land' and is punishable by death.

- *Fasad fil-ardh* ('spreading mischief or corruption in the land') Islam permits the death penalty for anyone who threatens to undermine the authority of the state or destroy the moral code of Islam.

What constitutes the crime of 'spreading mischief or corruption in the land' is not immediately clear and can be interpreted in several ways. It will usually involve apostasy, terrorism, piracy, rape, adultery or homosexuality.

Mohsen Kadivar is an Iranian philosopher who has criticized Iran for its use of capital punishment for apostasy (renouncing Islam) or insulting the Prophet Muhammad.

The members of an Islamic court must make all decisions on capital punishment, and evidence of guilt must be judged secure and convincing before a verdict is reached and sentence passed. While Islam remains firmly in favour of retaining capital punishment, there is a small but growing abolitionist view in support of the following points.

- The **Ulamas** (scholars who have trained for many years in Islamic law) do not always agree on the interpretation or authenticity of the sacred texts. Nor do they agree on the social context in which these texts should be applied.
- Shari'a law can be interpreted in many different ways, meaning that decisions can reflect the views of the people who make them rather than the proper legal decision. Shari'a has often been used to attack women and the poor.
- There are examples of accused people being sentenced and executed without the proper legal processes, such as a Shari'a court being assembled and legal representation being made for the accused, being followed. This behaviour is totally against Islamic law and contradicts its ideas of justice.

> **Ulama**
> refers to Islamic scholars, or a council of learned men, who hold government appointments in an Islamic state.

Task

Look at the figures below. Do you think that all countries should have to report its figures for executions? Give reasons for your answer. In 2014, the five countries with the highest rate of executions were:

- China: 3,000 (this is a low estimate; China does not report its figures)
- Iran: 721
- Saudi Arabia: 90
- Iraq: 61
- USA   35

Non-religious views on capital punishment

Non-religious people use many of the same arguments for or against capital punishment as religious believers. The major omission from these arguments is, of course, one that depends on the existence of God. So, for instance, non-religious people do not use the argument based on the sanctity of human life.

British Humanist Association

One non-religious organization that has discussed and written about punishment is the British Humanist Association. Some of the main arguments are as follows.

- Laws are necessary for the smooth running of society. They exist for the common good and can be changed when our ideas about society change.
- In a democratic society, people should obey the laws. If they think the laws are wrong, they should work within the democratic system to change them.
- Criminals should be treated impartially according to the law, have a fair trial, be able to defend themselves in court and be treated humanely in custody.

On capital punishment, the BHA says:

- Capital punishment is generally opposed by humanists because premeditated killing is wrong, even if it is carried out by the state.
- There is the possibility of executing an innocent person in error.
- Capital punishment is the sign that justice has failed.
- Capital punishment does not seem to deter murder. The USA, one of the few democracies to retain capital punishment, has one of the highest murder rates in the world, at around 1 per 10,000 of the population (in Britain, it is 1 in 100,000). The number of murders does not rise when capital punishment is abolished, and in fact there are 50 per cent more murders in US states with the death penalty than those without it.

World Coalition Against the Death Penalty

This is a non-religious international organization, set up in 2002, committed to the creation of local and national groups to campaign for an end to the death penalty. As part of this aim, they set up a World Day Against the Death Penalty, which is held on 10 October each year. Their website (www.worldcoalition.org) holds information, resources, a database of executions per year and other relevant information.

Amnesty International

Amnesty was set up in 1961 in Britain to 'conduct research and generate action to prevent and end grave abuses of human rights, and demand justice for those whose rights have been violated'. It is now a worldwide organization and influences both public opinion and governments to make changes to policies and actions if they infringe human rights. One of their key campaigns is to argue against use of the death penalty and to try to persuade governments to abolish it. It publishes annual figures for executions. Amnesty has no religious or political affiliations.

Tasks

1 Do you think that terrorists should be executed for their actions? Give reasons for your answer.
2 'The death penalty is used unjustly in some societies.' Do you agree with this statement? Give reasons for your answer.

TICK THE TOPICS

Now you should tick the relevant topics to check what you have learned in this chapter.

Sections	Topics	Tick
	What is a crime?	
	Should crimes always be punished?	
Punishment	Purposes of punishment	
	Christian views on punishment	
	Muslim views on punishment	
Capital punishment	Arguments for and against capital punishment	
	Christian views on capital punishment	
	Roman Catholic views on capital punishment	
	Muslim views on capital punishment	
	Non-religious views on capital punishment	

Sample questions

AQA Religious Studies A (8062)

1 Which one of the following best expresses the religious idea of justice?
   a) Impossible b) Desirable c) Attainable d) God-given   (1 mark)
2 Give two ways in which religious believers can help victims of crime.   (2 marks)
3 Explain two contrasting beliefs in contemporary British society about the death
   penalty.   (4 marks)
4 Explain two religious beliefs about punishment.   (5 marks)
5 'Criminals should be forgiven, not punished.'
Evaluate this statement. In your answer, you:
   • should give reasoned arguments in support of this statement
   • should give reasoned arguments to support a different point of view
   • should refer to religious arguments
   • may refer to non-religious arguments
   • should reach a justified conclusion.   (12 marks)

Edexcel Religious Studies B (1RB0)

a) Give three examples of crime.   (3)
b) Explain two theories of punishment.   (4)
c) Assess whether religious believers should criticize governments that use the death
   penalty.   (9)
d) 'Capital punishment should be used much more.'
Evaluate this statement, considering more than one point of view.   (12)

WJEC Eduqas Religious Studies (Full Course)

a) Giving one example, state what is meant by 'crime'.   (2)
b) With reference to one religion you have studied, explain views about forgiveness. (5)
c) From two different religions or two religious traditions, explain views on punishment. (8)
d) 'No religious believer should support capital punishment.'
Discuss this statement, showing that you have considered more than one point of view.
(You must refer to religion and belief in your answer.)   (15)
                                                                          (SPaG + 6)

14 Study Skills, Revision and Exams

In this final chapter, we will look at some practical hints that should help you to study and revise effectively and efficiently. We will also focus on how your examination will test your knowledge and understanding of the subject, as well as how and where you will use the skills of analysis and evaluation.

Study skills

Your teacher will certainly give you lots of advice and guidance about the most appropriate ways to study. To supplement this, I offer here some very brief general points about the sorts of things that should help you work effectively and efficiently. These will be relevant to whichever specification you are studying.

Organization

There will be several sections or parts in your course, such as the study of one or two religions, philosophy and ethics. It will be very useful to have a separate folder for each one, preferably in different colours, and labelled so that you know which folder is for which part of the course. Large folders, such as Lever Arch-type ones, are ideal for holding all your notes, handouts and work sheets. You will need dividers to separate topics, so, for example, in your philosophy folder you could have one section for arguments for the existence of God and another for the problem of evil. Your large folders should be kept in a secure place at home and should not be taken into school. You will need a small envelope folder that you can take into school to keep your week's work in. At the end of each week, you should get into the habit of transferring this into the large folder. In that way, if you should lose the smaller 'weekly' folder, you will only have to replace a small amount of material. If you were to take the large folder into school and it went missing, you could lose a whole term's work. A little organization at the beginning of the course is worth its weight in gold! Organization will help keep you on track and save you time, energy and stress later.

A place to work

You will need somewhere to do your homework, make notes or revise for a test or mock exam. The physical surroundings you have will have an impact on the quantity and quality of your work. As far as possible, you need to have an area at home that you can use each day. This should be a space where you can keep your folders and any textbooks you have, as well as a supply of paper and any exercise book you use for notes. A desk or table is necessary, which should be kept clear and without distractions (no cuddly toys or magazines). The area should be well lit. You will need pens, pencils, rulers, highlighters and erasers to hand in a pencil-case or box. You will need to turn your mobile phone off – not just to silent. There should not be a TV in the area, and your computer should be used only for legitimate, relevant research (NB: Facebook does NOT count as 'relevant research'!).

Set a time limit

It is a good idea to have a weekly timetable for working. You should build some flexibility into this, though, because you may have a special task to do one evening. When you get home from school, you will probably be hungry, so you should not aim to work straight away, as you will be concentrating on your stomach rather than the work. You will need to determine your workload, including homework, revision and other tasks, so you can calculate how much time you actually have. Any work done after 9.30 p.m. will probably not be of the same quality as that done earlier.

In setting a timetable, you will need to consider such things as the following.

- How long can you work effectively for?
- Remember you will have subjects other than RS that demand your attention.

- How long can you concentrate for? For most people, working for about 20 minutes then taking a break for 10 minutes is a manageable starting point. You can then build this up as you progress.
- You need to factor in breaks.
- During your break, you can text your friends, talk to your family or do something that is not related to work. You might go for a short walk. If you have a snack, make it a healthy one, such as fruit or nuts. Make sure you stay hydrated.

Making notes

During your course, you will have to develop a style of note-taking that suits you. There is no universally effective way of making notes. Some people use bullet points, others use diagrams, mind-mapping or spider diagrams. You should experiment with different types and see which one works best for you. The ultimate purpose is to have a short-cut to information and skills you have learned during your course, so that, when the examination is close, you do not have to trawl through every page of the textbook or all the handouts you have been given. Whichever method you use, try to keep your notes neat. Don't forget to keep them together in a folder.

The 'Tick the Topics' grids at the end of each chapter will help you to structure the notes you take from this textbook.

Revision

At various points during your course, such as when you have tests or mock exams, and obviously in the final few weeks before you sit the actual GCSE examinations, you will have to revise. Revision is the process where you go back over topics you have already studied so that you have them at the forefront of your mind. There are lots of ways you can revise; after all, different people learn and remember information in different ways. You will have to work out which is the most effective way for you. Your teacher will help you with this, but some hints are given below.

Revision timetables

- Some people like to have a detailed and extensive revision timetable planned weeks in advance.
- Others plan time slots for each evening and weekend and simply allocate subjects to each slot, deciding exactly what to do on each occasion by taking things from the top of their checklist.
- Others use their time slots even more flexibly: they decide on the subjects they fancy at the start of each session and work through their checklists as they go.

Mix the subjects or concentrate on one?

- Some people find it best to plan to do a mixture of different subjects during the course of each evening or day in short time slots.
- Others find it most effective to plan blocks of time over several days or evenings on one subject only.

Work to the clock or not?

- Some people find it best to work to strict time periods with fixed start and finish times.
- Others find that clock-watching is a distraction and that it is better to work on a given topic until it is finished.

You should create a blank timetable or planner to help you organize your time. Whatever your plan is, you should build in some flexibility: things may not always go as you expect them to. Only plan a week ahead: time spent revising is better than time spent replanning!

Make sure you achieve what you set out to do each session – it is demoralizing when you fall short of your targets. Revision should be positive! Build some breaks into your plan – you will have earned them. Get your parents involved by encouraging them to arrange a treat for you and to prepare snacks and drinks.

When to start revising

Sorting, setting up, organizing and planning revision should take place over the Easter holiday at the latest – earlier depending on when your actual GCSE exams begin. Allow plenty of time for filling in any gaps in your notes.

During the summer term, you should be spending your time making notes and learning. You should aim for two hours per night and three hours per day at weekends or holidays (including homework).

When your exams begin, you should be in 'exam mode', and each night you will be finalizing your notes or practising questions. By this time, you should be quite familiar with the material.

Breaking up the time

Some students find that they can begin revising and immerse themselves in the material for an extended period of time. More commonly, people work best in short bursts of about 30 to 40 minutes. If this works well for you, remember to plan breaks of 10 to 15 minutes. During breaks, you should have a drink and healthy snack (fruit and nuts), or you can ask your parents to test you on what you have been revising.

Most students work most effectively in the early evening. You should try to avoid studying late into the night, as you will just be tired the next morning and will not work effectively. At weekends, you should ask your parents to get you up early, when you will be at your most alert. Aim to do three sessions in the morning, then relax in the afternoon, perhaps getting some fresh air and exercise.

Writing notes

The most common way of learning is to rewrite notes in a condensed form. These do not have to be grammatically correct or in prose, but they should be neat, with clear headings and important points highlighted or underlined. If you do this, you will end up with the bare essentials. For example, if you are revising a topic such as human rights or arguments for the existence of God, try to condense your class notes down to five or six pages. At a later stage, try to condense them further, into a single page, perhaps using a diagram or grid for the essential information or ideas. You might underline your condensed notes to emphasize key ideas.

Active learning

The most effective way to learn anything is to question, sort, process or apply information, not to look at it passively. There are two challenges in this approach:

- push yourself to 'do' – you need to be determined to succeed, rather than just sitting looking at the pages;
- be imaginative – think about how you can process, use and apply information so that you can remember it. Try to be adventurous by using diagrams, lists, tables or charts instead of writing notes. Use different colours for contrasting ideas or put technical terms on 'post-it' notes and stick them around the room.

Finally, find a system that works for you and stick with it!

Understanding the examination

All the study you will do during the course will eventually be focused on a final examination. This is the place where you can show how much you know and understand about the topics you have studied. It is extremely important, therefore, that you appreciate exactly what it is that you have to do in the examination, and how to do this to the best of your ability, so that you achieve the highest grade you can.

In what follows, we will be looking at what each of the awarding organizations (exam boards) requires in terms of your knowledge and understanding and how they will assess this. We will see how each of the exam boards sets its questions and explain what this means for you. The good news is that, here, you will need to look at only one section – the one that deals with the specification you are studying.

You may already have noticed that, at the end of each chapter, there are sample questions for you to practise on. Because each of the exam boards has designed the style of questions for its particular specification, AQA-type questions are different from those of OCR and the other exam boards. Each sample question is clearly labelled with the exam board for which it is designed. This means that, for some chapters, there are sample questions for each of the exam boards, while for others (for example chapter 6, 'Religion and Science', and chapter 11, 'Global Relationships') there are questions for AQA and Edexcel but not for OCR, because these topics are not included in its specifications. This sounds more complicated than it actually is! As you begin to use the sample questions, you will understand easily how it works. Chapter 1, 'Religious Texts and Other Sources of Authority', covers a topic that is not specifically examined in any of the courses, and so there are no sample questions. However, it is important in helping you to understand how to use religious texts and other sources of authority.

Assessment objectives

An 'assessment objective' (AO) sounds rather technical, but it really just means what you are being tested on. AOs break down into four areas – knowledge, understanding, analysis and evaluation – all of which mean slightly different things. As you work through the course, you will learn what each means.

You will be assessed on two assessment objectives:

- AO1 – your knowledge of the course content and your ability to show how well you understand this and can explain it in your answers to the questions;
- AO2 – whether you can analyse and make judgements about aspects of the content, including their significance for and influence on religious and other people.

AO1 requires you to demonstrate your **knowledge** and **understanding** of religion and beliefs, including

- beliefs, practices and sources of authority
- the influence of religion and beliefs on individuals, communities and societies
- similarities and differences within and/or between religions and beliefs.

AO2 requires you to **analyse** and **evaluate** aspects of religion and belief, including their significance and influence.

Your answers to the AO1 questions are worth 50 per cent of the total marks for the paper, and your answers for the AO2 questions make up the other 50 per cent. You will also be expected to show how accurately you can use technical terms, such as 'human rights', 'discrimination', 'stewardship', sanctity of life', and so on. Your teacher will help ensure that you know all the relevant technical terms. You will get some help in this by looking at the glossary in this book.

In your answers, you should also refer to sources of religious wisdom and authority, including religious texts, where these are relevant. Reading chapter 1 of this book will help you to understand how these sources and texts are important.

You should also try to spell, punctuate and use grammar correctly and accurately in all your answers. Five per cent of the total marks for the examination are allocated to these aspects, which are specifically assessed in the extended answer questions.

AQA

Specification A, Component 2: Thematic studies

You will have studied up to four themes, chosen from:

A: Relationships and families
B: Religion and life
C: The existence of God and revelation
D: Religion, peace and conflict
E: Religion, crime and punishment
F: Religion, human rights and social justice.

For each of the themes, the structure of the questions will be the same:

1   a multiple-choice question, worth 1 mark (AO1)
2   a short answer knowledge question, worth 2 marks (AO1)
3   a question asking you to 'explain' something, worth 4 marks (AO1)
4   a question asking you to 'explain' something, worth 5 marks (AO1)
5   a long answer question asking you to 'evaluate' a statement, worth 12 marks (AO2).

You will have 1 hour 45 minutes to complete the paper. 50% of qualification.

Specification B: Perspectives on faith (Section 2)

You will have studied two themes chosen from:

A: Religion, relationships and families
B: Religion, peace and conflict
C: Religion, human rights and social justice.

For each of the themes, the structure of the questions will be the same:

1   a multiple-choice question, worth 1 mark (AO1)
2   a short answer knowledge question, worth 2 marks (AO1)
3   a question asking you to 'explain' something, worth 4 marks (AO1)
4   a question asking you to 'explain' something, worth 5 marks (AO1)
5   a long answer question asking you to 'evaluate' a statement, worth 12 marks (AO2).

You will have approximately 50 minutes to complete this section of the paper. (1 hour 45 minutes for the whole paper). 50% of qualification.

Short course Section B: Thematic studies: religious, philosophical and ethical studies

You will have studied two themes:

A: Relationships and families
B: Religion, peace and conflict.

For each of the themes, the structure of the questions will be the same:

1   a multiple choice question, worth 1 mark (AO1)
2   a short answer knowledge question, worth 2 marks (AO1)
3   a question asking you to 'explain' something, worth 4 marks (AO1)
4   a question asking you to 'explain' something, worth 5 marks (AO1)
5   a long answer question asking you to 'evaluate' a statement, worth 12 marks (AO2).

You will have approximately 50 minutes to complete this section of the paper. (1 hour 45 minutes for the whole paper). 50% of qualification.

Edexcel

Specification A: Faith & Practice in the 21st Century, Paper 3

You will have studied three areas, which may include 'Area of Study 3: Philosophy and Ethics', with the following:

A: Arguments for the Existence of God
B: Religious Teachings on Relationships and Families in the 21st Century.

The question structure is the same for each area of study – four questions, each of which is in four parts. You must answer all sections and all questions in each paper:

1   a short answer question testing factual knowledge, worth 3 marks (AO1)
2   another short answer question testing factual knowledge and your understanding of it, worth 4 marks (AO1)
3   a medium-length question testing your ability to make connections between different elements of the question, worth 6 marks (AO1)
4   an extended answer question testing your ability to weigh up different viewpoints and come to a reasoned conclusion, worth 12 marks (4 marks AO1; 8 marks AO2).

You will have 50 minutes for this section of the examination. 25% of qualification.

Specification B: Beliefs in Action (1RB0)

You will have studied two of a possible three areas:

A: Religion and Ethics
B: Religion, Peace and Conflict
C: Religion, Philosophy and Social Justice.

The question structure is the same for each area of study – four questions, each of which is in four parts. You must answer all sections and all questions in each paper:

1   a short answer question testing factual knowledge, worth 3 marks (AO1)
2   another short answer question testing factual knowledge and your understanding of it, worth 4 marks (AO1)
3   a medium-length question testing your ability to make connections between different elements of the question, worth 6 marks (AO1)

4 an extended answer question testing your ability to weigh up different viewpoints and come to a reasoned conclusion, worth 12 marks (4 marks AO1; 8 marks AO2).

You will have 1 hour 45 minutes for each of the two papers. Each paper 50% of qualification.

Short course B: Beliefs in Action (3RB0)

You will have studied two areas:

A: Religion and Ethics
B: Religion, Peace and Conflict.

The question structure is the same for each area of study – four questions, each of which is in four parts. You must answer all sections and all questions in each paper:

1 a short answer question testing factual knowledge, worth 3 marks (AO1)
2 another short answer question testing factual knowledge and your understanding of it, worth 4 marks (AO1)
3 a medium-length question testing your ability to make connections between different elements of the question, worth 6 marks (AO1)
4 an extended answer question testing your ability to weigh up different viewpoints and come to a reasoned conclusion, worth 12 marks (4 marks AO1; 8 marks AO2).

You will have 50 minutes for each of the two papers. Each paper 50% of qualification.

International GCSE (4RS0)

The notes here refer to Part 1: Beliefs and values. You will study four topic areas:

A: The universe, human beings and their destiny
B: Ultimate reality and the meaning of life
C: Relationships, families and children
D: Rights, equality and responsibilities.

The question structure is the same for all areas. Two questions are set for each topic area and you will answer one from each area. All the questions are in four parts:

1 a short answer question testing factual recall of a definition, worth 2 marks (AO1)
2 a medium-length question testing knowledge of an idea or theme, worth 5 marks (AO1)
3 a long answer question testing understanding and analysis, worth 8 marks (AO1 and AO2)
4 a medium-length question testing analysis and evaluation, worth 5 marks (AO2).

You will have approximately 1 hour 30 minutes for this part of the examination. (2 hours 30 minutes for the whole paper). 62% of the qualification.

OCR

Full course (J625)

You will have studied four themes:

A: Relationships and families
B: The existence of God, gods and the ultimate reality
C: Religion, peace and conflict
D: Dialogue between religious and non-religious beliefs and attitudes.

For each of the themes, the structure of the questions will be the same:

1 a short answer question testing AO1 factual information, worth 3 marks
2 a medium-length question also testing AO1 knowledge, worth 6 marks
3 a medium-length question testing AO1 and AO2, worth 6 marks
4 a long answer question testing AO1 and AO2, worth 15 marks.

You will have 2 hours to complete the paper. 50% of qualification.

Short course (J125)

There will be one examination paper for this course. It will be split into three sections:

A: Beliefs and teachings
B: Relationships and families
C: Dialogue between religious and non-religious beliefs and attitudes.

The questions in sections B and C will be divided into four parts:

1 a short answer question testing AO1, worth 3 marks
2 a medium-length question testing AO1, worth 6 marks
3 a medium-length question testing both AO1 and AO2, worth 6 marks
4 a long answer question testing AO1 and AO2, worth 15 marks.

You will have approximately 1 hour to complete these sections of the paper (2 hours for the whole paper). 50% of qualification.

WJEC Eduqas

Comments here relate to Route A, Component 1: Religious, Philosophical and Ethical Studies in the Modern World. In this component, you will have studied four themes (or just two themes for the short course: themes A and B below):

A: Issues of Relationships
B: Issues of Life and Death
C: Issues of Good and Evil
D: Issues of Human Rights.

Each question on the examination paper is made up of four parts: a), b), c) and d). There are four questions and you answer all of them. You will have 2 hours to complete the examination (1 hour for the short course). 50% of qualification.

1 Part a) is an AO1 knowledge question worth 2 marks. This will often ask you to 'state' or say 'what is meant by' a word or idea.
2 Part b) is also an AO1 knowledge or explanation question that will typically ask you to 'describe', 'describe ways in which' or 'explain views about' a religious or non-religious view on something.
3 Part c) is an AO1 question that will ask you to 'explain attitudes to', 'explain beliefs about' or 'explain attitudes about' an issue, belief or view.
4 Part d) is a question that includes both AO1 and AO2 skills. This is the extended question where your spelling, punctuation and grammar will also be assessed. There will be some knowledge you have to describe or explain, but there will also be an evaluation where you will have to express your own analysis and evaluation of an idea, belief or statement.

Glossary

A posteriori   The term '*a posteriori*' refers to a kind of argument based on evidence and experience.

Abortion   Abortion is the expulsion of a foetus from the womb.

Actuary   An actuary is an expert in the management of risk, usually future risks for individuals.

Aesthetics   Aesthetics is the name given to the study of 'beauty'.

Al-Adl   Al-Adl is one of the ninety-nine names of God in Islam, meaning 'the Just'.

Al-Fatihah   Al-Fatihah is the name given to the first surah in the Qur'an.

Allahu Akbar   Allahu Akbar is Arabic for 'God is great'.

Angels   Angels are heavenly, semi-divine beings who are seen, in both Islam and Christianity, as messengers of God.

Annulment   An annulment is a declaration in the Roman Catholic Church that a marriage never existed.

Anthropic Principle   The Anthropic Principle is the idea that the universe was designed by God in order that humans could thrive in it.

Anthropomorphism   Anthropomorphism is a way of giving God human characteristics, such as having a body, being able to speak, and so on.

Apocalyptic   Apocalyptic is a type of literature in the Bible that talks about the end of the world.

Apostles   The Apostles are the original twelve disciples of Jesus (minus Judas Iscariot), who became the leaders of the Christian Church.

Argument   An argument is a reasoning process that gives carefully stated evidence leading to a conclusion that can be agreed or disagreed with.

Authority   Authority is the power to give orders or enforce obedience. Internal authority is what makes someone or something important for who or what they are. External authority is given to people because of the position they hold.

Beatific Vision   The Beatific Vision, in Christianity, refers to a person's direct experience of God.

Belief   A belief relates to a set of ideas that are important to an individual or a group. It does not necessarily involve a divine being.

Bible   The Bible is the Christian holy book, consisting of sixty-six separate books – thirty-nine in the Old Testament and twenty-seven in the New Testament. Roman Catholics hold seven extra books in their Bible (the Apocrypha) that Protestants reject.

Big Bang theory   The Big Bang theory is the scientific theory that the universe began with a huge explosion which expanded over billions of years to create galaxies, solar systems and planets.

Blasphemy   Blasphemy is when someone uses God's name in an inappropriate way – e.g., to swear using God's name – to show lack of respect.

Brain death   Brain death, when there is no brain activity, is the modern definition of when a person is dead.

Burqa   The burqa is a style of clothing covering the body and face worn by many Muslim women.

Canon   Canon comes from the Greek word for 'measure'. It is the name given to the books in the Bible and are the 'measure' of Christian belief.

Canonization   Canonization is the process of making someone a saint. Recent examples include Mother Teresa of Calcutta and Padre Pio of Pietrelcina.

Capital punishment   Capital punishment is the sentencing to death and execution of someone for very serious crimes, such as murder.

Category mistake   A category mistake is a logical term where a person confuses the properties of the whole with the properties of a part.

Climate change   Climate change is an environmental concern affecting many countries and refers to changes in weather and climate patterns, including global warming, reduced rainfall and increased tidal floods.

Cohabitation   Cohabitation refers to a couple living together without being married.

Compassion   Compassion means showing a caring attitude towards someone.

Consanguinity   Consanguinity means being descended from the same ancestors.

Conscience   Conscience is a faculty that helps humans to reflect on their actions; it is seen as a guardian of a believer's moral health.

Conscientious objector   A conscientious objector is someone who refuses to fight in a war because of their pacifist beliefs.

Contingency   Contingency is a logical term used in some arguments for the existence of God to conclude that everything there is, except God, came into existence and will cease to exist at some point.

Conversion   A conversion is a form of religious experience that causes a person to change radically, typically from being atheist to being religious.

Cosmological   Cosmological means 'to do with the world' and is the name given to a group of arguments for God's existence based on cause and motion.

Counter-argument   Counter-argument is a term used when a person argues against someone else's position.

Covenant   A covenant is a special, mutually binding agreement between two or more people, or between God and his people.

Creationism   Creationism is the idea in fundamentalist Christianity that God created the earth between six thousand and ten thousand years ago.

Crime   A crime is an action that breaks a law.

Deep ecology   Deep ecology is a movement that encourages a commitment to respect the intrinsic values of nature and the interconnectedness of all species.

Deforestation   Deforestation refers to the deliberate policy of destroying large areas of forest, using the land for other purposes despite the dangers to the environment.

Design   Design suggests that something shows order, complexity and purpose, as opposed to random existence.

Deterrence Deterrence is a strategy to dissuade someone from doing something, such as attempting to stop a person from committing a crime.

Discrimination Discrimination is the act of putting prejudices into practice.

Divine command theory Divine command theory is the belief that what is right is commanded by God.

Divorce Divorce is the legal declaration that a marriage has ended.

Djinni A djinni is an invisible spirit in Islam which can affect humans.

Doctrine A doctrine is an official belief of a religion – for example, the Trinity in Christianity or the Five Pillars in Islam.

Dogma Dogma refers to key principles of faith, such as transubstantiation for Roman Catholic Christians or belief in angels and the day of destiny for Muslims.

Dualism Dualism is a philosophical position that says that humans are made up of two elements: body and soul.

Empirical Empirical means based on observations of what happens, and how, in the world around us.

Eschatological verification The eschatological verification is John Hick's idea that Christians will only know after death if God exists.

Eschatology Eschatology is doctrine and teaching about the end of the world.

Essence Essence refers to what is essential in a person – what cannot be taken away from someone if they are still to be a 'person'.

Euthanasia Euthanasia, literally meaning 'good death', refers to the practice of deliberately ending a very ill person's life without pain because that person wants to die. Euthanasia is currently illegal in Britain and many other countries, though it is legal in the Netherlands, Belgium, Ireland, Colombia and Luxembourg. Assisted suicide is legal in Switzerland, Germany, Japan, Albania and the US states of Washington, Oregon, Vermont, New Mexico, Montana and California.

Euthyphro dilemma The Euthyphro dilemma is a problem in ethics as to whether things are good because God says so, or if God says things are good because they are already good.

Evolution Evolution is the principle that living organisms change and develop over time so that only the fittest survive.

Ex cathedra *Ex cathedra* statements are considered to have apostolic and divine authority. Only the Pope may make this kind of statement.

Ex nihilo *Ex nihilo* is the Latin phrase for 'out of nothing' and refers to the idea that God created the universe from nothing.

Existentialism Existentialism is a philosophical movement that argues that humans are responsible for how their life develops, as there is no God to guide them in the choices they make.

Extended family In an extended family, several generations live together or within very close proximity to each other.

The Fall The Fall is the name given by Christians to explain the idea that humans were originally created perfect but then 'fell' from this state and became imperfect by going against God's will. Genesis chapters 2 and 3 tell the story of how Adam and Eve disobeyed God and their punishment for doing so.

Fallacy A fallacy is an error in logic or a mistake made in an argument.

Fasad fil-ardh   Fasad fil-ardh is a Muslim concept meaning 'spreading mischief in the land' and is punishable by death.

FGM   FGM is the abbreviation of female genital mutilation.

Fiqh   Fiqh refers to God-given knowledge and understanding to help Muslims live their lives. It also refers to Muslim principles of law.

Fitrah   Fitrah is the natural tendency for humans to believe in and worship God.

Five Pillars   The Five Pillars are the guiding principles of Islam: belief in one God, prayer, giving money to the poor, fasting during Ramadan and pilgrimage to Mecca.

Five Ways   The Five Ways is the name given to five arguments for the existence of God by St Thomas Aquinas.

Forgiveness   Forgiveness is a process by which a victim changes their negative emotions about something that has happened to them into positive ones and pardons those who have hurt them.

Free will   Free will is the idea that human beings are able to make their own decisions about what they do without being limited by outside factors.

Fundamentalist   A fundamentalist is a Christian who believes that many of the words in the Bible are literally true, though they may need some level of interpretation to make their meaning clear in the present day.

Gaia Hypothesis   The Gaia Hypothesis is James Lovelock's idea that the earth heals itself.

Gender prejudice   Gender prejudice involves thinking that one gender is superior to another.

Genocide   Genocide is the deliberate killing of a whole race of people, especially of a religious, cultural or ethnic group.

Glass ceiling effect   The glass ceiling effect describes the unseen barrier that prevents some people, typically women, from attaining certain jobs or roles.

God of the Gaps   God of the Gaps is a theory arguing that science provides almost all the answers to the origins of the universe, and that God is needed only to fill in the gaps that science cannot (yet) answer.

Hadd   Hadd is a punishment fixed in the Qur'an for sins against the rights of God.

Hadith   A hadith is an individual saying of the Prophet Muhammad. The plural form of this is ahadith.

Haram   Haram describes what is forbidden in Islam.

Harim   A harim is an area or zone set aside for a special purpose. One such use is the part of a house reserved for female members of the family. It can also refer to areas of the environment set aside for specific purposes.

Heaven   Heaven describes a state after bodily death reserved for those who have lived according to God's laws.

Hell   Hell describes a state after bodily death where those who have disobeyed God's laws spend eternity in pain.

Hima   Hima is the Muslim ecological practice of keeping a certain amount of land free from particular human and farming use.

Holy war   A holy war is a war fought for a religious purpose and is thought to be sanctioned by God.

Human   Human describes a member of the species *Homo sapiens*.

Human rights   Human rights are those rights that people have by virtue of being members of the human race, such as rights to life, freedom of belief and religion.

Human Rights Act   The Human Rights Act (UK, 1998) is a legal document that protects the rights of all humans.

Humanism   Humanism is a non-religious set of beliefs that promotes certain values, such as reason, to make decisions about how humans should live, without the need for God.

Hypocrisy   Hypocrisy means saying one thing but doing the opposite.

Iblis   Iblis is the Muslim name for the Devil.

Iddah   Iddah is the period that a woman must observe after the death of her husband or a divorce before marrying again.

Imago dei   is a Latin term meaning 'in the image of God'. Christians believe that all humans are created in God's image.

Immanence   Immanence refers to the idea that God is inside the universe and can make relationships with human beings.

Immortality   Immortality refers to the belief in an everlasting existence after the death of the body.

Incarnation   Incarnation is the Christian belief that God came down to earth in the form of a human being and lived a fully human life.

Infallible   Infallible means 'incapable of error'.

Infinite regress   Infinite regress refers to the idea that there is an unending chain of causes and effects, so that there was no beginning and there will be no end.

Isnad   Isnad is a 'chain' of comments on a hadith from several Muslim scholars.

Ius ad bellum   Ius ad bellum describes a set of criteria to show that embarking on war is morally justified.

Ius in bello   Ius in bello describes a set of criteria to be used to ensure that war is conducted in a 'just' manner.

Ius post bellum   Ius post bellum describes a set of criteria used to show that justice is maintained after the end of a war.

Jahannam   Jahannam is the Muslim name for Hell.

Jihad   Jihad is an Islamic term referring to the religious duty of Muslims to defend their religion. The term is Arabic for 'struggle'.

Just war theory   Just war theory attempts to show that some wars are necessary in order to defend justice.

Justice   Justice refers to people gaining what is fair or right.

Kalam   Kalam is a Muslim argument that claims that God may be known by the application of human reasoning, not just by direct revelation from God.

Kenosis   Kenosis is the Christian term for the 'self-emptying' of Jesus to redeem the sins of humans.

Kufr   Kufr is the Islamic term for disbelief in God.

Liberal   A liberal is a Christian who believes that the Bible contains errors because it was written by human authors trying to reflect on their understanding of God's nature.

Literalist   A literalist is a Christian who takes the words in the Bible as literally true, because they are believed to be the actual words of God and that no interpretation is needed.

Liturgy   The liturgy is the set order in which a Christian service of worship is conducted.

Logical behaviourism   Logical behaviourism is a philosophical view claiming that mental concepts can be explained in terms of behaviour.

Mahr   Mahr is a dowry paid by a Muslim husband to his wife as a sign of respect to her.

Malnutrition   Malnutrition means not having enough nourishment to develop properly.

Marriage   Marriage is the legal joining of two individuals in a mutually beneficial relationship. It is seen by many Christians as a sacrament.

Messiah   Messiah is the title of the person the Jews believed God would send to save them from evil and oppression. Christians understand this title and person to be Jesus.

Miracle   A miracle is claimed to be an action of God in the world for the benefit of an individual or group of people.

Monism   Monism is the philosophical view that all things in the universe are fundamentally linked together.

Monotheism   Monotheism is the belief that there is only one God. Both Christianity and Islam are monotheistic religions.

Mysticism   Mysticism is a form of religious experience where a person has a feeling of union with God.

Natural law   Natural law refers to the idea that God, when he created the universe, implanted certain fundamental laws that both nature and humans should obey.

Natural selection   Natural selection is Darwin's idea that animals and plants which are best adapted to their natural environment will survive and pass on their 'improvement' to the next generation.

Natural theology   Natural theology was the attempt by Christian scholars to find evidence of God's existence by looking at the natural world.

Necessity   Necessity is a logical term used in some arguments for God's existence to conclude that God *must* exist – that he cannot *not* exist.

Nuclear family   A nuclear family is one where a married couple of a man and a woman have their own children.

Omnibenevolence   Omnibenevolence refers to the idea that God is all loving and good.

Omnipotence   Omnipotence refers to the idea that God is all powerful.

Omnipresence   Omnipresence refers to the idea that God is always present.

Omniscience   Omniscience refers to the idea that God is all knowing.

Ozone layer   The ozone layer is a 'shield' of gas in the stratosphere that absorbs most of the sun's harmful UV radiation.

Pacifism   Pacifism is the view that it is always wrong to use violence against another person or nation.

Papal infallibility   Papal infallibility is a doctrine in the Roman Catholic Church which holds that, when the Pope speaks '*ex cathedra*', whatever he says has God's authority and becomes Christian doctrine.

Paradise   Paradise is another name for heaven or for a blissful afterlife in God's presence.

Patriarchal   Patriarchal is an adjective of 'patriarch', or 'father leader', and denotes a relationship in which the man is the dominant partner. It was the norm in biblical times and is still seen today.

Pharisee   A Pharisee was a member of a Jewish religious sect who opposed Jesus' attempts to reform Judaism. St Paul was trained as a Pharisee.

Philosophy   Philosophy means the love of wisdom, involving argument concerning reality, persons, ethics and religion, among many other things.

Physicalism   Physicalism is the belief that the entirety of the world is made up of physical substances without the need for any non-physical or spiritual elements.

Plenitude   Plenitude is Augustine's idea that the world is 'full' of all varieties of experience, events and objects and that there is more goodness than evil.

Pollution   Pollution refers to the introduction into the environment of contaminants that have a harmful or dangerous effect on humans or the natural world.

Polytheist   A polytheist is someone who believes in and may worship many gods.

Population pressure   Population pressure refers to the reduced ability of the environment to sustain the number of people, resulting in migration, decline or extinction of the population.

Poverty   Poverty can be defined as 'not having the minimum income to obtain the necessities of life'. The 'necessities of life' would include food, clean water and shelter. Poverty also means not having the opportunity of an education, access to healthcare or human rights.

Prejudice   Prejudice is 'pre-judgement', or forming an opinion without knowing all the facts.

Principle of Credulity   The Principle of Credulity is Swinburne's idea that how things seem to be is a good guide to how they are.

Principle of Sufficient Reason   The Principle of Sufficient Reason is Leibniz's idea that everything has a reason for why it is what it is.

Principle of Testimony   The Principle of Testimony is Swinburne's idea that what people say is probably genuine.

Privation   Privation is Augustine's idea that what might be called 'evil' is only a 'lack' of goodness.

Proselytism   Proselytism means attempting to convert people to a particular religious view.

Providence   Providence is the idea that God provides for and takes care of humans.

Punishment   Punishment refers to the actions taken against criminals (or those who have done wrong) as a consequence of their crime.

Purgatory   Purgatory describes an intermediate, temporary state after death in which a soul is prepared for entry into heaven.

PVS   PVS is an abbreviation of permanent vegetative state, a condition in which a person lacks brain function and has to be kept alive by machines.

QALYs   QALYs, an abbreviation of quality-adjusted life years, is a way of determining the cost benefit of someone's life.

Qur'an   The Qur'an is the Muslim holy book, believed to have been revealed to the

Prophet Muhammad. It consists of 114 surahs (chapters), each of which is subdivided into ayats (verses).

Racial discrimination Racial discrimination means treating someone differently because of their race.

Racial prejudice Racial prejudice means thinking that someone is of less value because of their race.

Rahim Rahim is one of the ninety-nine names of God in Islam, meaning 'the Merciful'.

Rahma Rahma is the Islamic concept of mercy.

Rape Rape refers to forced sexual relations with a person against that person's will.

Rapture The Rapture refers to the belief that, either before or at the same time as the second coming of Jesus Christ to earth, righteous Christians who have died and those still alive will be raised up to heaven.

Reincarnation Reincarnation is a dualist idea that, when someone dies, their soul moves into a different body, often carrying memories with it.

Religion Religion is usually associated with belief in a transcendent deity or deities, so Christians refer to 'God' and Muslims refer to 'God' or 'Allah'.

Religious experience A religious experience is when an individual or group believes that they have received a special message from God, typically by having a vision, conversion or mystical experience.

Replica theory Replica theory is Hick's idea of showing that it is logically possible for someone to disappear from one location and simultaneously reappear in another.

Respect Respect means treating people as individuals who have feelings, desires and rights.

Restitution Restitution describes a type of punishment that focuses on the criminal making up for the damages or harm they have done.

Resurrection Resurrection is the bodily form of the afterlife in both Christianity and Islam.

Retribution Retribution describes a type of punishment which seeks to inflict the same kind of suffering on a criminal as the criminal inflicted on their victim.

Revelation Revelation is the making known of something that was previously hidden.

Risalah Risalah refers to prophecy in Islam.

Sabbath The Sabbath is now a rather old-fashioned way of referring to Sunday (or, in some Christian traditions, Saturday, which is the Jewish Sabbath day), the special day of rest that used to be observed by Christians (some still hold to the tradition). It meant that Christians should not do any work on that day so that they could concentrate on worshipping God, reading the Bible and spending time with their family.

Sacrament A sacrament is described as 'an outward sign of an inner grace', or a ceremony that imparts special gifts to the believer. Roman Catholic Christians have seven sacraments, and Protestants share two of these (baptism and the Eucharist).

Salaam Aleikhum Salaam Aleikhum is an Arabic greeting, meaning 'peace be with you'.

Sanctity of life The sanctity of life is the view that human life comes from God and therefore must be protected and preserved.

Secularism Secularism is the principle that there should be a complete separation of the state from religious institutions.

Shahadah   Shahadah is one of the Five Pillars in Islam, the declaration of faith that there is only one God and Muhammad is his messenger.

Shari'a law   Shari'a law is the legal system derived from Muslim religious principles. It is practised in several Islamic countries.

Shaytan   Shaytan is the Muslim name for Satan.

Shi'a   Shi'a Islam is a branch of Islam made up of about 10 per cent of Muslims worldwide, most of whom live in Iran and Iraq.

Sin   Sin refers to something that is against the will of God.

Single-parent family   A single-parent family consists of one parent (usually the mother) plus children.

Spiritualism   Spiritualism is the belief that the spirits of dead people have the ability to communicate with the living.

Stewardship   Stewardship is the belief that humans have the responsibility to look after the created world.

Sufism   Sufism is a branch of Islam that focuses on mystical experience and personal relationship with God.

Summum bonum   *Summum bonum* is Kant's term for the 'highest good' of which humans are capable.

Sunnah   The Arabic word 'Sunnah' refers to the things the Prophet Muhammad said and did and how Muslims have put these into practice.

Sunni   Sunni Islam is the largest branch of Islam, with about 90 per cent of Muslims worldwide.

Surah   A surah is a major division (or chapter) in the Qur'an. There are 114 surahs.

Synoptic   Synoptic means 'seen together' and is used of the Gospels of Matthew, Mark and Luke, which have many similar stories about Jesus and his teaching. John's Gospel is quite different from these three. The synoptic Gospels may have had some sources in common.

Tawhid   Tawhid is the Muslim belief in the Oneness of God.

Terrorism   Terrorism is the unauthorized use of violence and intimidation against ordinary people in order to achieve political objectives.

Theodicy   Theodicy means an attempt to justify God's goodness despite the existence of evil in the world.

Theology   Theology is the study of God and his actions in the world.

Torture   Torture is the act of deliberately inflicting physical or psychological pain on someone for the benefit of the torturer.

Tradition   The word 'tradition' actually means *handing down* something to someone else. A capital 'T' is used for sacred Tradition to distinguish it from traditions that are just customs or habits.

Transcendence   Transcendence refers to the idea that God is outside and remote from the universe and beings in it.

The Trinity   The Trinity describes the Christian belief in one God who exists in three 'persons' – Father, Son and Holy Spirit.

Ulama   Ulama refers to Islamic scholars, or a council of learned men, who hold government appointments in an Islamic state.

Ummah   Ummah is the Arabic world for people or community and refers to the worldwide Muslim community.

Universal Declaration of Human Rights   The Universal Declaration of Human Rights was the declaration of the United Nations in 1948 that clarified basic human rights.

Vision   A vision is a form of religious experience in which the person 'sees' God or another holy figure.

War   A war is when nations take military action against each other.

Zakah   Zakah is the Muslim belief in giving to charity, which is one of the Five Pillars.

Illustration credits

Index